Les Routiers in Ireland Guide 2006

The Road to Good Food

Edited by Hugo Arnold

The restaurant, pub and accommodation
guide to quality, value and hospitality

Les Routiers is an association of independent, mainly owner-managed properties. However, membership is not automatic. Many applications are refused because every property displaying the Les Routiers sign must satisfy our rigorous quality criteria.

Published 2005 by:
Les Routiers Ireland Ltd
Ballykelly House
Drinagh
Wexford
Ireland
Tel +353 (0)53 58693
Fax +353 (0)53 58688

Book Trade Distribution:

Eason Wholesale Books
Furry Park Industrial Estate
Santry
Co Dublin
Ireland

Portfolio Books Ltd
Unit 5, Perivale Industrial Park
Horseden Lane South
Greenford
Middlesex
UB6 7RL
England

ISBN 0-9548797-2-4
Copyright © 2005 Les Routiers Ireland Ltd

For all enquiries and information about Les Routiers properties
telephone:+353 (0)53 58693
email: info@routiersireland.com
www.routiersireland.com

Front cover: Lacken House soup
Back cover: Blue Haven Hotel bedroom and Mint Restaurant main course

Editor:
Hugo Arnold

Production & Design Editor:
Margaret Jeffares

Contributing Editors:
Charlotte Coleman-Smith
Elizabeth Field

Editorial Assistant:
Suzanne Doyle

Design:
Karen Nolan Design
www.karennolandesign.ie

Feature Contributors:
Hugo Arnold
Charlotte Coleman-Smith
Elizabeth Field
John Wilson
Caroline Workman

Location Photography:
Failte Ireland
Kingdoms of Down
Causeway Coast & Glens
Belfast Visitor & Convention Centre
Fermanagh Lakeland Tourism
Carlow Tourism
Mark Nolan

Printed in Ireland by:
Walshe Print Ltd
59 O'Connell Street
Waterford
Ireland

For Les Routiers:

Managing Director:
Margaret Jeffares

Associate Food Consultant:
Hugo Arnold

Wine Consultant:
John Wilson

Operations Manager:
Susan O' Connor

Marketing Manager:
Melina Magourty

Marketing Assistant:
Alison James

Business Development Manager:
Colleen Bredican

Membership:
Olive Williams
Caroline Workman
Claire McNamara

A word from Margaret Jeffares

The 2006 guide, our 2nd edition brings Les Routiers Ireland to a new level and with it all our members, all our associates and partners. A great new horizon is dawning. Irish tourism is changing - both the people and their expectation - becoming more demanding and discerning, booking at the last minute and always looking for some type of offer. The Internet is here to stay and offers huge benefits, online booking chief among them. This is something we all have to embrace.

Tourism on the island of Ireland is like our weather ever changing and unpredictable. Yet with it there is enormous opportunity and constant change, characteristics that are vital in a world where people are constantly looking for change. Les Routiers offers something of the highest quality; people committed, hard working and forever improving their stalls in a world that can often seem determined to frustrate everyone's best efforts. We try hard, we work long hours, train staff and constantly reinvest and reinvent. Yet events outside of our control - world events, currency fluctuations, oil prices, terrorism - tumble in to upset the apple cart. We are strong willed individuals with high resolve we knuckle down and we survive. We analyse and we tweak and we change, we study what the visitor wants and expects and we try to satisfy, we rally around and we support one another and we wait for the sun to come out, the tide to come in and hopefully all our ships will rise, as the song says "We Will Survive". We are the best, and Les Routiers celebrates and champions the best. "The best of their type".

The "Road to Good Food", well, this is what we are all about. Food tourism is nothing new, but the term is being used throughout the industry as if this is some new development. We have been championing food tourism since our foundation in France in the 1930s; restaurateurs, delis, markets and indeed the Slow Food initiative are all about fresh food, real food, food that looks and tastes the way it should served by people not manuals in a way that enhances the whole crucial experience. Food, and health are right back on everyone's agenda, where they should be. Throughout this guide you will find members, individuals, striving to produce the best, allowing you the traveller to experience something that is totally unique.

Les Routiers origins are food; it is central to what we do. In a world where so much seems so short-lived, this is something to celebrate surely.

Margaret Jeffares
Managing Director

About this Guide

The Les Routiers in Ireland guide is about celebrating independence. In the following pages you will find establishments run by real people who have a passion for what they do. You will see it in a welcome, a gesture, in the ingredients on the plate, in the way a room is furnished or a pint is pulled. Individuality, in an era when we are surrounded by so much uniformity, makes for a refreshing change, a difference.

Standards are important and every Les Routiers member is assessed to ensure that you, the customer, is only ever confronted with surprises which delight; we are talking home-made bread, locally sourced ingredients, real cooking. Ireland is full of establishments doing just that, but many of them are hidden away, down the small roads of Ireland that have delighted travellers - and we hope you - for centuries.

Nora Brown, Grange Lodge

Real Hospitality

Peter & Anne O'Brien, O'Connor's Seafood Restaurant

This guide is all about finding those places, owners who genuinely want to see you. Our sign is about identifying independently owned establishments offering quality and something a little bit different and special.

Over the last few years there has been a change in the membership as we have sought out and found new members and said goodbye to those who have opted to tread a different course. It is significant however, that there has been very little change in the membership from last year to this. We have added more, but very few have departed. This is largely due to high standards and to a vote of confidence from you, dear reader, in your use of and expressed interest in the guide.

Graham & Mary Gaunt, Caragh Lodge

Local Foods

The use of local foods has become something of a success story for many members. Where once their source of supply involved many miles, increasing numbers are looking to local growers and breeders. This is having a huge knock-on benefit to local economies where producers are seeing a direct link to the market place and on to your plate. There is a new-found pride in indigenous Irish dishes and we have featured some of the more unusual ones. We may all know of Irish stew, but what of drisheen and Dublin coddle? That these dishes are appearing once again on Irish menus is something to be celebrated and enjoyed and we hope this guide will help you to do just that.

Which Wine?

Negotiating wine lists is never easy and it is a challenge we have understood and hope we have met with some advice from our resident wine consultant. Wine lists should aid and assist, but for those which do not help is at hand.

Drive and Dine

Travelling is as important as getting there. One innovation in this year's guide is a route map for some of the major journeys showing you where a crab salad, plate of home-cooked ham or bowl of Irish stew lies just off the main road. So you can avoid a plastic-wrapped sandwich in a service station and get in touch with the real Ireland.

Maurice Keller, Arlington Lodge

Hugo Arnold
Editor

Contents

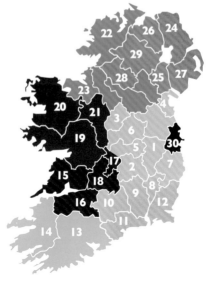

Regional Guide

How to use this Guide

Establishments are sorted first into one of nine regions then alphabetically by county, placename and establishment. For a quick search by region see the borders of the page edges. To find a particular establishment by its name, use the A-Z Index at the back.

Region | County

Place County

Establishment Name
Establishment type

Address
Tel. +353(0)65 7777777
Email. info@therestaurant.com
www.therestaurant.com

This cosy, bustling country restaurant, set in a quiet nook has a rustic cottagey décor. There are two small rooms on two floors, the former furnished in old-world Irish style, with exposed rafters, stone and subdued red rendered walls and hanging lantern-style lamps. The latter has a pine ceiling and timber floors. While the ambience is traditional

Rooms: 9 ensuite.
Double from €76. Single from €68.
Family from €90.
Closed: Mid Nov - mid Feb
Other Points: Non-smoking house. Garden. Children welcome. Car park.
Directions: Situated 0.75kms outside the village of Ballyvaughan on the N67 Lisdoonvarna road.

Telephone
Numbers include the international code for dialling Ireland from abroad. To dial from within Ireland start the number with the 0 in the brackets. To dial Northern Ireland from the Republic of Ireland replace the local area code 28 with 48. From outside Ireland dial all numbers except the (0) in the brackets.

Photograph
These have all been chosen and supplied by the individual establishments.

Les Routiers Awards
⭐ 2002 Award Winner
⭐ 2003 Award Winner
⭐ 2004 Award Winner
⭐ 2005 Award Winner

The Symbols

- Accommodation
- Restaurant
- Café
- Pub/Bar
- Daytime opening only
- Deli
- Wine
- Bakery
- Gourmet/Farm Shop
- Leisure Centre/Spa
- CS Craft Shop
- VC Visitor Centre

Prices

Set meals usually consist of three courses but can include more. Where no set lunch or dinner is offered, we give the price of the cheapest main course on the menu. House wine prices are by the bottle. Prices are meant as a guideline to the cost of a meal only. All prices include VAT. In Northern Ireland prices are given in sterling £.

Hours

Times given are opening times and annual closures.

Food serving hours

Times when food serving hours differ from above.

Rooms

For establishments offering accommodation the number of rooms is given, along with the lowest price for double and single rooms. Where this price is per person it is indicated. Prices usually include breakfast. You can check prices by calling our Central Reservations Office. Tel. +353(0)53 58693.

Other Points

Children: Although we indicate whether or not children are welcome in a pub or hotel, we do not list facilities for guests with babies; we advise telephoning beforehand to sort out any particular requirements.

Disabled: As disabilities vary considerably we advise that you telephone the hotel or restaurant of your choice to discuss your needs with the manager or proprietor.

Credit cards: Very few places fail to take credit cards. Check with individual establishments.

Directions

These have been supplied by the individual establishments.

Booking Information

Our **Central Reservations Office** staff will be happy to deal with any reservations or enquiries you may have. We can suggest or tailor-make personal itineraries, book all accommodation, restaurants, pubs and cafés and show you where to find real Irish hospitality.

Accommodation Rates & Reservations

Ballygarry House Hotel

Rates are based upon two people sharing a standard double/twin room and usually include breakfast. Rates for single and family rooms have been quoted wherever possible. Some properties will also have superior rooms and suites. We have endeavoured to reflect accurate rates for 2006. Rates are a guide and subject to change without notice, please re-confirm rates when booking.

You can contact us directly

Central Reservations:

Office hours Mon-Fri. 9.00am-5.30pm
Tel. +353 (0)53 58693
Fax. +353 (0)53 58688
Email. reservations@routiersireland.com
Web. www.routiersireland.com

Cancellations

When booking please check individual deposit and cancellation policies. Each property has its own cancellation policy and we recommend that you familiarise yourself with each prior to booking.

Ireland at Your Fingertips

Book Online

Be sure to visit our newly redesigned website, now with more information and easier navigation.

You can view up to the minute details on our members, read about special offers, book your car hire, see the best places to visit, choose from a number of great itineraries and make instantaneous reservations – all with the click of your mouse.

Online access to your one-stop guide to Ireland

Les Routiers Ireland
The Road to Good Food

www.routiersireland.com

Professional Travel Planning

Finding the best in Ireland isn't easy. Individuality in an era when we are surrounded by so much uniformity makes for a refreshing change, a difference.

Les Routiers, "The Road to Good Food", offers over 160 carefully selected, quality, independent hotels, guesthouses, country houses, B&Bs, farmhouses, castles, restaurants, pubs and cafes throughout the island of Ireland, all "Best of Their Type". You can experience what is truly Irish, stay and eat in places that are run by real people who have a passion for what they do. You will see it in a welcome, a gesture, in the ingredients on the plate, in the way a room is furnished or a pint is pulled.

For all your travel needs, visit www.routiersireland.com and register your details online now, to receive news updates, special offers and tailor made itineraries.

- Comprehensive information on where to stay and eat throughout the island of Ireland
- Quality lunch or coffee breaks along the road
- Over 40 of the best places to visit
- Central reservations team for all your special requirements
- Online booking facility for accommodation and restaurants - with independent reviews
- Sophisticated map and location search
- Route planning
- Fast and efficient tailor-made itineraries

Book online www.routiersireland.com

Be on call.

The world of tourism and leisure.
The ultimate people business.
Where service is priority number
one at all times.

As the bank of choice for many
Irish businesses involved in tourism
and leisure, it's a world we know
a lot about at AIB. In fact we're
the bank that more businesses
choose to be with.

So why not put our knowledge of
your business world to the test?

**Drop into your nearest branch
or visit www.aib.ie/business**

be with

Gift Vouchers
The Perfect Present

Give your friends, family or colleagues a true Irish experience in those often hard to find "real" places, run by people who have a passion for what they do, where hospitality is genuine - a refreshing change, a difference.

Vouchers can be purchased in values of €50 and €100 plus a 10% service charge for gift wrapping, postage and handling.

Purchase Online www.routiersireland.com

And, why not purchase the Les Routiers in Ireland Guide to accompany your gift voucher, at a special reduced rate. For further assistance or information please telephone +353 35 58693 or email info@routiersireland.com

Join Club Routiers

Keep up to date with all the news at Les Routiers Ireland. Special offers, Suggested Itineraries, the Best Places to Visit, regular electronic newsletters.

Annual Membership €9.99

Join now and receive the 2006 Les Routiers Touring Map of Ireland for FREE.

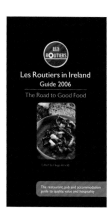

Les Routiers in Ireland Guide 2006

Receive a copy of this wonderful guide of carefully selected properties, all "best of their type", a one-stop shop for your Irish travel plans.

Special reduced price to all Club Routiers members Only €12.95 plus postage and packaging

Pre-order the 2007 edition before November 2006 and receive a further 10% discount.

Les Routiers in Ireland Touring Map

A map of Ireland showing you the best places to stay, eat and visit while driving in Ireland. You can soak up some genuine Irish hospitality, taste Irish soda bread and eat locally sourced ingredients - "real" cooking, the best that Ireland has to offer.

Only €3.95 plus postage and packaging to all Club Routiers members

Alternatively, buy both now for only €10.00 – almost 50% of a saving

To find out more or place your order, contact us on +353 53 58693 OR Email: info@routiersireland.com

The Les Routiers annual awards are a celebration of those members who, in the panel's opinion, excel and go the extra mile. The Nominations are open to all Les Routiers members who are assessed throughout the year using set guidelines. Because of the cross-section of properties, the awards embrace and epitomize our slogan "best of their type" which allows the small simple restaurant to compete with the most lavish of restaurant. The final decision rests with the panel and editor and the first and final impressions along with the "wow factor" are paramount in the final decision.

To gain entry as a member of Les Routiers a property must fit the Les Routiers criteria. Independence and breadth of choice mark out the highly regarded group of members who go through an assessment process before being recommended. Over 160 properties have made the grade, having been carefully selected for their quality, individual hospitality, good food and value for money. Only these properties are entitled to display the Les Routiers sign.

In the course of assessment some members stand out as surpassing our entry standards. These members are nominated and begin the award process. All nominations are based on recommendations by our independent assessment team who are tasked with defining what and how a particular member may stand out and therefore qualify for an award.

The following nominees and award winners have impressed with the quality of their product, their attention to detail or sheer hospitality. Its all about going that extra mile in an age when uniformity is too often the order of the day.

Each award nominee is presented with a Certificate and the winner receives a Waterford Crystal "Crookhaven Carafe".

Waterford Crystal Visitor Centre

Bed and Breakfast of the Year

Glasha Farmhouse

Ballymacarbry
Co. Waterford

"This is not the normal bed and breakfast experience, but a wonderful retreat in an incredibly unique farmhouse environment, the breakfast was truely unforgettable with wonderful extra touches."

Gone are the days when the bed and breakfast was considered second best. Our nominees offer first class accommodation with a friendly, but unobtrusive service. The bedrooms and reception areas combine a comfortable home from home feel with stylish interiors. As most are owner-managed they guarantee an interactive Irish experience.

Nominees

Raglan Lodge
Tara Lodge
The Heron's Cove
Viewmount House

Sponsored by

Waterford Crystal
Kilbarry, Waterford
Tel. + 353 (0)51 332500
Email. visitorreception@waterford.ie
www.waterfordvisitorcentre.com

Restaurant of the Year

The Lime Tree
Kenmare, Co Kerry

"This atmospheric restaurant is stylish, restrained and yet full of welcome enthusiasm."

While the food is crucial, service is no less important. A restaurant has to perform on many levels, more perhaps than it has in the past. It has to entertain, excite, but also comfort and calm. the sense of occasion needs to be there, but not so much that the diner feels ill at ease. The restaurant of the year must be a keen supporter of fresh, local produce in season, serving imaginative but unpretentious dishes.

Nominees

Chapter One
Fitzpatrick's Restaurant
O'Grady's on the Pier
Restaurant David Norris
Restaurant H2O
The Gallery Restaurant
The Tannery Restaurant
White Gables Restaurant

LaBrea
BAKERY.

Bringing bread to life

For more information on
our breads contact us at:
irelandinfo@labreabakery.com

Hotel
of the Year

Ballygarry
House Hotel
Tralee, Co Kerry

"on entering the warm homely reception you are immediately aware of the distinctive style, from its extraordinarily attractive rooms to exceptional service."

All our hotels are independently run and this is evident in their friendly, personal service, individually designed interiors and quality accommodation. Our nominees successfully combine individual hospitality with a high standard of decor and many thoughtful extras.

Nominees

Abbeyglen Castle
Arlington Lodge
Loch Lein Country House
Madison's Hotel

PERFECTLY
PRACTICAL YET
ELEGANT

**Professional restaurant cutlery from Villeroy & Boch,
in finest 18/10 stainless steel. With a range of designs to meet
every mood, every theme and every occasion.**

Country House of the Year

Delphi Lodge
Leenane, Co Galway

"The Marquis of Sligo did it in style as does Peter; the all encompassing dining experience, from the layout to the exceptional cuisine. This is a true jewel."

Rural bliss? Style, comfort and elegance and yet something of a welcoming feel were key attributes we were looking for in this category. Country House implies a sense of getting away but the real jewels make a statement so you know you have arrived at something special. Country Houses can often imply grandeur as you imagine sweeping up the drive. We were looking for the detail of what happens after this, the detail that provides you with a really excellent visit.

Nominees
Caragh Lodge
Carrygerry Country House
Coxtown Manor
Inch House & Restaurant

Guesthouse & Restaurant of the Year

Aherne's
Youghal, Co. Cork

"the Fitzgibbon family mark is evident in all aspects of this wonderful property."

The restaurant is certainly key in this award, yet the guesthouse element is an integral part and both must work together. We were looking for a synergy between both elements of this exciting category that reflected the commitment of the owners. What happens in the dining room has to be carried through the rest of the operation.

Nominees

Íragh Tí Connor
McGrory's of Culdaff
Redbank House & Restaurant
The Old Schoolhouse Inn

Importer of French Food & Wines

Sponsored by

Barrell of Grapes
Carrowmeer, Newmarket-on-Fergus, Co Clare
Contact Jacques Hubert
Tel./Fax. +353 (0)61 368915
Email. info@barrell-of-grapes.com
www.barrell-of-grapes.com

Café Restaurant of the Year

La Dolce Vita
Wexford Town

"Roberto's abundant character, his passion for good food and wine dictates the overall experience and offers as authentic a slice of Italy as you will find anywhere in Ireland."

Relaxed, accessible, easy to use and yet with fantastic food, first-class service and a friendly outlook are the kinds of characteristics we are looking for in a great café. The menu need not be long, but the ingredients and their execution have to be first class. The surroundings may be basic or indeed more than but the attention to detail is there. The winner and indeed the nominees - have turned casual into something to shout about.

Nominees

Angela's Restaurant
Blackberry Café
Isaacs Restaurant
Nash 19 Restaurant
The Yellow Door

Sponsored by

James Nicholson Wine Merchant
27a Killyleagh Street, Crossgar, Co Down, BT30 9DQ
Contact Charles O'Reilly (mob +353 872 463 778)
Tel. +44 (0)28 44830091. Tel. Lo-call from ROI 1890 667799
Email. info@jnwine.com
www.jnwine.com

Food Pub of the Year

The Thatch Bar & Restaurant
Birr, Co Offaly

"A genuine well-run country pub with superb food and hospitality."

A food pub must still be a pub, a place to go for a pint, which has a bar. It is the atmosphere, which says it all, however. You walk in the door and what hits you is something friendly and welcoming, a sense of joining something very social. If you choose to eat food then what is presented is of the first order but there is nothing pretentious about it. Food that will complement a glass of beer as well as a glass of wine. Food to be enjoyed in a casual way.

Nominees
Kennedy's Bar & Martha's Vineyard Restaurant
Linnanes Lobster Bar
McAlpin's Suir Inn
The Tankard Bar & Restaurant

Sponsored by

Dawn Meats Food Service
Kilmacthomas, Co Waterford
Contact Michael Wall
Tel. +353 (0)51 295296. Fax: +353 (0)51 295295
Email. Michael.wall@dawnmeats.com
www.dawnmeats.com

Wine List of the Year

Kelly's Resort Hotel & Spa
Rosslare, Co Wexford

"This was a list that had me salivating at the turn of every page, a list that showed passion and huge commitment of time; a list that offered the customer exceptional value."

We were looking for wine lists that offer the customer choice, value and interest. They did not not have to be long, nor did they have to be comprehensive. They did need to be made up of well-chosen quality wines at every price level, wines that reflected the food on offer. We looked for a selection of wines available by the glass or half-bottle. But most of all we wanted to see the passion and interest of the proprietor.

Nominees

Chapter One
Café Paradiso
Ely Wine Bar
Nick's Warehouse
The Tea Room at the Clarence

Sponsored by

FEBVRE

Febvre & Company
Highfield House, Burton Hall Road
Sandyford Industrial Estate, Dublin 18
Contact Colin Sheil
Tel. +353 (0)1 216 1400. Fax. +353 (0)1 295 9036
Email. info@febvre.ie www.febvre.ie

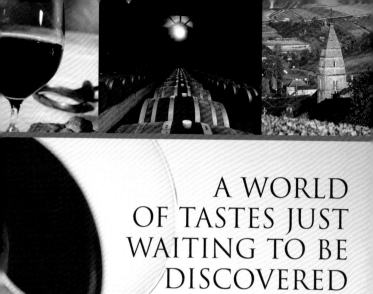

A WORLD OF TASTES JUST WAITING TO BE DISCOVERED

Febvre is a family owned business, built on a commitment to provide discerning Irish palates with a selection of carefully chosen wines from around the world.

We bring you these wines through our close links with grower-producers, both large and small, who share our desire to uphold the traditions of quality and good taste for which family owned vineyards are renowned.

FEBVRE

Highfield House, Burton Hall Road,
Sandyford Industrial Estate, Dublin 18.
Tel: (01) 216 1400   Fax: (01) 295 9036
Email: info@febvre.ie

Special Award

Barça
Lismore, Co Waterford

"Attention is in the detail, and from that a smooth, sleek, professional operation has arrived. A real surprise of the best kind."

It is a mark of our industry and how it has developed that every year more and more members appear that do not necessarily fit easily into any one category. Cafés that are bars that are restaurants that are art galleries that also offer bedrooms are increasingly to be found, or some combination that sets them apart. While being unusual is important for consideration in this award, the real test is about the quality of the offer, how it is delivered and expressed.

Sponsored by

Waterford Crystal
Kilbarry. Waterford
Tel. + 353 (0)51 332500
Email. visitorreception@waterford.ie
www.waterfordvisitorcentre.com

Locally Produced Food Supporters Award

Redbank House & Restaurant
Skerries, Co Dublin

At the core of every menu lie the ingredients used to make the dishes. This award seeks to celebrate those establishments that work hard to foster links with local growers and producers. This route is not easy; supply often being erratic and dependent on seasonal variations. Yet when it works there really is something to celebrate. a freshness and vitality that efficient distribution has done much to erode.

"Terry's clear understanding of Irish produce and his ability to incorporate these seasonal ingredients in his kitchen daily, sets him apart"

Nominees

Arlington Lodge
Café Paradiso
Chapter One
Country Choice
Ely Wine Bar
Farmgate Café & Restaurant
Farmgate Restaurant & Country Store
Glin Castle
Nick's Warehouse
O'Connell's of Ballsbridge
Sqiql Restaurant

Sponsored by

Les Routiers Ireland
Les Routiers Ireland, Ballykelly House, Drinagh, Co Wexford
Tel. +353 (0)53 58693. Fax. +353 (0)53 58688
Email. info@routiersireland.com
www.routiersireland.com

Host
of the Year

Mrs Jackie Kennedy Toner
Lacken House & Restaurant, Kilkenny

"Friendly enthusiasm delivered with real passion and professionalism."

For an industry as focused on food as ours is we can often overlook the fact that at its heart lie people. This award celebrates an individual who excels at turning this fact into a key attribute. Being a good host is a complex and often fraught occupation. How to be friendly and yet efficient, how to welcome and yet offer space, how to suggest without crowding. The winner of this award can do all of this and more.

Book your Hertz car online and save!

Hertz and Les Routiers Ireland have come together to guide you along the road to great Irish hospitality. Click www.hertz.ie or www.routiersireland.com

Book online & quote CDP 601776* to claim special 10% Les Routiers discount!

Hertz, #1 for great value, low-cost car rental.

Chilled Rose
for all cold meats
£9.99

WORLD CHEESE
AWARDS
2005

Award
Winnin
Chees

Mossfield Organic Farm · Goa
GOLD
SILVER

Gouda Mossfield Cheese made in Birr and winner of British gold Leven Prize 2005

Crozier Sheep's Milk Natural yoghurt.

LOCAL FARMHOUSE BUTTER UNPASTEURISED

LOCAL FARMHOUSE BUTTER UNPASTEURISED

Country Choice, Nenagh

Guesthouse of the Year

Old Bank House
Kinsale, Co. Cork

"it sets itself apart with a distinctive style, from its comfy bedrooms to its exquisite breakfasts."

The winner of this award combines that rare ability to furnish their establishment as if it were as a home and yet have others to stay. As the term suggests, the establishment is still very much a house overtly not a hotel. As a guest you should feel and experience this difference. It is a difficult balance to achieve and yet when done well can provide a real point of difference.

Nominees

Aberdeen Lodge
Ariel House
Lotamore House
Rusheen Lodge

Sponsored by

Hertz
Ferrybank, Co Wexford
Tel. +353 (0)53 52512 (Reservations Ireland)
Tel. +353 (0)1 6767476 (Central Reservations)
www.hertz.ie

Newcomer of the Year

Browns Restaurant, Bar & Brasserie
Derry City

"Ivan Taylor is his own man, creating menus that are much less predictable with a genuine attempt to give familiar dishes a Browns facelift."

Each year we have a flood of new members, some have been in business a long time, others have only just started. This award celebrates the member who we feel has really brought something special, something that makes them clearly stand out from the crowd. That something is rarely one thing, more often it is a combination of factors hard to put your finger on exactly but which add up to a really memorable experience.

Nominees
Admiralty Lodge
Andersons Food Hall and Café
Aubergine Gallery Café
Eden
Hayfield Manor Hotel
Les Gourmandises Restaurant

Wine Person of the Year

Mr Ian Brosnan
Chapter One, Dublin

We were not looking for a wine expert, instead, we wanted someone with a deep love of wine, someone who knew and could talk enthusiastically about their wine list. We wanted someone comfortable talking to a wine lover, but also with the ability to advise the less knowledgeable without talking down or patronising; someone who understood that wine and food are one of life's great pleasures, and could give the diner that extra touch.

"he had an enthusiasm that was infectious; most of all he had a quiet confidence that would put any customer at their ease."

Nominees

Aundria Cameron, Shanahan's on the Green

Jackie Kennedy Toner
Lacken House & Restaurant

Kevin McMahon, Ely Wine Bar

Laetitia Tricard
The Tea Room at the Clarence

Maurice Keller, Arlington Lodge

Mirco Fondrini, Farmgate Café & Restaurant

Nick Price, Nick's Warehouse

Paul O'Brien, Barrtra Seafood Restaurant

Sponsored by

GHS Classic Drinks Limited
Unit 5, OC Commercial Park, Little Island, Cork, Ireland
Contact Hugh Murray
Tel. +353 (0)21 451 0066. Fax. +353 (0)21 4355504
Email. sales@classicdrinks.ie www.classicdrinks.ie

EATING
YOUR WAY
THROUGH
IRELAND

Food tourism is one sure way to discovering some of the many culinary treats dotted around this wonderful island. **Hugo Arnold** *shares some of the secrets and reveals a heartfelt passion expressed by many.*

Lacken House & Restaurant, Kilkenny

Discovering a country through its food often labelled food tourism is undoubtedly one of the most rewarding ways of exploring and area. You get to meet interesting people, go to out-of-the-way places, frequently going through doors not open to the general public and you get to eat well.

We live in an age of vast differences and nowhere is this more true than in culinary Ireland. We have our cheap supermarkets, so-called delis (they are nothing of the sort) and awful pubs yet dotted around the country are people with real passion and commitment, dedicated to giving you, the visitor, the best of Ireland. Perfect pubs, welcoming bed and breakfast establishments, superb hotels and cafes where everything is prepared with love and with pride.

Powersfield House
Dungarvan

Order monkfish at QC's in Kerry and owner Kate Cooke will tell you with some pride that it came off her family's trawler that morning. When you eat at the Farmgate Café in the English Market in Cork city, owner Kay Harte will have shopped for the ingredients that morning from the stallholders below. Order beef or pork in any form from Country Choice in Nenagh and all of it will have come from owner Peter Ward's family farm, along with most of the other ingredients on the plate.

Food defines us, and while the net has been thrown wider and the influences are global there has also been a reawakening in Ireland about our own indigenous foods and all that is great about them; from salmon to scallops, honey to real cream. Why not discover Ireland through the people who grow, make and cook the kind of food we want to eat, food that has never seen the sight of a factory let alone a production line. Many of those people are featured in the following pages.

Café Paradiso, Cork

Restaurant H20

This whole approach means vegetables grown in the garden, or bought from the farmer down the road, local fish, beef that has been properly hung and pork from pigs treated with respect and love. Jam made from fruit from the garden or honey from privately kept bees. It can mean beer brewed out the back, cheese from a neighbour or smoked salmon that arrives wrapped in greaseproof paper and still warm, rather than in plastic from miles away.

There is excellence in every corner of Ireland and our sole aim is to find it and share it with you. Individuality can be a good thing and when it is, when it is the best, our job is to help you find it.

Ireland is full of empty countryside but up the odd lane, across that lough there are people making individually crafted food. Many sell at local markets, many also welcome visitors. You can visit and see beer being made at Franciscan Well Brew Pub, you can see salmon being smoked at The Burren Smokehouse or watch Burren Gold cheese being made. There is a network of small producers out there who believe in what they do with a passion and want nothing more than to meet others who share their love of individuality.

Hayfield Manor Hotel, Co

In an age of so much mass manufacture the art of the individual is something to be celebrated. Hard to find? Not if you come with us. Using this guide and talking to Les Routiers members will open up a hidden Ireland that has strong links with its past - remember this is an island of butter and milk, beef, pork and lamb and seas still rich in fish - but an eye to the future. A future that is about sustainability, locality, identity. Don't rush, you might miss something delicious but if you are short of time we'll get you there with a minimum of fuss. ∎

Your wine says
connoisseur.

Your cheese says
gourmet.

What exactly does
your bread say?

Great meals start with great bread.

In 1989, Nancy Silverton set out to create a bread worthy of the finest meal. La Brea Bakery was born when Nancy carefully combined flour, water and organic grapes to create a unique 'starter' dough that evolved to become the essense of La Brea Bakery bread.

This unique dough and the gourmet ingredients used to flavour it, were critical elements in the phenomenal success of La Brea Bakery Breads in the United States. This exciting range is now available in Ireland for your enjoyment!

Above: La Brea Bakery White Country Oval

Bread, like wine is a product of fermentation, a process critical in the development of a loaf's overall character. The key to the La Brea Bakery method is our signature 'starter' dough, which contains naturally occurring yeast that causes the bread to ferment and rise very slowly.

Left: La Brea Bakery Founder, Nancy Silverton

This unrushed leavening process creates the distinctive characteristics that set our bread apart from the rest. It's a difference you will notice from the first bite - the enticing flavour, distinctive crust and unique texture, that delivers an experience that can only be achieved through a passion and commitment to creating the perfect loaf.

Above: La Brea Bakery Raisin & Pecan Oval

"Take heed, oh bread eaters... this loaf sets the standard."

The Washington Post

Whether its our Roasted Garlic Loaf, perfect with pasta or risotto dishes or our Olive Oval, which is a delight just on its own, you'll find a La Brea Bakery bread of size and flavour to compliment any meal.

So what exactly does our bread say? Well, the quality speaks for itself. Enjoy!

Above: La Brea Bakery Rosemary Olive Oil Round

WINE
WITHOUT
THE FUSS

Drinking wine should be a pleasure yet too many establishments and lists seem hell-bent on making the task difficult.

Wine consultant John Wilson lends you a guiding hand and a five-point route to real satisfaction.

John Wilson is a consultant specialising in wine and is author of the annual and much-respected The Wine Guide. He writes a weekly wine column in the Sunday Tribune and is a regular contributor to Wine Ireland and Food and Wine Magazine.

When a wine waiter offers you a taste of wine, you are not being asked if you like the wine. You are checking to see that the wine is free of faults. These days, thanks to modern technology, it is rare to come across a faulty wine. Beware of anything that looks cloudy, or smells of vinegar. Deposits and sediment,

Locks Restaurant

although not pleasant to look at, are not a fault, and can actually be an indication of a wine made in a non-interventionist manner.

The fault you are most likely to come across is corked wine. Industry experts reckon that between 1-5% of wines are contaminated by a faulty cork, giving the wine a musty, rank smell, often called 'dirty dishcloths'. There is no way of knowing a wine is corked until it is opened. If a wine has a Stelvin closure, or screw-cap, it cannot be corked. More and more producers are using them as a quality control measure, and not as a money-saving measure.

If you suspect a wine is faulty, send it back. Your wine waiter should accept this without quibble, and offer another bottle of the same wine.

FIVE KEY ROUTES TO NEGOTIATING A WINE LIST

1. I try to go off the beaten track - nearly every famous wine area has a lesser-known, better value alternative - Châteauneuf-du-Pape has Gigondas, Bordeaux has Bergerac, Sancerre has Menetou-Salon, Rioja has Navarra, and Chianti Classico has Rufina and Colli Senesi. A well-chosen good wine list will have plenty of less expensive options.

2. I check out the descriptions - bland sentences such as 'a well-made wine of superior quality' means nothing. Precise descriptions, with useful information as to weight, alcohol, dryness of a wine, as well as food matches can be a real help.

3. In my experience, the best value wines tend to be in the €30-40 price bracket. Working backwards, this provides the winemaker with enough money to produce something of real quality.

Noel Delaney, Andersons Foodhall & Café

Quay Cottage, Westport

4. I am happy to ask my wine waiter for advice. It will soon become apparent whether they know their stuff or not. If they do, I go along with their suggestion - and quite often make a new and exciting discovery.

5. I look for countries and regions that offer value (there are so many) - places like South Africa, the Languedoc and South-west France, Navarra, Portugal, the south of Italy. Drinking the same wines from the same few regions is a certain route.

John Wilson
Les Routiers Wine Consultant

DISHES
TO DIE FOR

Passion, commitment and attention to detail can all be used to describe Les Routiers establishments.

But what about when you get home? Here a few members share their favourite recipes.

Penny Plunkett, Chef/Proprietor of
La Maison des Gourmets

TROPEZIENE
(From St Tropez)

225g (8oz, 1 cup) butter
8g (1/4 oz) baker's yeast
1 tbsp warm water
15g (1/2 oz, 1 tbsp)
granulated sugar
pinch of salt

2 tbsps cold milk
250g (9oz, 2 cups) flour
2 eggs
almonds

Soften 8oz (1 cup) butter at room temperature.
Crumble 1/4 oz baker's yeast and stir into one
tablespoon of warm water. In a separate container
stir 1/2 oz (1 tablespoon) granulated sugar and a
pinch of salt into 2 tablespoons cold milk. Sieve 9oz
(2 cups) flour, make a well in the centre, and place
the yeast mixture and one whole egg in the well.
After working in a little flour, add the sugar and salt
mixture, and another egg. Continue to work the
dough until it becomes smooth and elastic. It should
stretch easily. Mix a third of the dough with the
softened butter, then add the second and finally the
remaining third of the dough to the mixture. Shape
like a ball and flatten dough. Sprinkle with almonds
and brush with egg. Bake for 15-20 mins at 200°C
(checking towards the end of cooking). Cool then
cut through centre and pipe pasty cream inside.
Slice, sprinkle with icing sugar and serve.

Emer Murray, Chef/Proprietor of Goyas

LEMON MERINGUE PIE

Quantity for 1 x 10 inch round loose bottomed Quiche tin one and half inches deep.

Pastry case baked blind.

Filling

10 oz of castor sugar and three and half oz of cornflour, 1 teaspoon of salt – mix this together. Bring 15 fluid oz of water to the boil – add to sugar mix in two parts.

Bring to the boil gradually stirring very often as it is prone to sticking. When at the boil turn down the heat to the lowest setting and cook out for 12 minutes - NOT STIRRING.

Add the juice and zest of three lemons, 4 egg yolks, half oz of butter and mix it through. Pour into a bowl and leave to cool fully. Turn filling into pastry case which must be still in its tin.

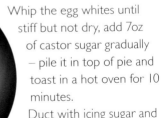

Whip the egg whites until stiff but not dry, add 7oz of castor sugar gradually – pile it in top of pie and toast in a hot oven for 10 minutes.
Duct with icing sugar and enjoy!!

Peter Caviston, Proprietor of
Caviston's Food Emporium

ROASTED MONKFISH FILLETS

WITH ROAST RED PEPPER AND OLIVE OIL DRESSING

1 lb (454 g) fillet of monkfish
1 red pepper
1 bulb garlic
1/2 pint of extra virgin olive oil
flat leaf parsley

Cut fish into 4 pieces approx. 4 oz (112 g). Dust lightly with seasoned flour. Heat pan with olive oil (small amount) until quite hot. Brown fish for 30 seconds on each side. Transfer to hot oven at 200°C for 4 minutes. Roast red pepper and bulb of garlic in the oven for 20 minutes. Set garlic aside. Skin and de-seed pepper. Chop pepper into strips. Add roasted cloves of garlic and pepper to the olive oil. Heat until just boiling and serve over fillets of monkfish. Garnish with parsley and sea salt.

David Norris, Chef/Proprietor of
Restaurant David Norris

Parma Ham and Melon

with spiced chutney juices and mint syrup

1 small galia melon.
1 small charentais melon
8 slices parma ham
1 jar good chutney
1 bunch fresh mint
30g sultanas (soaked in whiskey)
1 teaspoon chilli flakes
225 ml water

Dissolve sugar with water and boil for one minute. Liquidise the chutney and add enough syrup to thin it down to sauce consistency. Over a medium heat reduce remaining syrup until quite thick. Roughly chop mint, add to syrup then liquidise for two to three minutes until a good green colour is achieved. Pass through a fine sieve and reserve in a small pot. Gently heat the chutney juices with the sultanas and chilli flakes. Remove from heat and chill. Chill mint syrup. Cut melon into eight even wedges and arrange with parma ham as shown. Spoon over the chutney juices and spoon around the mint syrup. Garnish with fresh mint. Serves 4

David Fitzgibbon, Chef/Proprietor of Aherne's

POACHED TURBOT & PRAWNS
WITH A CHABLIS CREAM SAUCE

200g fillet of turbot
5 cooked peeled fresh prawns
75ml white wine
1 lemon
1 onion
75ml cream
4oz butter
herbs: chives, coriander, parsley

1. Poach the fillet of turbot in wine, water, lemon wedges & herbs.
2. When turbot is cooked (opaque in colour), remove from liquid & reduce liquid to ½ of its volume, add a little cream and whisk in 4oz of butter.
3. Replace the fillet of turbot in the sauce add prawns & reheat gently.
4. Add chopped herbs then serve with fresh parsley & lemon wedge.

Monkfish could be substituted for turbot.

Paul Rankin, Chef Proprietor of Cayenne,
Roscoffs and City

SPAGHETTINI MOLLY MALONE

Wonderful cockles and mussels thrive all around the coast of Ireland. They often suit a good splash of cream or a few knobs of butter, but for Paul Rankin this treatment with white wine, garlic, and olive oil is his favourite. We heard once that it's a recipe Molly brought back after having a fling with Marco Polo on her holidays.

Serves 4

8 tablespoons extra virgin olive oil
1 large red chilli, seeded and finely chopped
4 garlic cloves, chopped

1 kg (2lb 4oz) mussels
1 kg (2lb 4oz) cockles
250 ml (9 fl oz) dry white wine
3 tablespoons onion, finely chopped
2 fresh parsley stalks

450 g (1 lb) spaghettini
2 tablespoons roughly chopped fresh parsley

Place the chilli (reserving a little to garnish), garlic and oil in a small bowl and cook in the microwave on full power for 1 minute. Alternatively, warm over gentle heat in a small saucepan for about 5 minutes. Set aside.

Wash and scrub the cockles and mussels carefully, scraping off the beards from the mussels. Rinse in plenty of clean water, and discard any mussels that are open and do not close when tapped with a knife.

Bring the wine, onion, and parsley stalks to the boil in a large saucepan over high heat. Add the cockles and mussels, cover, and boil vigorously for 3-4 minutes, or until all the cockles and mussels have opened. Discard any mussels that remain closed. Drain into a colander with a bowl underneath to catch all that precious cooking liquid. Reserve the broth and, as soon as they are cool enough, remove about two-thirds of the cockles and mussels from their shells. Place both the shelled cockles and mussels and the ones in their shells in a saucepan and pour the reserved broth over them, leaving behind the last few spoonfuls of liquid as that will be quite gritty.

Cook the spaghettini in plenty of boiling, salted water according to the packet instructions.

Meanwhile, heat the cockles and mussels in the broth, adding the chilli and garlic oil to the pan. Add the herbs, reserving some of the chopped parsley to garnish. Do not allow to boil or continue to cook as the cockles and mussels will toughen.

Drain the spaghettini, toss the pasta with the cockles and mussels mixture, sprinkle over the reserved chilli and parsley, and serve at once in warm bowls.

Key Events

Festival St Patrick's Day Festivals	Throughout Region March 13 - 17	
Equestrian Powers Irish Grand National	Fairyhouse April 16 -18	
Equestrian Budweiser Irish Derby Festival	Curragh June 30 - July 2	
Gardens Wicklow Gardens	Wicklow May 1 - Aug 14	
Sport Ryder Cup	K Club Sept 22 - 24	

East Coast & Midlands

| **Milltown** Co Kildare | 🅿 ✕ 🍷 |

Hanged Man's
Pub and restaurant

Milltown, Newbridge, Co Kildare
Tel. +353 (0)45 431515
Email. pm_keane@yahoo.ie

This meticulously kept pub and restaurant is scenically situated by a river five miles outside Newbridge. Owner Pat Keane has thirty years experience in the trade and runs a professional establishment, with superbly attentive, smartly uniformed staff. Inside, stone fireplaces, black cauldrons and simple, polished black tables are lit by scores of fairylights and candles. Two dining rooms lead off the main pub, and the view over the river through a large glass window brings a sense of tranquillity. A modern Irish menu with some international inclusions - loin of kangaroo with honey and red wine jus - proudly acknowledges local producers. A typical menu might bring wild mushroom salad with black truffle oil and panfried blackened fillet of seatrout with yogurt and mango dressing. The short wine list includes a single estate red from Uruguay and Lebanon's Chateau Musar.

Prices: Lunch: (2 courses)from €25. Dinner main course from €18. House Wine from €18.
Food Served: 17.00-21.30 Mon-Sat. 12.00-21.30 Sun.
Cuisine: Modern Irish with a twist.
Other Points: Covered balcony/deck. Garden. Car Park. Beside the Grand Canal and walking distance to Pollardstown Fen (National Nature Reserve).
Directions: 5 minutes from Newbridge. South on Main St. in Newbridge. Turn right at Post Office & Bank of Ireland. Pass Newbridge Railway Station on right. Turn right in Milltown Village, 300 yards on right.

Nearest Golf Courses

K Club Tel. +353 (0)1 6017200
Laois Tel. +353 (0)502 46533
Longford Tel. +353 (0)43 46310
Louth Tel. +353 (0)41 9881530

Nearest Racecourses

Curragh Racecourse Tel. +353 (0)45 441205
Fairyhouse Racecourse Tel. +353 (0)1 8256167
Kilbeggan Racecourse Tel. +353 (0)506 32176
Punchestown Racecourse Tel. +353 (0)45 897704

The Irish National Stud and Gardens | *Place to visit*

Tully, Kildare.
Tel. +353(0)45 521617 or 522963
Fax. +353(0)45 522964
Email. japanesegardens@eircom.net
www.irish-national-stud.ie

The role of the National Stud is; standing commercial stallions for breeders providing facilities to have their stock boarded on a long or short term basis, mares foaled, stock prepared for all sales, organising a five month residential training course in Horse Breeding for young people each year.

However, it also provides guided tours of the Stud for groups and individuals. **One admission charge** covers entrance to the Stud along with the Japanese Gardens and St. Fiachra's Garden, which are both, located within the Tully estate. The World famous Japanese Gardens were created between 1906-1910 by the owner of the Tully Estate Col. William Hall Walker. The gardens were laid out in their paths of beauty by the Japanese Gardener Tassa Eida and his Son Minoru. They were planned to symbolise the 'Life of Man' from the cradle to the grave and the significance of the Japanese Gardens is not only horticultural but also religious, philosophical and historical. In 1946 the Irish National Stud Co. was formed having taken over the running of the farm from the British Government who had been running it since 1915 when Col. Hall-Walker presented the estate to the British Government in return for the title Lord Wavertree. The tourism facility at the Irish National Stud became so popular with International and Irish visitors that in 1999 St. Fiachra's Garden was built to celebrate the Millennium. This garden has 4 acres of woodland and lakeside walks and the centre of the garden is dominated by fissured limestone Monastic cells which feature hand crafted Waterford Crystal rocks and plants such as ferns and orchids.

Other Points
Restaurant and Craft Shop, Picnic Area and Free Car & Coach Parking.

Hours
Feb 12 to Nov 1, daily 9.30 - 17.00
Thereafter groups only by booking.

Admission Charged

Directions
The Irish National Stud is situated off the M7 and the R 415 just outside Kildare town approximately 30 miles south of Dublin.

Portlaoise Co Laois

The Kitchen & Foodhall
Daytime restaurant, café and food shop

Hynd's Square, Portlaoise, Co. Laois
Tel. +353(0)502 62061

Established 23 years ago, this charming, friendly and buzzy spot in the centre of Portlaoise town is awash in delicious aromas and lovely window displays. It is perennially popular with both local habituees and motorists passing through town. Old-fashioned and homely, it has two large front windows, two entrances and a small outdoor eating area. Within, its three unpretentious slate-floored rooms on two floors feature cosy open fireplaces, and restaurant seating for 175. A long cold unit, tablecloth-covered buffet tables and pine shelves are laden with an extensive self-service array of Irish and imported specialty foods, patés and terrines, salads, pastas, cold deli meats, preserves, chocolates, breads, scones, and desserts all made on the premises by proprietor Jim Tynan. The restaurant's wholesome specialties include roast Hereford prime beef with organic vegetables

Prices: Lunch main course from €10.50. House Wine from €10.99.
Food served: 9.00-17.30 Mon-Sat.
Closed: Sundays, 25 Dec-3 Jan incl. Good Friday & bank holidays.
Cuisine: Traditional Irish/Mediterranean.
Other Points: Children welcome.
Directions: Entrance on Church Street beside the courthouse or through Hynd's Square off Main Street.

or a selection of salads from the buffet. Wines from the shop can be bought for the restaurant without a corkage charge.

The Kitchen & Foodhall

Longford Town Co Longford

Aubergine Gallery Café
Town centre restaurant and café

17 Ballymahon St, Longford
Tel.+353(0)43 48633

This family-run café in the centre of Longford is somewhat off the beaten track, above a ladies' clothes shop - but it's well worth a dedicated detour. Co-proprietor and chef Stephen Devlin offers a truly creative menu using organic herbs and summer vegetables grown by his parents. There are great vegetarian options such as a mixed vegetable and mozzarella burrito with avocado and mango, or a mezze with olives and breads. The lunchtime soup - parsnip, rosemary, olive and feta, say - and sandwich is a good deal at under 6 euro. Sunday lunch might bring popcorn shrimp with piquant dressing, followed by smoked bacon chop with braised red cabbage and whiskey caramel sauce, or fillet of salmon and prawn Kiev with pistachio crust. All dishes are chalked up on a blackboard in the small bar area, which leads into a long, narrow restaurant fitted with leather banquettes.

Prices: Lunch main course from €7.95 Dinner main course from €15.95. House Wine from €16.50.
Food Served: 12.00-17.00 Tue. 12.00-17.00 & 18.00-20.00 Wed, Thur. 12.00-16.00 & 18.00-21.30 Fri, Sat. 14.00-20.00 Sun.
Closed: Mondays, Good Friday, 25, 26 Dec & 1 Jan.
Cuisine: Modern Irish/ Mediterranean.
Other Points: Children welcome over 5 years.
Directions: On Ballymahon St, (left as you are heading West) over The Old White House Pub. (entrance on right of ground floor shop.)

A short wine list leans towards France, with six half bottles.

Longford Town Co Longford

Viewmount House
Country house bed and breakfast

Dublin Road, Longford
Tel. +353(0)43 41919
Email. info@viewmounthouse.com
www.viewmounthouse.com

This is a most appealing 1750s Georgian house, set amid four acres of lovely wooded gardens. Formerly owned by Lord Longford, the house has graceful architectural details including a white "flying staircase" which leads to six ample bedrooms furnished with large antique beds, tasteful woven rugs and garden views. Bathrooms are good-sized and well appointed. James and Beryl Kearney's warmth and attention to detail is evident throughout the house. Breakfast, served in a unique vaulted dining room with pine woodblock flooring, Georgian blue walls and crisp white linens, includes freshly squeezed orange juice or fruit salad, homemade muesli with natural yogurt, and a choice of a "full Irish" breakfast, scrambled eggs and smoked salmon, cheese/mushroom omelettes, or pancakes topped with pecans and maple syrup, served with crispy

Rooms: 6 ensuite. Double/twin from €100. Single from €60.
Closed: Never
Other Points: Non-smoking house. Garden. Car park. Children welcome.
Directions: Coming from Dublin leave the N4 at first roundabout towards Longford town. After (30) speed limit sign you see Viewmount House sign. Turn very sharp left and the house is on your right - five hundred metres.

bacon. This is an ideal base to explore the midlands, the River Shannon and Carrigglas Manor; eight championship golf courses are within a 30-mile radius. Children welcome.

Carlingford Co Louth

Ghan House
Coastal country house & restaurant

Carlingford, Co Louth
Tel. +353(0)42 937 3682
Email. ghanhouse@eircom.net
www.ghanhouse.com

Paul Carroll's attractive Georgian country house and cookery school stands in walled grounds in a lovely village close to Carlingford Lough. The small lake to the front catches the reflection of the long, white, two-storey building and breathtaking views of Slieve Foy encircle the house. Inside, a large hallway with old timber floors and an open fireplace create an atmosphere of warmth and comfort which permeates the house. The twelve ensuite bedrooms, all with mountain views, are furnished with family antiques and filled with fresh flowers and old-fashioned attention to detail. The restaurant offers intimate dining in classic surroundings, with homebaked bread and dishes such as ceviche of tuna loin with spicy lime dressing, or roasted local red legged partridge setting the elegant tone. The cookery school attracts high calibre guest chefs and the impressive

Rooms: 12 ensuite. Double from €180. Single from €75.
Prices: Dinner main course from €27.50. House Wine from €18.50.
Food Served: Fri, Sat, Sun (booking recommended) and at any other time by prior arrangement.
Closed: 24-26, 31 Dec. 1-6 Jan.
Cuisine: Modern Irish.
Other Points: Garden. Dogs welcome in stable. Children welcome. Cookery school.
Directions: 1 hour from Dublin & Belfast Airports, 15 minutes from N1, signposted to Medieval Carlingford. Ghan House is a tree length away from Carlingford.

programme of events includes fishing trips on Carlingford Lough, whiskey tasting and eight-course gourmet nights.

Jenkinstown Co Louth

Fitzpatrick's Bar & Restaurant
Country pub and restaurant

Jenkinstown, Rockmarshall,
Dundalk, Co Louth
Tel. +353(0)42 9376193.
Email.fitzpatricksbarandrestaurant@
eircom.net
www.fitzpatricks-restaurant.com

Danny and Dympna Fitzpatrick's country pub and restaurant is well positioned on the Carlingford Road, five miles from Dundalk and next to the Cooley mountains, Carlingford Lough and several fine beaches. There's a consistently warm welcome at Fitzpatrick's - the interior is bedecked with retro artefacts and old advertisement placards, making for a laidback, nostalgic atmosphere, perfect for a quiet pint or cosy Sunday lunch - and this, combined with an extensive menu of dependable favourites, adds up to a winning formula. Bistro starters range from Oriental duck pancakes and prawn cocktail to grilled Carlingford crab claws and garlic mushrooms. Main courses such as steak and Guinness pie, chicken Kiev, grilled steaks and fish and chips with mushy peas are complemented by specials such as roast rack of lamb with a Madeira

Prices: Lunch main course from €10.50. Set Sunday lunch €22.50. Bar snack from €19. Dinner main course from €25. House wine from €18.50
Hours: Bar 12.30-23.30 Mon-Wed. 12.30-24.30 Thurs-Sat. 12.30-23.00 Sun.
Food served: 12.30-22.00 Tue-Sun.
Closed: Mondays except for Bank Holidays and high season. Good Friday and 25 Dec.
Cuisine: Modern Irish.
Other Points: Garden. Children welcome. Car park. Winner - Dining Pub of the Year 2004.
Directions: Go north through Dundalk, take the Carlingford Road, Fitzpatrick's is approx. 5 miles down the Carlingford Road on the left hand side.

and rosemary jus and baked fillet of hake with a velouté of monkfish. All breads and petits fours are homebaked and vegetables are locally grown.

Ghan House

| Tullamore Dew Heritage Centre | *Place to visit* |

Bury Quay, Tullamore, Co Offaly
Tel. +353(0)506 25015
Fax.+353(0)506 25016
Email. tullamoredhc@eircom.net
www.tullamore-dew.org

The Tullamore Dew Heritage Centre, housed in the 1897 Bonded Warehouse, relates the story of Tullamore Dew Whiskey/ Irish Mist Liqueur and the development of Tullamore town. Visitors can wander through the various recreated working stations of the distillery such as malting, bottling or cooperage areas and learn how the whiskey was made. Throughout the tour, visitors can interact with the artefacts, admire bees collecting honey for the production of Irish Mist, try out outfits worn on canal barges in the 1850's and learn about the history of Tullamore Town. Audiovisual presentation, guided and self guided tours, complimentary tasting of Tullamore Dew Whiskey or Irish Mist Liqueur.

Other Points
Coffee Shop, Restaurant, Fully licensed bar, Tourist Office and Gift Shop.

Hours
May to Sept: Mon to Sat 9.00 - 18.00
Sun 12.00 - 17.00
Oct to Apr: Mon - Sat: 10.00 - 17.00
Sun 12.00 - 17.00

Admission Charged

Directions
Located on the banks of the Grand Canal. Just 6 minutes off the N6 at Kilbeggan, on reaching Tullamore, take an immediate right after the bridge and drive along the quay. From the N52, drive through the town and take a left before the Grand Canal

Mullingar Co Westmeath

Gallery 29 Café
Daytime café and restaurant

16 Oliver Plunkett Street, Mullingar,
Co Westmeath
Tel. +353(0)44 49449
Email. corbetstown@eircom.net

Ann and Emily Gray's popular café makes the most of its handsome black-painted 19th-century façade and refurbished interior featuring seating for 50 people. This delightful eatery has a lively open kitchen, and tempting displays of the Grays' home-baked goodies: breads, scones, muffins, baked puddings, tarts and gateaux. Hearty breakfast favourites include pancakes with lemon and sugar; or baked potato cake with tomato and crispy bacon. The lunch menu offers delicious soups; a large choice of sandwiches on freshly baked focaccia bread or demi baguettes; and hot dishes like bacon, mushroom and Mozzarella cheese quiche with fresh herbs, served with a selection of house salads. Of course, there's always room for coffee and a

Prices: Lunch main course from €8.95-€10.90.
Closed: Sun & Mon. 25 Dec to 10 Jan.
Food Served: 9.00-18.00 Tue-Sat.
Cuisine: Modern Irish with European/Asian twist.
Other Points: Children welcome. Fully air-conditioned.
Directions: Take any of the three exits from the Mullingar bypass to the town centre. Gallery 29 Café is about fifty yards from the Market Square on the main street.

homemade pastry. Ann and Emily's philosophy of creating "good honest food cooked with passion" shows in all their offerings.

Avoca Co Wicklow   CS VC

Avoca Café at The Old Mill
Daytime café and shop

The Old Mill, Avoca, Co Wicklow
Tel. +353(0)402 35105
Email. info@avoca.ie
www.avoca.ie

Owned and operated by the Pratt family, Avoca Handweavers is well-known for its beautifully woven throws, rugs, scarves, clothing, accessories and handcrafts. Much of the fabric seen in this, and all the other Avoca stores, is woven here at a restored mill dating from 1723. It is the oldest working mill in Ireland, and visitors are welcome to see the entire weaving process first-hand by taking a free tour of the mill. The store also carries soft furnishings, toys, gifts and food from the Avoca Pantry range. A self-service café, like all the other Avoca cafés, is renowned for its wide selection of high-quality, homemade food: tomato and roasted pepper soup; shepherd's pie; chicken and broccoli encroute; home-cooked ham; oak-smoked trout; sweet chilli salmon; and chicken breast

Prices: Main course from €10.95. House wine from €19.
Food Served: 9.00-17.00.
Closed: 25, 26 December.
Cuisine: Traditional and modern Irish.
Other Points: Garden. Children welcome. Car park. Historic working mill.
Directions: Turn off the N11 at Rathnew and follow the signs to Avoca.

with sesame. Mouth-watering desserts include home-baked scones with butter and preserves, and strawberry meringue roulade. The picturesque village is the fictional home of the BBC's popular "Ballykissangel."

A MAN FOR ALL SEASONS

Evan Doyle is all about seasonality. Committed to organic and wild food he has cut a swathe through preconceptions about what food is about. Charlotte Coleman-Smith meets a man with a very important message.

'This is no passing whim, it's a commitment for life,' says Evan Doyle. In 1992, the head chef of the Strawberry Tree restaurant, then in Killarney, decided to cook exclusively with organic or wild food.

For the past fourteen years he has kept doggedly to this promise, and it's a stance which has won him many admirers.

The Strawberry Tree is now the flagship restaurant of BrookLodge, a hotel and spa in the heart of the Wicklow countryside - complete with village pub, shops and farmers' market - which Evan founded with his brothers, Eoin and Brendan in 1999.

The Lodge is a one-stop rural idyll, a chance to recharge the batteries by way of excellent food, a great night's sleep and a pint of microbrewed beer over the Sunday papers. With the help of German chef Norman Luedke, Evan is still pushing the boundaries in his quest to source a totally organic menu, 365 days a year. 'We got our organic licence two years ago', he explains, 'So now, everything you eat here, from the bread on the table to the sugar with your coffee is organic. And if it's wild - I have a penchant for wild leaves and herbs - then we say so.'

This takes meticulous planning and it's extremely seasonal - so, no year-round lamb, no asparagus in January. And there is still work to do. 'I imported 30% of our food last year,' says Doyle. 'The onus is now on the government to develop this country as a grower of organic food - after all, we're supposed to be the 'green island'!' ■

Blessington Co Wicklow

Grangecon Café
Daytime café, restaurant and foodshop

Kilbride Road, Blessington,
Co Wicklow
Tel.+353(0)45 857892
Email. grangeconcafe@eircom.net

Jenny and Richard Street opened this lovely little daytime café five years ago. Hidden away in a sleepy village among verdant countryside, close to the N81, it's a gem of a place with a firm commitment to all things organic, homemade and local. Specialist produce is on show all around, with farmhouse cheeses, homecooked hams and lunch dishes in a display cabinet. The owners admit to keeping things simple to keep down costs, but customers - including those who come to stock up on Grangecon's excellent ready-meals - are the richer. Aside from delicious homemade soup, there are sandwiches, meltingly good quiches, sausage rolls made from organic pork, salads - baked St Tola cheese with roasted red pepper, mixed leaves and toasted pine nuts - and shepherd's pie. On the sweet side, there are freshly baked apple pies and brownies, with Illy coffee,

Prices: Lunch main course from €7.50.
Food served: 9.00-16.00 Mon.
9.00-17.30 Tues-Sat.
Closed: Sundays. 25 Dec - 1 Jan.
Cuisine: Simple.
Other Points: Children welcome. Dogs welcome.
Directions: Left at the Downshire House Hotel in Blessington, the café is three doors down on the left.

Crinnaughton apple juice and ginger beer to round things off.

Bray Co Wicklow

Barracuda Steak & Seafood Restaurant
Coastal restaurant

Strand Road, Bray, Co Wicklow
Tel. +353 (0) 1 276 5686
Email. barracuda@eircom.net
www.barracuda.ie

This light, airy restaurant is situated above the national aquarium, with a great view over Bray seafront through its floor-to-ceiling windows. The large dining area is divided up into smaller sections, and the relaxed atmosphere makes it ideal for a weekend lunch or brunch. The menu brings familiar, well-loved dishes, such as seafood chowder, Caesar salad and crab cakes, all of which are well produced and presented. For brunch, there are a range of eggy options including Eggs Benedict and Eggs St Charles - smoked cod with poached egg and béarnaise sauce. Dinner - last orders are at 11pm - includes fillet, rib-eye and sirloin steaks, Dover sole meunière and specials such as Barracuda garlic chicken. There are also some substantial soups for an informal lunch, and after-

Prices: Lunch 2 courses €16.95
Dinner main course from €16.95-€29.
House wine from €18.95.
Food Served: 12.00-15.00 &
17.00-23.00 Mon-Fri. 12.00-17.00 &
18.00-23.00 Sat-Sun.
Closed: Good Friday, 25, 26 Dec.
Cuisine: Steak and seafood.
Other Points: Children welcome.
Directions: From Dublin on N11. Take exit for Bray. Turn left at Royal Hotel, go over train tracks. Take a right at seafront, restaurant on the left.

noon tea, served until 6. All wines on the wide-ranging list are available by the glass. On the ground floor, there's a laid back lounge area with soft seating.

Enniskerry Co Wicklow

Powerscourt Terrace Café
Daytime café and shop

Powerscourt House and Gardens,
Enniskerry, Co Wicklow
Tel. +353(0)1 2046066
Email: info@avoca.ie
www.avoca.ie

Powerscourt House and Gardens is situated 12 miles south of Dublin and is one of the world's great Italianate gardens, stretching over 47 acres. The Powerscourt Terrace Café, owned by the Pratt family of Avoca Handweavers, is located in the 18th century Palladian house overlooking the estate's gardens and fountains with breathtaking views to Sugarloaf Moutain. The bright, airy eatery is self-service and extends to a large outdoor eating area that buzzes in good weather. The menu changes daily and might include beef and Guinness stew, Lakeshore pork, Spanish meatballs and chicken and broccoli crumble, as well as a selection of quiches, and wine in quarter, half and full bottles. An extensive range of homemade desserts bring raspberry tart, apple pie, strawberry roulade, chocolate fudge cake and deli-

Prices: Main course from €10.95
House wine from €15.
Food served: 10.00-17.00. Sunday until 17.30.
Closed: 25, 26 December.
Cuisine: Traditional and modern Irish.
Other Points: Children welcome. Outdoor terrace. Car park. Private dining.
Directions: 2 miles from Enniskerry Village.

cious scones - perfect for tea after a walk round the gardens or a browse through the wonderful Avoca shop for gifts, clothes and deli produce.

Kilmacanogue Co Wicklow

Avoca Terrace Café
Daytime cafe, shop and garden centre

Kilmacanogue, Bray, Co Wicklow
Tel. +353(0)1 2867466
Email.info@avoca.ie
www.avoca.ie

Situated in 11 acres of gardens in the old Jameson (of whiskey fame) estate, just 30 minutes from Dublin at the gateway to scenic Wicklow county, this Avoca shop, like all the others in the enterprise, combines great shopping with delicious, country-style eating. As in all the stores, this one sells its own range of clothing for men, women and children; throws, scarves and hand-knit designer sweaters; toys; accessories; pottery and books. It also has a garden centre. The foodhall's specialty food offerings include deluxe flavoured olive oils and vinegars, fancy chocolates, and Mongetto pasta sauces. The attractive self-service terrace café with outdoor seating has a strong wholefoods, salads and international orientation. Typical tasty dishes include freshly baked breads, carrot and coriander soup, home-cooked ham with a selection of salads, roasted Mediterranean vegetables,

Prices: Main course from €11.45.
House wine from €15.
Food served: 9.30-17.30 Mon-Fri.
10.00-17.30 Sat-Sun.
Closed: 25, 26 December.
Cuisine: Traditional and modern Irish
Other Points: Garden and outdoor terrace. Children welcome. Car park. Craft shop. Highly Commended - Café of the Year 2003. Winner - Café of the Year 2004.
Directions: On the N11 signposted before Kilmacanogue village.

Mexican chilli beef, and assorted quiches and pizzas. Save room for the strawberry and fresh cream roulade, cheesecake, and chocolate cakes.

Macreddin Village Co Wicklow

The BrookLodge Hotel & Wells Spa
Country house hotel, spa, organic restaurant and pub

Macreddin Village, Co Wicklow
Tel. +353(0)402 36444
Email. info@brooklodge.com
www.brooklodge.com

An hour from Dublin and nestled in the Wicklow hills, this peaceful and welcoming country house hotel, owned by three brothers Eoin, Evan and Bernard Doyle, is situated 3km outside Aughrim. Surrounded by well-groomed lawns, the hotel has its own chapel as well as a bakery, pub, brewery, shop and stables. The bedrooms, suites and open spaces are luxurious and comfortable, with fresh flowers and open fires adding to the "switch off" factor! If you did need more encouragement to leave the rat race behind, you can step into 'The Wells Spa' for some professional pampering or treatments, or you can just spend some alone time in their indoor to outdoor pool, gym or outdoor hot tub! The hotel's main restaurant 'The Strawberry Tree' is the only certified Organic restaurant in Ireland. You can enjoy delights such as marinated wild haddock with roast fennel, wholegrain mustard crusted rack of lamb, rosemary jus or for a less formal approach you can opt for 'The Orchard' where you can get open organic focaccia pizza, crab and hake crumble or just simply an organic potato and leek soup

Rooms: 64 ensuite. Double from €180-€260. Junior Suite from €240-€320.
Prices: Set Sunday lunch €40. Set dinner from €60. Bar snack from €10. House wine from €25.
Opening Hours: Bar: 12.30-23.30 Mon-Thur. 12.30-00.30 Fri & Sat. 12.30-23.30 Sun.
Cuisine: Modern Irish organic.
Other Points: Garden. Children welcome. Dogs welcome. Car park. Equestrian centre and stables. Leisure centre and spa.
Directions: In Aughrim, you will see a church on your right hand side of the road, follow the road to the right by the church, continue straight to the "T" juntion at the top of the road, take a right and continue for approximately 1.5 miles. The hotel is on the left hand side after the bridge.

with homemade bread. Gold River Farm nearby grows over 7 acres of organic vegetables just for the hotel.

Local Farmers' Markets

Athy Farmers Market & Craft Fair
Every Sunday from 13 February.
Birr, The Full Moon Market
Every third Saturday
Blessington Market
Saturdays 2.30pm - 4.30pm
BrookLodge Market, Macreddin Village
First & third Sunday.
Castle Bellingham Market
First Sunday of month 11am - 6pm.
Naas Market *Saturdays 10am - 3pm*
Tullamore county Fair *Saturdays 9am - 4pm.*

Brewing
MAGIC

To some it is beer, to others it is the greatest drink on earth. As microbreweries come of age in Ireland Charlotte Coleman-Smith tracks down pints with a difference.

Next time you stumble into your local and ask for a pint of 'the usual', think again. In pubs around Ireland, there are an increasing number of intriguing new beers at the bar, made by dedicated craftspeople who care about creating ales with a distinct character and flavour. Their mission is to challenge our drinking habits and provide an alternative to the 'coloured, alcoholic water' some of them believe we're far too happy to knock back.

The story of microbrewing is not a new one. For centuries, every town in Ireland had its own brewery - in late eighteenth-century Dublin alone, there were a dozen along the river Liffey. At the turn of the twentieth century came the multinationals, and with them a monopoly over the beer industry which forced out smaller producers, curtailing choice and spreading bland uniformity. In the UK, a groundswell of protest culminated in the 1970s with the foundation of the Campaign for Real Ale (CAMRA); there are now thousands of microbreweries throughout the country. In the US microbrewing activity peaked in the 1980s and continues at a steady pace. In Ireland, microbreweries were slower to set up stall - perhaps because the average pint was carefully controlled by giants such as Guinness, and standards were

reasonable, even if choice was next to nil.

The Porterhouse - a pioneering enterprise and perhaps the best known brewpub in Ireland - opened in Bray in 1989, with a second premises following in Temple Bar seven years later. But it was not until the mid-nineties that the new wave of microbreweries really gathered momentum. It's not hard to see why this was a long time coming. The ethos of the microbrewery - to use local, natural ingredients and traditional methods - is a commitment which requires passion, dedication and expert knowledge from the publican since the yeast they contain is still alive. Overheads are high, the process is time-consuming, but rewards can be rich.

'There's a human element now in the making of beer', says Brendan Burke, manager of the Biddy Early Brewery in Ennis, County Clare, established ten years ago by Dr Peadar Garvey. 'Not every batch works, but that's part of the experience.' Visitors see this process in action and are naturally more curious about sampling the small range of beers, which include a stout, a lager, a sweet Irish ale and a cask-conditioned ale. No wonder, when natural ingredients such as wild bog myrtle and Carrigeen moss - a fining agent, picked from the seashore close by - are involved. When brewmaster Niall Garvey developed Black Biddy, it was the first new stout in Ireland to emerge in over 200 years, a considerable achievement in the history of beermaking. Recently, the Brewery opened up a restaurant, serving dishes with beery twists - fish in a beer batter made from Blonde Biddy, for example, or a wintry, Black Biddy beef stew.

The fact that food is now mentioned in the same breath as beer is a new challenge for the microbrewer. The Kinsale Brewing Company, known for its distinct, easy-drinking lager, is developing beers specifically to complement food. 'We're taking inspiration from 'champagne beers, which come in tall bottles and are made for serving and pouring with a meal,' says Cathal Kiely, who founded the brewery in 1997 with his uncle and father. 'Our wheat beers will use coriander and orange peel - perfect with seafood, which of course we have in abundance here'.

Innovation draws, inevitably, from tradition. The O'Haras of the Carlow Brewing Company - founded in 1996 - were keenly aware of this when they created their award-winning beers. 'The Barrow valley was once a major hop- and malt-growing area', says Kay O'Hara. 'So our location and its history is a major part of our identity.'
The landscape is still littered with old malthouses, many since converted into trendy apartments. Recipes are new, but share characteristics, and names, with beers once enjoyed by ancient Celts. Hence, Curim Gold Celtic Beer draws its name from a Celtic wheat beer and Molings Traditional Red Ale, from a seventh-century local saint.

Despite keen local interest in speciality beers, there are still remarkably few microbreweries in Ireland. Those that exist find a large proportion of their interest comes from the American market, and many beers are crafted specifically for this purpose. But vital support also comes from closer to home. Twice a year, the Franciscan Well Brew Pub (see page 126) in Cork city organises hugely popular beerfestivals in its beer garden - the largest in Cork, according to Russell Garet, director of business operations. These festivals, apart from being huge fun, create important opportunities for networking in a niche market where contact with customers and others in the brewing fraternity is crucial. As Garet points out, 'It's really important for us to foster the spirit of innovation. Unlike industrial breweries, there's no economy of scale - we don't take shortcuts. And, of course, quality is paramount.' ■

Carlow Brewing Company

Key Events

Comedy Kilkenny Cat Laughs	Kilkenny June 1 - 5	
Music International Festival of Light Opera	Waterford Sept 17 - Oct 2	
Arts Clonmel Junction Festival	Clonmel July 1 - 9	
Arts Kilkenny Arts Festival	Kilkenny Aug 12 - 21	
Opera Blackstairs Opera Festival	Enniscorthy July 7 & 8	
Opera Wexford Festival Opera	Wexford Oct 20 - Nov 6	

South East

Carlow Town Co Carlow

Barrowville Townhouse
Period guesthouse

Kilkenny Road, Carlow Town
Tel. +353(0)59 9143324
Email. barrowvilletownhouse@eircom.net
www.barrowvillehouse.com

This Georgian gem, set amid beautiful walled gardens, is just a 3-minute walk from Carlow town centre, and a good base for touring the 17th century Altamount House and Gardens, Browns Hill Dolmen, Carlow Castle, Bagenalstown, the Barrow River Valley and Kilkenny. Several excellent golf courses are also nearby. Its 7 comfortable ensuite bedrooms boast large, wide period windows; a mix of antique and modern fitted furnishings and paintings; soft, warm colour schemes, and well-appointed bathrooms. An elegantly proportioned drawing room, with its grand piano, comfortable seating, open fire, and abundance of interesting books, provides a lovely spot for relaxation. Owners Randal and Marie Dempsey have run their fine guesthouse for 16 years, during which they've become known for their hospitality.

Rooms: 7 ensuite. Double from €95-€100. Single from €50-€60. Triple from €125-€130. Discount for stays of 3 nights or more.
Other Points: Non-smoking house. Garden. Car park.
Directions: From travelling south on the N9, 300 metres from the town centre at the traffic lights on the right. Travelling north, 50 metres before the first set of traffic lights on the left.

Marie's luscious breakfasts, laid out buffet-style in an elegant vine-clad conservatory overlooking semi-formal gardens, include smoked salmon, local cheeses, lamb's liver or kidney, as well as homemade scones, breads and preserves.

Leighlinbridge Co Carlow ★

Lord Bagenal Inn
Waterside hotel and restaurant

Leighlinbridge, Co Carlow
Tel. + 353(0)59 9721668
Email. info@lordbagenal.com
www.lordbagenal.com

Situated on the banks of the River Barrow, four miles from Carlow town, this hotel has been owned and run by James Kehoe and his family for twenty-six years. It makes good use of its watery location with its own private marina. Pass through a flower-decked courtyard into a large, low-ceilinged bar with wooden beams and open fires, and sup a pint of O'Hara's stout - one of a selection from a local micro-brewery. The wine list is impressive, with a good balance of new and old world classics. The restaurant, a well-lit space hung with James's private art collection, offers a creative menu, rooted in traditional favourites: signature crispy coated bacon ribs with chunky sweet and sour sauce, for example, followed by roast cod with mussels and leeks in a saffron cream, and chocolate marquise. A children's menu and popular carvery lunch offer good value. The 12 ensuite bedrooms are smart and spacious.

Rooms: 12 ensuite. Double from €125. Single from €87.50. Family room - rates on request.
Prices: Lunch main course from €8.75. Sunday hot buffet lunch from €10.50. Dinner main course from €22. Bar menu from €7.95. House wine from €18.
Food Served: 12.00-22.00 Mon-Thurs. 12.00-22.30 Fri & Sat. 12.00-21.00 Sun.
Closed: 25 Dec.
Cuisine: Modern Irish.
Other Points: Children's play area. Private marina. Car park. Winner - Pub Wine List of the Year 2003.
Directions: Just off the main N9 Dublin/Waterford road in Leighlinbridge.

KILKENNY HIBERNIAN HOTEL

Kilkenny City Co Kilkenny

Kilkenny Hibernian Hotel
City centre hotel & restaurant

1 Ormonde Street, Kilkenny,
Tel. +353(0)56 7771888
Email. info@kilkennyhibernianhotel.com
www.kilkennyhibernianhotel.com

This converted Victorian bank in the shadow of Kilkenny castle is a buzzing focal point in this sociable city. It combines vibrant bars and cosy snugs with an atmospheric restaurant, 46 comfortable bedrooms and many original features. The smartly decorated bedrooms, including penthouses with jacuzzi baths, are all en-suite, with carved mahogany headboards and top-drawer soaps and shampoos. The Hibernian Bar with its leather sofas and wooden floors serves a 'Modern Irish' menu throughout the day, while the more upbeat Morrisons is a lively place for a nightcap. The Jacob's Cottage restaurant is an elegant, subtly-lit dining room, serving a range of contemporary dishes using fresh Irish produce. Starters could include slow-roasted pork belly with savoy cabbage, bacon and apple compote, followed by pan-fried hake with bok choi, harissa and basil butter, or roast rack of Wicklow lamb. The wine list has a good selection from France and the New World.

Rooms: 46 ensuite. Double from €100. Single from €80.
Prices: Lunch main course from €10.95. Set Sunday lunch €22.50. Dinner main course from €15.25. Bar snack from €7.95. House wine from €19.75
Food served: Bar:12.00-20.00 Sun-Thurs. 12.00-17.00 Fri-Sat. Restaurant: 12.30-14.30 & 18.30-22.00 Mon-Sat. 12.30-15.00 & 18.30-21.00 Sun.
Closed: Christmas Eve night & Christmas Day.
Cuisine: Modern Irish.
Other Points: Children welcome. Secure public car park adjacent to hotel.
Directions: From N10 travel to Waterford road roundabout on ring road, take exit to city centre. Hotel is located on corner of Patrick St. and Ormonde St.

Local Farmers' Markets

Cahir Market *Saturdays 9am - 1pm*
Carlow, Potato Market *Saturdays 9am-2pm*
Dungarvan Market *Thursdays from 9.30am - 2pm*
Enniscorthy Market *Saturdays 9am - 2pm*
Kilkenny Market *First and third Sunday of every month*
Waterford Market *Saturdays 10am - 4pm.*
Wexford Market *Fridays from 9am - 2pm*

Kilkenny City   Co Kilkenny   ★ ★

Lacken House & Restaurant
Victorian house and restaurant

Dublin Road, Kilkenny
Tel. +353(0)56 7761085
Email. info@lackenhouse.ie
www.lackenhouse.ie

Trevor Toner and Jackie Kennedy Toner are now in their fifth year at this established period house and restaurant. Situated on the edge of Kilkenny, Lacken House - an attractive, ochre-coloured Victorian dower house - is a relaxing place to stay, with 12 uniformly comfortable and quiet bedrooms and a superb dining room. Local and seasonal produce are top priorities on a sophisticated menu of modern Irish and European dishes. Starters might include Lacken wild nettle and fish soup with fried crab claws and toasted croûte; while dishes such as pan-fried south-east skate wing with mini capers, or roast cushion of French veal with lemon hazelnut and garlic butter are elegant main courses. Desserts bring sumptuous treats such as homebaked chocolate cake, or pineapple sorbet with a tasting of foie gras, white truffle foam, apple and rosemary sauce. The wine list is comprehensive and affordably priced, with an extensive range of dessert wines.

Rooms: 10 ensuite. Double from €150. Single from €75. Family from €75 pps (based on 3 sharing). DB&B from €109 pps.
Prices: Main course dinner from €23.50. House wine from €21.
Food served: 18.30-21.30 Tue.-Sat. 18.00-21.00 Sundays of bank holiday weekends.
Closed: 24-27 December.
Cuisine: Modern Irish, European.
Other Points: Non-smoking house. Children welcome. Car park. Private dining room. Highly Commended - Guesthouse with Restaurant of the Year 2003. Winner - Host of the Year 2005.
Directions: In Kilkenny city on the main Carlow to Dublin road (N10).

Kilkenny City   Co Kilkenny

Marble City Bar
Contemporary city centre pub

66 High Street, Kilkenny
Tel. +353(0)56 7761143

Eamon Langton's successful bar in the heart of Kilkenny is hard to miss with its eye-catching, stained-glass window of undulating red and white stripes. This is the most stylish joint in which to enjoy your morning rashers. Come at 10am, though, for the MCB full Irish breakfast, and you may end up staying all day. International hotshot designer, David Collins, has created a striking, low-lit space with brown leather seating opposite a long bar, widening at the rear to accommodate tables. The lack of daylight gives the sense of a cosy microclimate where one could chat, eat and drink all day long. Rub shoulders with a mix of sharply dressed locals and tourists, and enjoy a pint, a hot chocolate or a café latte. Lunch brings bistro-style dishes such as smoked haddock risotto cakes and confit of

Prices: Main course from €8.50. Dinner main course from €10. Bar snack from €4.50. House wine from €20.
Food served: 10.00-20.30 daily.
Closed: Good Friday and 25 Dec.
Cuisine: Modern Irish.
Directions: On the main shopping street, after the Town Hall, 150 metres on the same side.

pork sausages with creamy potatoes and red wine gravy. Service is sleek and attentive.

Cashel Co Tipperary

Hill House
Georgian bed and breakfast

Palmers Hill, Cashel, Co Tipperary
Tel. +353(0)62 61277
Email. hillhouse1@eircom.net
www.hillhousecashel.com

From every room of this historic and comfortable Georgian home, which dates back to 1710, you have spectacular views of the timeless Rock of Cashel. Overlooking the town of Cashel on Palmers Hill, you are in walking distance to the many bars, shops, restaurants, as well as museums and medieval abbeys. This luxurious B&B, which is owned and run by Carmel Purcell, has been extensively refurbished and lovingly restored to its former glory. Genuine Georgian antiques and heirlooms, combined with high ceilings and open fires not to mention a fine array of old books, have a calming and welcoming effect for the weary traveller. There are five ensuite bedrooms, all spacious and unique, painted with bold and vibrant Georgian colours. You can expect a warm and friendly welcome at Hill House and of course a hearty home cooked breakfast which will set you

Rooms: 5 ensuite. Double from €100. Single from €60. Family from €150.
Other Points: Bedrooms non-smoking. Children welcome over 10 years old. Garden. Car park.
Directions: Located just 10 minutes from the town centre.

on your way should you feel the urge to play golf, go hiking in the mountains or forests nearby or maybe its fishing that takes your fancy. Whatever it is, Hill House will make your visit to Cashel a memorable one.

The Symbols

 Accommodation
✕ Restaurant
● Café
🍺 Pub/Bar
◉ Daytime opening only
🥩 Deli
🍷 Wine
🥐 Bakery
🍶 Gourmet/Farm Shop
🎿 Leisure Centre/Spa
CS Craft Shop
VC Visitor Centre

Les Routiers Awards

⭐ 2002 Award Winner
⭐ 2003 Award Winner
⭐ 2004 Award Winner
⭐ 2005 Award Winner

Cashel   Co Tipperary   ⬦ ✕ ☊ ⬤ CS

Horse & Jockey Inn
Hotel and restaurant

Near Cashel, Co Tipperary
Tel. +353(0)504 44192
Email. horseandjockeyinn@eircom.net
www.horseandjockeyinn.com

Tom Egan's famous inn at the heart of
Ireland's horse country has been trading
continuously for over 250 years and is a
popular meeting spot for jockeys, trainers
and anyone involved in this cherished
industry. The interior is spacious and
welcoming, and the plentiful racing
memorabilia contributes to the elegantly
sporting atmosphere. The menu reflects
the earthy roots of the establishment; a
Sunday lunch of prime roast sirloin of beef
and Yorkshire pudding followed by sherry
trifle will please traditionalists, but there
are also appealing chicken, fish and vegetarian options. Elsewhere, classics such
as Irish oak smoked salmon salad, duck a
l'orange and grilled lamb cutlets provide
further robust sustenance. There's a good
range of hot sandwiches, including Hot
Joint of the Day, and grilled Cashel Blue
and ham on homemade soda bread with
cranberry preserve. The thirty comfortable,
contemporary bedrooms are individually

Rooms: 30 ensuite. Double from
€160. Single from €85. Family from
€170.
Prices: Set Sunday lunch €25. Lunch
main course from €9.50. Dinner main
course from €13.90-€23.80. Bar snack
from €7.50. House wine from €16.
Food Served: Daily in bar 10.30-
22.00. Lunch last orders 15.30 Mon-
Sat. 14.30 Sun. Dinner last orders 21.30
Mon-Sat. 20.30 Sun.
Closed: 25 December.
Cuisine: Traditional Irish & European.
Other Points: Garden. Children
welcome. Car park. Gift shop.
Directions: Midway between Cork
and Dublin on the N8. Five miles north
of Cashel.

furnished and some have disabled access.

Clonmel   Co Tipperary   ✦ ✕ ☊ ◉

Angela's Restaurant
Town centre restaurant & coffee shop

14 Abbey Street, Clonmel, Co Tipperary
Tel. +353(0)52 26899

Angela Ryan, former chef to the Australian
ambassador to Ireland, now runs this small,
daytime restaurant and café in the centre
of Clonmel, opposite the Franciscan friary.
Arched windows and doors are painted a
smart shade of blue and a matching canopy
shelters a couple of pavement tables where
business lunchers and shoppers can watch
the world go by. The interior is simple, with
kitchen tables and chairs and a blackboard
announcing the day's specials. The Sicilian
chef brings Mediterranean flair to a varied
menu which starts with breakfast, and
includes fresh asparagus panzarotti with
tomato, basil and parmesan; and bruschette
with Cooleeny cheese. Homemade roasted
onion and potato soup, and Hungarian beef
goulash are tempting options for a rainy
day. Delicious sandwiches - ploughmans,
Italiano, BLT - can be ordered on a range of

Prices: Lunch main course from €8.50
House wine €7.90 (half bottle).
Food Served: 9.00-17.30 Tue-Sat.
Closed: Sunday, Monday. Good Friday,
Christmas and New Year.
Cuisine: Eclectic with Italian
influences.
Directions: Opposite Friary church
close to the river Suir.

breads including oatbran and linseed and
crusty white. A good choice of salads is
based around seasonal organic produce.

Ballymacarbry Co Waterford

Glasha Farmhouse
Farmhouse accommodation

Glasha, Ballymacarbry, Via Clonmel,
Co Waterford
Tel.+ 353(0)52 36108
Email.glasha@eircom.net
www.glashafarmhouse.com

Olive and Paddy O'Gorman have run this
attractive guesthouse, on a working dairy
farm, since 1995, although the place has
been in the family for several generations.
The nineteenth-century farmhouse has
been sensitively modernised, and has a
lovely landscaped garden of rose beds
and water features. The O'Gormans are
excellent hosts, and Olive's homecooking is
a real treat. Magnificent breakfasts include
scrambled eggs wrapped in smoked salmon
and garnished with fresh flowers; pancakes
with bacon and maple syrup; farmhouse
cheeses; fresh berries and homebaked apple
and raisin muffins. There are tea-and-coffee
making facilities in the spacious bedrooms,
little chocolates to nibble by the bedside
and jacuzzi baths in some rooms. The views
of the surrounding mountains are stunning.
A typical five-course dinner might bring

Rooms: 8 ensuite. Double from €100.
Single from €60. Family from €120.
Prices: Set dinner €25-€35 (residents
only).
Food Served: Last orders 19.30-20.00
Mon-Sat.
Closed: 1 Dec - 28 Dec.
Cuisine: Modern Irish.
Other Points: Large garden and patio
area. Car park. Children welcome over
12 years old. Winner - Bed & Breakfast
of the Year 2005.
Directions: Glasha is situated off the
R671 between Clonmel and Dungarvan.
There are three signs for Glasha on
the R671.

black and white pudding on a bed of apple
coulis, homemade soup, poached monkfish
in a creamy red pepper sauce and warm
lemon pudding.

Ballymacarbry Co Waterford

Hanora's Cottage
Country guesthouse and restaurant

Nire Valley, Ballymacarbry,
Co Waterford
Tel. +353(0)52 36134/36442
Email. hanorascottage@eircom.net
www.hanorascottage.com

Hanora's Cottage started life in 1891 as a
tiny two-roomed stone house beside the
river in the lovely Nire valley. Now a ten-
roomed guesthouse and restaurant, its' been
in the same family ever since. Mary Wall,
her son, Eoin, and daughter-in-law, Judith,
run a successful operation and their focus
remains excellent homecooking, a warm
country house welcome, and the provision
of peace and tranquillity for visitors to this
breathtaking region, known for its magnificent walks. To this end, all rooms have
jacuzzi baths, while superior rooms have
double tubs. Eoin, and Judith, also a superb
cook, are committed to using local produce.
Sumptuous breakfasts include freshly
baked breads, Irish cheeses and poached
fruits. A typical dinner could feature rack
of spring lamb with wild mint hollandaise,

Rooms: 10 ensuite. Double from €150-
€250. Single from €85.
Prices: Dinner main course from €24.
House wine from €17.
Food Served: Last orders for dinner
21.15 Mon-Sat.
Closed: Christmas week.
Cuisine: Modern Irish.
Other Points: Non-smoking house.
Children welcome over 10 years old.
Garden. Car park.
Directions: From N25 follow
signpost for R672, Hanora's Cottage is
signposted off R672.

followed by fresh lemon tart with crème
anglaise. The wine list is adventurous, and
carefully sourced.

The Belfry Hotel, Waterford

Barça, Lismore

Cheekpoint Co Waterford

McAlpins Suir Inn
Waterside seafood restaurant and bar

Cheekpoint, Co Waterford
Tel. +353(0)51 382220/182
Email. frances@mcalpins.com
www.mcalpins.com

Dunstan and Mary McAlpin's charming harbour-front inn, in the quiet fishing village of Cheekpoint, just seven miles from Waterford, has been a pub for close to 300 years. Owned by the same family since 1971, it's now well known for its excellent, simply prepared seafood and the nostalgic, pared-down atmosphere created by its low ceilings, wooden tables and country-style plates. Locals and guests from much further afield crowd the pub at peak times to try specialities such as seafood pie, King scallops in cheese and white wine, crab baked in fennel sauce and generous platters heaped with the freshest seafood. Curried chicken breast, vegetarian bake and pan-fried beef fillet balance the predominantly fishy menu, and there are homemade desserts for those with hearty appetites. Wild salmon is from the river Suir, and there's a small wine list, which leans towards fish-

Prices: Dinner main course from €10.95. House wine from €16.
Food served: 17.30-21.45 Tue-Sat.
Cuisine: Seafood and meat dishes.
Other Points: Children welcome over six years old. Winner - Dining Pub of the Year 2003.
Directions: From Waterford city follow the signposts to Dunmore East passing the hospital. Continue for two miles until you reach the Passage East turn off; follow signs for Cheekpoint. Continue straight down to the harbour and McAlpin's is on the left hand side facing the river.

friendly whites. No reservations are taken, but the fine food justifies any wait.

Dungarvan Co Waterford

Powersfield House
Country guesthouse

Ballinamuck, Co Waterford
Tel. +353 (0)58 45594
Email. powersfieldhouse@cablesurf.com
www.powersfield.com

With its gracious, Georgian-style lines, lovely mature gardens, on-site cookery school, and location just outside Dungarvan in one of the prettiest and most golfer-friendly areas of West Waterford, Eunice Power's delightful, five-year-old guesthouse boasts many of the comforts of a much grander establishment. Its warm, inviting lounge is antiques-furnished and decorated in restful beige and gold, while each of the 6 light-filled bedrooms are individually decorated in tasteful colours with fresh floral arrangements. Smart bathrooms feature fluffy towels, spacious showers (some have baths), and a tempting basket of toiletry "goodies." Don't miss Eunice's delectable breakfasts and dinners, which might include Greek yogurt with granola, bananas and Cappagh Runny Honey; local Helvic smoked salmon with scrambled eggs; mussels and monkfish in a Thai broth

Rooms: 6 ensuite, Double from €110. Single from €60. Family from €120.
Prices: Set dinner from €28-€38.
Food served: Dinner by arrangement for residents.
Closed: Christmas to mid-Jan.
Cuisine: Contemporary Irish food, focusing on local organically grown ingredients.
Other Points: Non-smoking bedrooms. Garden. Children welcome. Car park.
Directions: Take the main Killarney road R672 from Dungarvan, second turn left, first house on the right

with wild rice; and hot chocolate pudding with vanilla ice cream. Powersfield House offers a great escape at excellent value.

Dungarvan Co Waterford ✕ ᵀ

The Tannery Restaurant
Coastal restaurant

10 Quay Street, Dungarvan,
Co Waterford
Tel. +353(0)58 45420
Email. tannery@cablesurf.com
www.tannery.ie

Situated on the quayside in a former grain store, latterly a leather factory, Paul and Maire Flynn's restaurant is a successful blend of traditional and contemporary styles, with rusted iron beams and wood floors merging with unfussy table settings, clean lines and muted colours. Paul and his team produce inspirational food: this is one of those places where dishes really are as uplifting as you hope they will be when you pore over the carefully sourced menu, where the only frustration is that you must make a choice. Dinner might begin with asparagus and brioche pie with truffle scented egg, tomato and avocado salad followed by roast rump of lamb with mild garlic cream, piquillo peppers and cocobeans, and crispy cannelloni of rhubarb fool. One of Ireland's best.

Prices: Lunch main course from €12.50. Set Sunday lunch €27. Dinner main course from €24. House wine from €19.50.
Food served: Lunch 12.30-14.15 Tue-Fri. Sunday lunch 12.30-14.30. Dinner 18.30-21.30 Tue-Sat. 18.30-21.00 Sunday evenings peak season and bank holidays.
Closed: End Jan/beginning Feb.
Cuisine: Modern Irish.
Other Points: Private dining room.
Directions: Located end of Main Street beside Old Market House building.

Dunmore East Co Waterford ✕ ᵀ ★

The Strand Inn
Seaside restaurant

Dunmore East, Co Waterford
Tel.+353(0)51 383174
Email. strandin@iol.ie
www.thestrandinn.com

This attractive 16th-century inn, right on the beach overlooking Hook Lighthouse, has been owned by Edwina and Mike Foyle for over 35 years. Once a notorious haunt for smugglers, it's now known for its fine seafood, much of which is landed at the harbour opposite. In summer, guests can enjoy the inviting outdoor patio, surely one of the most idyllic settings for a glass of chilled white wine and an expertly cooked catch of the day - be sure to book in high season. The daily changing menu might bring potato cakes stuffed with smoked salmon, with a cucumber salsa, followed by fresh scallops tossed in butter in a white wine, ginger and cream sauce. Meat dishes include roast Dromcollogher duck served with orange sauce, or roast pork fillets stuffed with a garlic salami farcie with cider and apple sauce. The global wine list is reasonably priced, and there are daily vegetarian specials.

Prices: Main course from €12.95. House wine from €16.
Hours: 12.30-14.15 (until 16.00 Wed-Sat). 18.30-22.00. Restaurant closed January and Tuesday & Wednesday November to March.
Cuisine: Modern/French
Other Points: Children welcome over ten years old. Car park. Joint winner - Dining Pub of the Year 2002.
Directions: From Waterford follow directions to Dunmore East. As you enter the village the inn is on the left after the garage.

Grannagh Castle Via Waterford

The Thatch
Country pub

Grannagh Castle, Kilmacow,
via Waterford, Co Waterford
Tel. +353(0)51 872876

David Ryan's small, thatched pub is scenically situated opposite the seventeenth-cen-
tury Grannagh Castle, on the banks of the
river Suir, just two miles from Waterford
City. Inside, it's a cosy spot, offering
traditional music once a week, live music
at weekends and decent pub food, prepared
fresh every day using Irish produce. A
blackboard lists daily specials, and homemade starters might include paté of the day
with melba toast and Cumberland sauce,
or soup with freshly baked brown bread.
There's a choice of steaks, including prime
Irish sirloin, and red meat is the theme of
the Thatch Mixed Grill, a generous plate
of bacon, egg, sausage, tomato, black and
white pudding, steak and potato cake;
smaller appetites can take on the Mini
Grill. Fish of the day comes with Thatch
salad and baked potato, and there's a range
of sandwiches and paninis, including a
vegetarian special of roast pepper, sun-dried

Prices: Lunch main course from €9.
Bar snack from €3.50. Dinner main
course from €11.50. House wine from
€16.
Opening hours: 10.30-23.30 Mon-Thur,
00.30 Fri & Sat, 23.00 Sun.
Food served: Morning coffee 10.30-
12.30. Lunch 12.30-15.00. Bar menu
15.00-21.00.
Closed: Good Friday, 25 December.
Cuisine: Modern & Traditional Irish.
Other Points: Car park. Beer garden.
Directions: Located two miles from
Waterford City on the Limerick road op-
posite the river Suir and Grannagh Castle.

tomato, Cashel Blue, pesto and mayo, with
many familiar dishes such as soup of the
day, omelettes, salads and open sandwiches
also available.

Lismore Co Waterford ★

Barça
Wine bar and restaurant

Main Street, Lismore, Co Waterford
Tel. +353(0)58 53810
Email. barcawine@eircom.net

Ciara and Jane Gormley's Spanish tapas
bar and restaurant offers great atmosphere
with its bare floorboards, white panelling,
plain wooden tables, profusion of paintings,
and cosy bar with high leather barstools.
Choose from a group of bite-sized tapas
(appetisers) at €3.50 each - anchovies
Andalusia, meatballs in tomato sauce,
mixed roast peppers crostini, duck rillettes
on toasted croûtons, chorizo croquettes over
caramelised onions - with a glass of chilled
Hidalgo fino sherry, or a bottle of good
red wine. The dinner menu overlaps the
tapas selection; you could order a tapas as a
starter, followed by chef Stephane Tricot's
simple but tasty free-range chicken breast
with a fricassee of carrots, courgettes, and
potatoes, or rib-eye steak with a Merlot
and shallot sauce. Desserts include mille-
feuilles with mixed berries over a bourbon
vanilla custard crème. A well-chosen wine
list, showcasing both French, Spanish and
New World selections, includes a good

Prices: Lunch main course from €6.50.
Bar snack from €3.50. Dinner main
course from €16. House wine from €19.
Opening hours: 11.00-late Tue-Sat.
12.00-22.00 Sun.
Food served: 12.30-14.30 & 18.00-
22.00 Tue-Sat. Sunday Brunch 12.30-
16.00. Tapas 16.00-20.00.
Closed: January. Generally closed Mon
but subject to seasonal changes. Please
check in advance.
Cuisine: Tapas and continental.
Other Points: Garden. Winner -
Special Award 2005.
Directions: Barça is on the main street
in Lismore, which is on the N72
Waterford to Killarney road.

choice of cavas, ports and sherries.

Waterford City Co Waterford

Arlington Lodge
Georgian hotel and restaurant

John's Hill, Waterford
Tel. +353(0)51 878584
Email. info@arlingtonlodge.com
www.arlingtonlodge.com

Maurice Keller is Arlington Lodge, his presence and his greeting transcends this elegant country house with its antique furniture and Georgian architecture into a home. Located in historic Waterford city, near the Crystal factory, it offers tranquillity and charm. Purchased from the Catholic Church in 1997, following three years of extensive refurbishment, Maurice and his team opened for business in 2001. Each of the 20 bedrooms have queen-sized or king-size beds, and some have four poster beds and fireplaces. All are individually decorated with antiques, paintings and lush draperies in soft warm colours. The elegant Robert Paul restaurant features crisp white linens, silver candelabra and fresh flowers. The chef's modern specialties include roast rack of Comeragh lamb, home-smoked Guinea fowl, pan-seared fillet of herb-crusted hake, and home made bread and butter pudding. The wine list, which is comprehensive also, reflects Maurice's passion and interest in wines. A bar menu of soups, sandwiches, salads, steaks and desserts is available in the cosy William Morris bar. Breakfast at Arlington is an experience, fresh fruit, fresh breads and croissants, fruit compôtes, homemade jams adorn the buffet and from the kitchen offerings such as Waterford Blaa, a locally produced bun, toasted with a poached egg on each side finished with

Rooms: 20 ensuite. Double from €150. Single from €110.
Prices: Dinner main course from €24.50. Set Sunday lunch from €24.50. Bar snack from €4.50. House wine from €19.
Food served: Restaurant 19.00-21.00 Mon-Sat. Bar 12.00-20.00 daily.
Closed: 25-27 Dec.
Cuisine: Modern Irish. Seafood and steak specialities.
Other Points: 5 mins. walk from city centre. Garden. Car park. Winner - Award for Excellence 2002.
Directions: Go over bridge in Waterford, turn left down the quay. At third set of traffic lights from the Tower Hotel turn left. Continue to next set of lights, go straight through up John's Hill for approx. half a mile, Arlington Lodge is on the right. From Cork, straight through roundabout just after Waterford Crystal, take a right turn at the second set of lights straight up to John's Hill.

melted Cheddar cheese, full Irish breakfast are but a few of the treats available. A perfect way to start the day.

Nearest Racecourses

Clonmel Racecourse *Tel. +353 (0)52 22611*

Gowran Park Racecourse
Co Kilkenny. Tel. +353 (0)56 7726225

Tramore Racecourse
Co Waterford. Tel. +353 (0)51 381425

Wexford Racecourse
Tel. +353 (0)53 42307

Arlington Lodge, Waterford

Waterford City Co Waterford   ✗ ✗

Fitzpatrick's Restaurant
City centre restaurant

Manor Court Lodge, Cork Road,
Waterford
Tel. +353(0)51 378851
Email. fitzrestaurant@iol.ie

Billy Fitzpatrick is the chef and co-owner of this fine dining restaurant. Inside the low, white and grey stone building, the decor is warm and bright, with intimate lighting, soft yellow walls, wooden floors and modern, sculptural plants. Billy has an impressive resumé, which includes a stint at Michelin-starred Chewton Glen in the UK. His menu, though influenced by the French-oriented cooking of may top European restaurants, retains an individual style with a wide choice of dishes across the Early Bird, Sunday lunch and à la carte menus. Elegant starters might bring Paella stuffed mussels with saffron soup, while main courses include chargrilled ribeye of beef with pancetta potatoes, chive & pink peppercorn butter or supreme of chicken with a lasagne of provencal vegetables and a trio of sauces. Stylish desserts include Crème brûlée with almond tuiles and

Prices: Dinner main course from €16.50. House wine from €19.
Food served: 12.00-15.00 & 17.00-21.00 Sun. 17.00-22.00 Tue-Sat.
Closed: Mondays, Good Friday, 24-25 December.
Cuisine: Modern Irish with international influences.
Other Points: Garden. Children welcome. Car park.
Directions: On the Tramore/Cork road (N25) in Waterford city.

vanilla cream or chocolate marquise gateau with a caramel sauce. The wine list includes some well-priced house bottles.

Waterford City Co Waterford   ✗ ◆ ✗ ◉ CS VC

Gatchell's Restaurant at Waterford Crystal
Daytime café and restaurant

Kilbarry, Waterford
Tel. 051 332575
Email.visitorreception@waterford.ie
www.waterfordvisitorcentre.com

Nicky O'Brien's restaurant, inside the sleek, modern Waterford Crystal visitors' centre, is named after Johnathan Gatchell, the original owner of Waterford Glasshouse in the 1800s. It serves traditional Irish food to the steady stream of guests who tour the bustling factory next door. The large, airy space is impressively contemporary in feel, and illuminated by natural light pouring through floor-to-ceiling windows. Everything is made on the premises and sourced locally where possible; vegetables come from a farm in Annestown, fish from Kilmore Quay and daily fresh Waterford 'Blas' from a nearby bakery. The concise menu brings soups such as Irish potato or turnip and bacon, while main courses include glazed loin of bacon with mustard mashed potato, cabbage and parsley sauce, Irish stew, and beef, Guinness and orange

Prices: Lunch main course from €9.75. House Wine from €5.
Food served: 8.30-17.30 daily from 18 Mar to 31 Oct. 9.00-16.30 daily from 1 Nov-16 March. Breakfast and afternoon tea served.
Closed: Christmas & St Patrick's Day.
Cuisine: Modern Irish.
Other Points: Children welcome, Car park.
Directions: Gatchell's Restaurant is located inside Waterford Crystal Visitor Centre, close to WIT on the main Cork Road (N25)

casserole. There's a fish option of salmon and prawn fishcake, and desserts such as Chocolate and Baileys roulade and rhubarb and orange crumble.

Waterford City Co Waterford ✗ ♈

Restaurant Chez K's
City centre restaurant

20-21 William Street, Waterford
Tel. +353 ()51 844180
Email. info@chez-ks.com
www.chez-ks.com

Niall and Maria Edmondson have created a relaxing, ambient space for their contemporary Irish restaurant. The attractive dining room, complete with piano, is popular among locals and guests from further afield, including the occasional celebrity. Diners can peruse the menu in the bar, or from comfy sofas in the reception area. Chef Shane Curtin uses only the freshest local seafood and all pastries, breads and desserts are homemade. Dinner might bring starters of home-smoked duck with herb-crusted lentil bake and cassis jus; or seared scallops with crushed garden peas, Serrano ham and citrus beurre blanc sauce. Eclectic main courses include lime-marinated breast of chicken with wild mushrooms and leeks, smoked bacon and parmesan cream, or tempura of monkfish with spiced pear and pineapple chutney. Steaks from the grill are served with wholegrain mustard mash. To

Prices: Dinner main course from €16. House wine from €20. Early Bird Menu available.
Food served: 17.30-22.00 Mon-Sat. 16.00-21.00 Sun.
Closed: Middle 2 weeks of January.
Cuisine: Contemporary Irish, French and European flavours.
Other Points: Children welcome. Pianist every Saturday night.
Directions: Turn left at Tower Hotel to Dunmore East. The restaurant is located 400 yards on the left.

finish, there's crème brûlée of the day, or an exquisitely comforting apple and rhubarb crumble.

Nearest Golf Courses

Carlow Golf Club *Tel. +353 (0)59 9131695*
Clonmel Golf Club *Tel. +353 (0)52 24050*
Kilkenny Golf Club *Tel. +353 (0)56 776 5400*
Mt. Juliet Estate Golf Club
Co Kilkenny. Tel. +353 (0)56 777 3000
Rosslare Golf Club *Co Wexford. Tel. +353 (0)53 32203*
Waterford Golf Club *Tel. +353 (0)51 876748*
West Waterford Golf Club *Tel. +353 (0)58 43216*

Waterford City Co Waterford

The Belfry Hotel
City centre hotel

Conduit Lane, Waterford
Tel. + 353(0)51 844800
Email. info@belfryhotel.ie
www.belfryhotel.ie

This comfortable, modern hotel in the centre of Waterford is owned and managed by the Reid family. It stands on the former grounds of Blackfriars Abbey, hence its name, and the smart cream and black exterior blends sympathetically with the surrounds. Inside, the hotel is decorated in low-key contemporary style, with 49 spacious ensuite bedrooms fully equipped with all mod-cons including internet access, satellite tv, large beds and bright, modern bathrooms. The Chapter House bar, with its stylish pillars of exposed brick, is a congenial place to meet for a drink; it also serves a tempting lunch and menu of dependable favourites. There's seafood chowder or the hotel's homemade soup, and a good range of toasted sandwiches and panninis. More robust dishes include joint of the day, bangers and mash and fisherman's pie, as well as homemade lasagne. There are hard-to-resist desserts such as warm orange and chocolate chip bread and butter pudding.

Rooms: 49 ensuite. Double from €100. Single from €75. Family room - rates on request.

Prices: Lunch main course from €8.50. Dinner main course from €14.95. Bar snack from €4.50. House wine from €16.50.

Hours: Bar 10.30-23.30. 10.30-00.30 Fri-Sat. 11.30-23.00 Sun.

Food served: Bar food 12.00-21.00 Sun-Thur. 12.00-19.00 Fri-Sat. Restaurant 18.30-21.30 Fri-Sat.

Closed: 24-30th December.

Cuisine: Modern Irish.

Other Points: Children welcome.

Directions: Follow the N25 along the quay, the hotel is located in Conduit Lane which is almost directly opposite the clock tower on the quay.

Ballycross Apple Farm
Near Wexford Town.
Tel. 053 35160

Wexford Festival Opera
The annual Wexford Festival Opera is one of the jewels in the crown of Ireland's arts programme. It runs for eighteen days during the last two weeks of October and the first week of November. Telephone 053 22144

Walking Tours
Walking Tours Kilkenny:
Tynan Tours. Tel. 087 265 1745.
Walking Tours Waterford City:
Jack Burtchaell. Tel 051 873711.

Hanora's Cottage, Ballymacarbry

Lismore Castle Gardens and Art Gallery | *Place to visit*

Lismore, Co Waterford
Tel. +353 (0)58 54061
Fax. +353 (0)58 54896
Email. administrator@lismorecastlearts.ie
www.lismorecastle.ie
www.lismorecastlearts.ie

Prince John first built a castle in Lismore in 1185, although much of the current building dates from the 17th and 19th centuries. Within the walls of the castle, the gardens at Lismore provide spectacular views, and a remarkable yew walk where Edward Spenser is said to have written the 'Faerie Queen'. While wandering the gardens, visitors are invited to enjoy several pieces of contemporary sculpture, and the West Wing of the Castle has been developed as a gallery for contemporary art (open at selected times). Lismore Castle is the Irish home of the Duke of Devonshire and his family, and may be rented fully staffed to guests.

Other Points
Tourist Information Office. Craft and Souvenir Shop.

Hours
15 Apr - 01 Oct: 13.45 - 16.45
Jun, Jul & Aug 11.00 - 16.45 (11.00 - 18.00 during exhibition period).

Admission Charged

Directions
Located on the outskirts of Lismore Town, within 2 minutes walking distance of the Main Street. Garden & Gallery entrance is through the Castle Riding House. Lismore is situated on the N72, main route from Rosslare to Killarney via Waterford.

Lismore Heritage Centre | *Place to visit*

Lismore, Co Waterford
Tel. 00 353 (0)58 54975/54855
Fax. 00 353 (0)58 53009
Email. lismoreheritage@eircom.net
www.discoverlismore.com

Situated in the centre of the town, is a must for those who wish to experience the rich history of the town and its surroundings. Your host Brother Declan (alias Niall Toibin) will take you on a fascinating journey through time in "The Lismore Experience" - an exciting multi lingual audio-visual presentation, which tells the story of the town since St. Carthages arrival in 636AD. Also exhibition galleries on Monastic, Norman and Medieval Lismore including a history of Lismore Castle and a science exhibition room on the life and works of Robert Boyle, "the Father of Modern Chemistry" who was born at Lismore Castle. Guided tours of this monastic town leave the Heritage Centre at appointed times each day.

Other Points
Tourist Information Office. Craft and Souvenir Shop.

Hours
All year: Mon - Fri 9.30 - 17.30
Apr-Sept: Sat 10.00 - 17.30
Sun 12.00 - 17.30

Admission Charged

Directions
Located in the centre of Lismore directly across the road from both Lismore Hotel and the Millennium Park. Lismore is situated on the N72, main route from Rosslare to Killarney via Waterford

Waterford Crystal | *Place to visit*

Kilbarry, Waterford City, Co Waterford
Tel. +353(0)51 332500
Fax. +353(0)51 332716
Email. visitorreception@waterford.ie
www.waterfordvisitorcentre.com

Waterford City is the home of Waterford Crystal manufacturing plant and Visitor Centre, nestling on the South East coast of Ireland, The Visitor Centre has become one of the most popular tourist venues in the country, and its manufacturing plant gives visitors an opportunity to see first hand how Waterford Crystal is crafted, from molten crystal to the finished masterpiece.

The factory tour begins with a 'Living with Waterford' presentation, a short pre-view of Waterford's manufacturing and its products. The video presentation will have given you some idea of what to expect, but nothing compares with the atmosphere of the furnace room; the noise, the air, the heat and the activity. You will see red-hot molten crystal take shape, in a miracle of light, heat and skill. Watch carefully as our craftspeople transform glowing balls of crystal into elegant bowls & vases.

Your guide will then take you through our World Sports Dept. where a selection of our current most prized trophies are on display. There are many opportunities on this tour to have your photography taken, please remember to bring your camera.

As you move to the cutting area, the atmosphere changes from the roar of furnaces to the whirr of diamond-tipped cutting wheels. It's an exciting sound which becomes all the more fascinating when you see the steady hand of our Master cutters. At the end of your factory tour, it's time to step back in time to meet our Master craftsmen in person and see them exercise their skills close up. The Workshop has been specially created to provide a relaxed atmosphere for our visitors to meet these Masters.

The Waterford Crystal Gallery is home to the world's largest display of Waterford Crystal, beautifully displayed in a bright, elegant showroom. In addition, you can see displays of Wedgwood, John Rocha at Waterford Crystal and Marquis by Waterford Crystal. The Gallery also includes a Craft and Jewellery Gift Store. We look forward to welcoming you to Waterford Crystal.

Other Points
Guided Tours, Craft & Jewellery Store, Restaurant and Car & Coach Parking. For group reservations please contact reception.

Hours
Visitor Centre Retail
Jan to Feb: daily 9.00 - 17.00
Mar to Oct: daily 8.30 - 18.00
Nov to Dec: daily 9.00 - 17.00
Factory Tours
Jan to Feb: Mon - Fri 9.00 - 15.15
Mar to Oct: daily 8.30 - 16.15
Nov to Dec: Mon - Fri 9.00 - 15.15

Admission Charged

Directions
Our visitor centre is approximately a five-minute drive from Waterford City on the N25 to Cork.

Arthurstown Co Wexford

Marsh Mere Lodge
Waterside bed and breakfast

Arthurstown, New Ross, Co Wexford
Tel. +353(0)51 389186
Email. stay@marshmerelodge.com
www. www.marshmerelodge.com

Maria McNamara's elegant and tastefully decorated bed and breakfast is made all the more special by the warmth of her welcome. Overlooking King's Bay and the Hook Head lighthouse, it's in a superb setting, and breathtaking sea views can be enjoyed from the pretty, flower-filled terrace in summer, or before a roaring fire from the cosy gallery sitting room in winter. The sitting room is filled with antiques, Persian rugs and attractive oil paintings and is the perfect place to take stock or plan excursions around this scenic area. Exceptionally comfortable bedrooms are all individually designed, and take their names from the pictures and portraits displayed in them; thus, for example, there's the 'romantic' Countess Howe room, or the

Rooms: 4 ensuite. Double from €80. Single from €40. Family from €90.
Other Points: Bedrooms non-smoking. Garden. Children welcome. Dogs welcome. Car park.
Directions: From Wexford take R733 to Arthurstown Via Wellingtonbridge From Waterford take Passage East Car Ferry to Ballyhack (Wexford). Turn right for 1km we are the 1st house on the left.

'tranquil' Poor Poet's room. Tiled bathrooms have fluffy towels and good quality toiletries.

Duncannon Co Wexford

Sqigl Restaurant
Seaside restaurant

Quay Road, Duncannon, New Ross, Co Wexford
Tel. +353(0)51 389188
Email. sqiglrestaurant@eircom.net

Cindy Roche's contemporary restaurant is housed in an old building with historical links to the town's military fort. Head chef Denise Bradley is committed to sourcing local produce, and seafood is fresh off the boat. The modern Irish menu could start with warm fish terrine with lobster sauce and a mango red pepper salsa, or chicken satay with summer leaves, sauté potatoes, pine nuts and parmesan shavings. Main courses bring fillet of Irish beef with spring onion champ, or spice-crusted fillet of monkfish with saffron couscous. The value menu includes a short selection of well-priced wines, and two organic bottles feature on an interesting global list.

Prices: Dinner main course from €18.50. House wine from €15.50.
Food served: From 19.00-21.00 Tue-Sat.
Closed: Good Friday. 24-26 December. Closed for 6 weeks from 3 January.
Cuisine: Modern Irish & Seafood.
Other points: Al fresco dining on balcony weather permitting.
Directions: From Wexford take the R733 (22 miles). From New Ross take the R733 (14 miles).

Gorey Co Wexford

Poole's Porterhouse
Town centre pub and restaurant

78 Main Street, Gorey, Co Wexford
Tel. +353(0)55 21271
www.pooles.ie

Eric Poole is head chef and owner of this
atmospheric pub and restaurant in the
centre of Gorey. The welcoming interior
has been recently refurbished and the
theme is tastefully nostalgic, with Victorian
memorabilia, cast-iron signs, antique books
and so on. The menu, served in the bar and
restaurant, offers a good range of snacks,
sandwiches and salads, as well as some
delicious homemade desserts and freshly
baked bread. Other, more substantial offerings might include pan-fried Kilmore Quay
crab claws in a garlic and chive cream
sauce, followed by supreme of chicken
with herb stuffing on boxty potato cake
with parsnip crisps, or pan-fried fresh water
prawns in provençal sauce. Seafood is
freshly caught, and all other produce locally
sourced, where possible - with the exception, perhaps, of the chargrilled kangaroo
steak. Live traditional music takes place
twice weekly in the main lounge, with a DJ

Prices: Lunch main course from €10.
Dinner main course from €12.50-€22.
House wine from €18.
Opening hours: 11.00-23.30 Mon-Thur.
11.00-00.30 Fri-Sat. 12.30-23.00 Sun.
Food served: Throughout the day.
Lunch last orders 14.30 Mon-Sat and
15.00 Sun. Dinner last orders 21.00
Sun-Thur and 21.30 Fri & Sat.
Closed: Good Friday & 25 Dec.
Cuisine: Contemporary Irish.
Other Points: Children welcome over
4 years old.
Directions: Take the N11 to Gorey
town. The pub is located mid-way on
the main street.

and cocktails in the large cellar bar.

New Ross Co Wexford

Kennedy's Bar & Martha's Vineyard Restaurant
Town centre pub and restaurant

5 South Quay, New Ross, Co Wexford
Tel. +353(0)51 425188
Email. kennedysbar@eircom.net
www.kennedyspub.com

This landmark bar, opened in 2002 by local
businessmen Barry Kent, honours the most
famous Irish-American in history, John F.
Kennedy. President Kennedy's people came
from this area, and it's said that the grand-
father of the Kennedy clan drank his last
pint of Guinness here before leaving New
Ross for America. The interior is old-world with a twist,
while the restaurant style is American beach
house in tones of sand and muted blue.
The bar menu is fairly traditional - you'll
find chowder, Thai fishcakes, nachos and
omelettes. More unusual is a low-calorie
selection of wraps, salads and chicken
dishes, including chicken fillet burger.
Things become rather more modern in the
popular upstairs Martha's Vineyard restaurant. Choose from Japanese-style chicken
skewers, vegetarian samosas, or warm

Prices: Lunch main course from €8.50.
Dinner main course from €13. Bar snack
from €8.50. House wine from €12.
Food served: Bar: 12.00-15.00 & 17.00-
20.00 daily. Restaurant: 18.30-21.00
Fri & Sat. 12.30-15.00 Sunday lunch.
Closed: Good Friday.
Cuisine: Contemporary Irish.
Other Points: Children welcome until
19.30.
Directions: Follow all signs to
Dunbrody Famine Ship, the bar is
directly across the road.

balsamic chicken and nectarine salad. Main
courses include a vegetarian pasta with
fresh oregano, cherry tomatoes, mushroom
and basil cream.

Rosslare Co Wexford ⚓ ✕ 🍷 🅿 🕸 ★ ★

Kelly's Resort Hotel & Spa
Resort hotel and spa

Rosslare, Co Wexford
Tel. +353(0)53 32114
Email. kellyhot@iol.ie
www.kellys.ie

The standards just keep rising at this unique, fourth-generation family-owned resort, situated along five miles of safe sandy beach in Ireland's "sunny southeast." Families return year after year for facilities that include two indoor swimming pools, tennis, a Canadian hot tub, sauna and steam rooms, as well as a sparkling new 14,000-square-foot SeaSpa featuring aqua aerobics, personal training and an enticing range of pampering body treatments. Kelly's 116 bedrooms are tasteful and comfortable; many have sea views and/or balconies. Other amenities include numerous attractive public rooms, a supervised crèche and gallery lounge. At Beaches restaurant, head chef Jim Aherne's opulently traditional specialties include oak-smoked Wexford trout Raifort; grilled wild Atlantic salmon with fennel and mousseline sauce, and passion fruit cheesecake. The more casual La Marine, under head chef Eugene Callaghan, offers a mix of European and fusion dishes, with luscious desserts including a coconut snowball with marinated pineapple. The splendid wine list is meticulously sourced.

Rooms: 116 ensuite. Double from €150. Single from €85. Family room - rates on request.
Prices: Set lunch €25. Set dinner €42. Lunch main course from €13. Dinner main course from €19. Bar snack from €6. House wine from €20.
Hours: Bar 11.00-23.30. 11.00-00.30 Fri-Sat. 12.00-23.00 Sun.
Food served: Restaurant 13.00-14.00 & 19.30-21.00 daily.
Bar food 12.00-17.00. 12.00-16.00 Sun.
Cuisine: Irish, French and Italian.
Closed: 11 Dec-17 Feb.
Other Points: SeaSpa-thermal spa, holistic treatment and pure relaxation. Health and fitness programmes - a range of indoor and outdoor pursuits. Children welcome. Tennis courts. Car park. Garden. Winner-Hotel of the Year 2003. Winner - Wine List of the Year 2005.
Directions: Follow the N25 from Rosslare Europort (5 miles) turning off at the sign for Rosslare Strand. The hotel is located in the centre of the holiday resort.

Kelly's Resort Hotel & Spa

Wexford Town Co Wexford ✗ ✦ ▼ ✦ ◉ ★

La Dolce Vita
Daytime Italian café, restaurant, deli and wine bar

6/7 Trimmers Lane, Wexford
Tel. +353(0)53 70806
Email. bigpons@eircom.net

This colourful Italian restaurant, tucked away on a pretty, tree-lined side street in the centre of Wexford, is as authentic a slice of Italy as you'll find anywhere. Ligurian-born Roberto Pons and his wife, Celine, have created an atmospheric space simple and clean, with a tiled floor and light wooden furniture offsetting the shelves of oils, pasta, chocolates, and the cold displays of salamis, mortadellas, parmesans and homemade tiramisus. Outside, smart red-and-green canopies and tables and chairs make an inviting first impression. Roberto's menu, and the interesting wine list, reflects the huge diversity of food in his country, with several dishes from his native region, including gnocchi Verdi al burro e salvia (spinach and ricotta gnocchi with butter and sage) and troffie con scampi e zucchini (pasta with prawns and courgettes). Freshly

Prices: Main course from €8.50. House wine from €13.
Food served: 9.00-17.30 Mon.-Sat. Hot food 12.00-16.00
Closed: Sundays. Closed Christmas for 4 days.
Cuisine: Italian.
Other Points: Children welcome. Winner - Café Restaurant of the Year 2005.
Directions: Located off Main Street, facing ruin of Selskar Abbey.

baked Italian bread is served with olive oil. Do save room for traditional desserts including panna cotta and orange and lemon tart.

Wexford Town Co Wexford ✗ ✦ ▼ ✦ ◉ CS ★

Westgate Design
Daytime restaurant, café and shop

22a North Main Street, Wexford
Tel. +353(0)53 23787
Email. darronjordan@yahoo.com

This craft shop and restaurant on Wexford's main shopping street is run by the Jordan family. The split-level, ground floor dining area is self-service, offering homemade scones, breads, cakes and pastries, and 20 freshly made salads each day. Specials, such as goats' cheese and apple tart, roast stuffed pork steak and battered hake, are chalked up on a blackboard. In addition, there are homebaked quiches and Mediterranean tarts, baked potatoes with various fillings and homemade soups. There's a good selection of sandwiches and paninis, and Irish breakfast is served all day. For the sweet tooth, there are fabulous homemade desserts, including chocolate fudge cake, lemon cheesecake and summer fruit tart, and healthy fruit smoothies, made to order. The atmosphere is relaxed - although

Prices: Main course from €8.50. House wine from €12.
Food served: 9.00-18.00 Mon.-Sat.
Closed: Sundays. 25, 26 December.
Cuisine: Traditional Irish.
Other Points: Children welcome. Commended - Café of the Year 2003.
Directions: On the Main Street in Wexford town.

lunchtimes can be busy - and the interior light, bright and airy. The craft shop, which you enter at street level, sells an interesting range of designer pottery, furniture, jewellery and much more.

DINNER IS SERVED.

With greyhound stadia in Cork, Clonmel, Dublin (Shelbourne Park and Harold's Cross), Dundalk, Enniscorthy, Galway, Kilkenny, Lifford, Limerick, Longford, Mullingar, Newbridge, Thurles, Tralee, Waterford and Youghal... you're never too far from great food and a great night at the dogs!

The thrill, the excitement and the rush of adrenaline will leave you breathless. The restaurants, bars and atmosphere will, on the other hand, leave you speechless.

For restaurant reservations LoCall **1850 525 575**. Visit www.igb.ie for further information.

THE DOGS - ALWAYS TOP FORM

Irish Greyhound Board
Bord na gCon

Announcing the **$1,000,000 WORLD GREYHOUND CHAMPIONSHIP** in Cork's Curraheen Park Greyhound Stadium in Summer 2006 - the first race ever of it's kind, featuring greyhounds from Australia, UK, USA and Ireland. Visit www.igb.ie further details.

HISTORIC DELIGHTS

Irish stew, Dublin coddle, and bread and butter pudding have gone the way of analogue watches, vinyl LPs, and

manual typewriters. Elizabeth Field checks out some Les Routiers members for traditional Irish fare.

Elizabeth Field is a freelance writer specialising in food

But for those who seek traditional Irish fare, characterised by humble ingredients prepared carefully and respectfully, there are vestiges of an old Irish food culture in various eateries around the country.

In Cork city, Kay Harte's Farmgate Café, located above the 200-year-old English Market, offers an array of regional and historical dishes - all prepared from ingredients sold in the colourful, sprawling ground-floor food emporium. Kay's finnan haddie features the West Cork Smokehouse's freshly smoked, dye-free Atlantic haddock, which she poaches in milk with thyme and onions and serves with "skin and all" jacket potatoes, a Cork specialty.

Kay also offers a delicious corned mutton that "older people might recognise from years ago." Her English Market butcher salts the meat for 4 to 5 days, after which Kay stews it in a large pot with onions, carrots, celery and water, and serves it with caper sauce and the ubiquitous jacket potatoes. Traditionalists will also enjoy her stewed tripe with onions, milk and drisheen (a regional blood pudding); Irish stew; as well as homemade bread and butter pudding, rhubarb compôte with fresh strawberries, and seasonal fruit tarts.

Ray, a somewhat stringy but tasty white flatfish beloved by Dubliners, shares top billing with sweet, flaky cod, among other fish available in the "chipper" department of the venerable McDonagh's Seafood House in Galway town. Start your meal, perhaps, with a half dozen sea-fresh, briny Clarenbridge oysters on the half shell, served au naturel of course. "A pint of Guinness (from the pub next door) would be handy," says proprietor P. J.McDonagh.

Peter Chessman's delightful cooking at the Rathmullan House in Rathmullan, Co Donegal, revolves around fresh, local and seasonal ingredients. His noisette of Rathmullan lamb with a goat's cheese and spinach tartlet is to die for, as is his freshly caught Lough Swilly black sole, simply grilled whole on-the-bone. Monaghan quail is given an exotic Asian twist by tea-smoking it and serving it with a spicy-sweet chorizo and mango salsa.

The popular Kitchen & Foodhall in Portlaoise is the place to go for old-fashioned Irish baked goods and desserts. Jim Tynan makes a traditional brown scone with white flour, bran, and kibbled wheat, while his white soda bread is made exclusively from fresh buttermilk, flour and soda - "no commercial compounds." His piece de resistance, however, is his

½ doz. oyster €10 – 1 doz. €18

Irish Lamb Stew €10⁵⁰

Lamb's Liver & Bacon €10⁵⁰

Tripe & onions – with drisheen option €8⁵⁰

Shepherd's Pie €10⁵⁰
served with vegetables or salad

Farmgate Café, Cork

bread-and-butter pudding, whose mousse-like lightness comes from using a minimum amount of bread. "It's just 4 slices of white bread, fresh cream, local eggs, sugar and butter," says Jim. Tea bracks, rhubarb-apple crumbles, whiskey fruit cakes and Christmas puddings and cakes are also home-made.

Top-flight Dublin restaurateurs Ross Lewis, Martin Corbett and their new chef, Garrett Byrne, of Chapter One, are known for their impeccable ingredients, straightforward cooking style, and abundant hospitality. Updated Irish classic dishes include West Cork ham with celeriac and mustard; loin of lamb with slow-cooked shoulder; and pig trotter boudin with red wine and raisin jus. Don't miss their exceptional range of Irish cheeses, and, for a special treat, their divine Irish coffee, prepared tableside.

Tempting homely old-fashioned sweets are well-represented at the Avoca Handweavers Restaurant and craft shop in Kilmacanogue, Co. Wicklow, just outside Dublin. Spectacular apple and blueberry crumbles, raspberry tarts, lemon cheesecakes, frangipane almond-strawberry cakes, passion-fruit tarts, chocolate and orange cake and buttered scones present the eater with a difficult choice. A homemade roulade, a.k.a. pavlova, features a flat meringue base rolled with copious amounts of whipped cream, strawberries, raspberries, blueberries and blackberries. It's probably the best pavlova in Ireland, if not on Earth. ▪

Key Events

Festival St Patrick's Day Festivals	Throughout Region March 13 - 17	
Festival Puck Fair	Killorglin Aug 10 - 12	
Food Bantry Mussel Fair	Bantry May 1 - 31	
Jazz Guinness Cork Jazz Festival	Cork Oct 27 - 30	
Film Cork Film Festival	Cork Mid Oct	

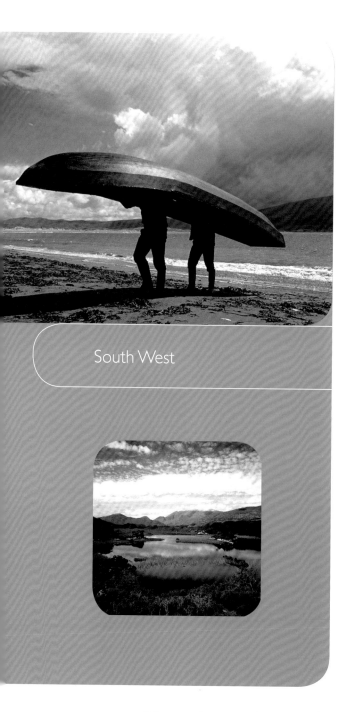

South West

Bantry Co Cork

O'Connor's Seafood Restaurant
Seafood restaurant and bar

The Square, Bantry, Co Cork
Tel. +353(0)27 50221
Email.oconnorseafood@eircom.net
www.oconnorseafood.com

West Cork boasts some of Ireland's finest scenery: sparkling bays, pastoral fields and charming villages. In Bantry town don't miss the friendly, unpretentious, and consistently value-wise O'Connor's. After over 30 years in the O'Connor family, the business was taken over by Peter and Anne O'Brien in 2003, and they have maintained standards. The nautical-themed restaurant has a lobster and fish tank near the entrance, a cosy bar and comfortable booths. All fish and seafood is local. Try the house specialty - mussels - prepared 3 ways: grilled in the half-shell with garlic butter and breadcrumbs; mariniere with wine and cream; or steamed in Murphy's stout. You can splurge on a lobster; and non-seafood specialties include Irish sirloin steak, roast loin lamb, and roast Skeaghanore duck breast. The Early Bird menu served between 6 - 7 p.m.

Prices: Lunch main course from €10. Dinner main course from €19. House Wine from €18.50.
Food Served: 12.15-15.00 daily, 18.00-22.00 Mon-Sat. 18.00-21.00 Sun from May to November.
Closed: Sundays & Monday evenings November to April.
Cuisine: Traditional/Modern Irish/ Seafood Specialities
Other Points: Children welcome before 20.00.
Directions: On the square in Bantry across from the fountain, beside Bantry Bay Hotel.

is a great value, and the reasonably priced wine list offers a global selection.

Blarney Co Cork

  ★★

Blairs Inn
Country pub and restaurant

Cloghroe, Blarney, Co Cork
Tel. +353(0)21 4381470
Email. jblair@blairsinn.ie
www.blairsinn.ie

This family-run, flower-decked pub, sits in a tranquil riverside setting, only five minutes from Blarney castle. John and Anne Blair have established a deserved reputation for their warm hospitality and fine food. Anne, together with chef Raphael Delage, cooks up a stylish menu based around the finest ingredients, including seafood from Kenmare and local farm produce. An interior of low ceilings and wooden furniture is the rustic setting for lunch and dinner, in the appropriately named Snug, or the Pantry. For lunch, there might be warm tartlet of organic goat's cheese, smoked salmon and leek, followed by roast stuffed loin of pork with cider and apple sauce and, among a dozen desserts, fresh meringues with cream and wild berry ice cream. In the evening, a bar menu of substantial choices, including Irish stew, offers good value, while a pricier carte brings sophisticated dishes such as

Prices: Lunch main course from €11.75. Dinner main course from €18.95. Bar snack (evening menu) from €11.25. House wine from €19.95.
Food served: 12.30-15.30 & 18.30-21.30 daily.
Closed: Good Friday and 25 Dec.
Cuisine: Modern and traditional Irish.
Other Points: Children welcome until 19.30. Garden. Car park. Joint Winner - Dining Pub of the Year 2002. Winner - Pub Host of the Year 2003.
Directions: Five minutes from Blarney on the R579.

baked lemon sole stuffed with crab, with a white butter sauce.

Blarney Co Cork

Maranatha Country House
Period bed and breakfast

Tower, Blarney, Co Cork
Tel. +353(0)21 4385102
Email.douglasvenn@eircom.net
www.maranathacountryhouse.com

Douglas and Olwen Venn's delightful Victorian house, situated up a long driveway lined with mature trees, shrubs, and manicured lawns, is a warm, welcoming, antiques-filled oasis full of many surprises. Its six en-suite bedrooms, overlooking the gardens, are quite spectacular: enormous, lavish confections done out around large and ornate beds, with flamboyant, painted wardrobes, and yards and yards of draperies, cushions upon cushions upon cushions. Bathrooms are on the large side with good-quality towels. The Royal Suite, featuring a king-size, four-poster bed, and its own circular jacuzzi, is perfect for romantic couples. Breakfast is served in the bright new, flower-filled conservatory, with trellises and floral-patterned tablecloths, accented by crisp pink napkins. There are abundant local activities, from visits to the Blarney Castle, shopping at the famous Blarney Woollen Mills, to fishing,

Rooms: 6 ensuite. Double from €68-€120. Family room from €78 + children half price.
Closed: Dec-Feb
Other Points: Non smoking bedrooms. Garden. Children welcome. Car park.
Directions: Approximately 3 km from Blarney, on the R617 heading towards Tower and Killarney, look for yellow & white cottage with white picket fence. Our sign is beside this on the right hand side, drive up the hill to Maranatha.

walking, swimming and golfing at one of several 18-hole courses.

Clonakilty Co Cork

An Sugán
Town centre pub and restaurant

41 Wolfe Tone Street, Clonakilty, Co Cork
Tel. +353(0)23 33498
Email.ansugan4@eircom.net
www.ansugan.com

The O'Crowley family have been serving up freshly cooked seafood at this landmark pub for over 20 years. The eyecatching pink building, with its traditional shop front, stands on a prominent corner site at the centre of Cork's black pudding capital, Clonakilty. Appropriately enough, redblooded starters such as a terrine of Clonakilty puddings and chicken liver paté share centre stage with fishy dishes such as smoked salmon and crab parcels and the house seafood chowder. Surf and turf main courses include salmon-stuffed chicken breast and the seafood salad brings together a generous list of fresh local fish and shellfish. The cosy bar, with its whitewashed walls, red carpet and exposed beams, has plenty of relaxed seating and an open fire; there's also a kitchen-style dining room with a spruce tiled floor and pine tables

Prices: Lunch main course from €9.50. Dinner main course from €12.90 Bar Snack from €6.90. House Wine from €18.
Opening Hours: 12.30-23.30 Mon-Sat, 12.30-23.00 Sun.
Food Served: 12.30-21.30 daily.
Closed: Good Friday, 25,26 Dec.
Cuisine: Seafood
Other Points: Children Welcome, Garden.
Directions: On entering the town from Cork, go straight through roundabout to the centre of town and An Sugan is on your left.

and chairs - the perfect place to tuck into homely classics such as apple pie and sticky toffee pudding.

Clonakilty Co Cork

Gleesons
Town centre restaurant

3 Connolly street, Clonakilty, Co Cork
Tel. +353(0)23 21834
Email. gleesonsrestaurant@eircom.net
www.gleesons.ie

Robert and Alex Gleeson are the husband-and-wife team behind this excellent town centre restaurant. The aubergine facade with its pretty windowboxes and potted bay trees makes for an elegant welcome; inside, the decor is plain but stylish, with dark wood tables and slate place mats, cream walls, and chairs upholstered in contrasting purple stripes. Robert, formerly a chef at London's Dorchester hotel, produces a creative menu of bistro classics-with-a-twist, using the freshest local ingredients. Tomato and Parmesan tart with warm shorescape smoked haddock, or coconut and lemon risotto cakes with grilled squid and lime and coriander dressing are typically inventive starters. Elsewhere, there's baked fillet of beef with turmeric herb crust and a port wine sauce and, to finish, ricotta and chocolate tart with peach ice cream. Alex's warmth of character sets the tone for the relaxed atmosphere; her expert knowledge

Prices: Lunch main course from €9.50. Dinner main course from €19.50. House Wine from €18.00
Food Served: Lunch 12.30-14.30 Tue-Fri July & August. Dinner 18.00-21.30 Tue-Sat & Sundays in July & August
Closed: Mondays. Closed Sundays except July & Aug. 3 weeks in Jan & Feb.
Cuisine: Modern Irish/French
Other Points: Children over 7 welcome. Parking nearby.
Directions: Located on Connolly Street adjacent to Scannell's Pub. The restaurant is located almost directly opposite the junction with Kent Street, location for Old Mill Library and Town Hall.

of wines - she was banqueting manager at the Dorchester - brings to life a most interesting, well annotated wine list.

Cobh Co Cork ★

Knockeven House
Country house bed and breakfast

Knockeven, Rushbrooke
Cobh, Co Cork
Tel. +353(0)21 4811778
Email. info@knockevenhouse.com
www.knockevenhouse.com

Pamela and John Mulhaire's exceptional Victorian house was the deserved winner of this guide's 2004 Bed and Breakfast award. A family-run business, which the Mulhaires only started up the previous year, it's an elegant retreat, remarkable for the impeccable good taste and attention to detail throughout, particularly in the choice of luxurious fabrics and antique furniture. Set on a hill in a residential area among mature gardens, the handsome, cream-painted house partly overlooks the bay. The drawing room, with its open fire and abundance of natural light, is a beautiful space in which to relax. The adjoining dining room is smartly furnished with a polished oval table and chairs covered in pretty, dusty pink fabric. The four ensuite bedrooms have been decorated in restful pinks and greens, while fine bedlinen and

Rooms: 4 ensuite. Double from €120. Single from €75. Family room - price on request.
Other Points: Garden. Car park. Winner - Bed & Breakfast of the Year 2004.
Directions: N25 in direction of Rosslare, Wexford/Waterford and take Cobh exit 624. Pass Fota Wildlife Park, over the bridge turn right at Great Island garage, sharp left and first right avenue to Knockeven House.

fluffy bathrobes provide a haven of comfort. An excellent night's sleep is rounded off with homemade breads and preserves, and a full Irish breakfast.

Marantha Country House, Blarney

Knockeven House, Cobh

Cobh Co Cork ⭐

WatersEdge Hotel
Waterside hotel and restaurant

Next to Cobh Heritage Centre
Cobh, Co Cork
Tel. +353(0)21 4815566
Email. info@watersedgehotel.ie
www.watersedgehotel.ie

This bright yellow-painted, modern 19-room hotel nestles conveniently between the road and the harbour, amid historic Cobh's Victorian architecture. Michael and Margaret Whelan's establishment exudes cheery comfort in its large, well-appointed, colourfully decorated bedrooms, many of which have French doors which open out over the veranda to the sea below. All water-based activities, such as sailing and windsurfing are available minutes away from the hotel, together with tennis, horse riding, angling and harbour cruises. The Jacob's Ladder restaurant was named for the ladder used by Harbour Pilots when boarding ships entering and leaving port. Tastefully decorated with a contemporary mint-and-terracotta colour scheme, its strong suit is seafood - homemade seafood chowder, fresh tiger prawns with garlic sauce, poached black sole with thyme butter, as well as excellent poultry and meat

Rooms: 19 ensuite. Double from €110. Single from €75. Family from €140.
Prices: Lunch main course from €10.95. Dinner main course from €18. House wine from €19.
Food Served: Breakfast 7.30-10.00. Lunch 12.30-15.00 (summer). Dinner 18.00-21.00 (winter), 18.00-21.30 (summer).
Closed: After lunch on 24 - 27 Dec incl.
Cuisine: Modern Irish & seafood.
Other Points: Children welcome. Car park. Winner - Hotel of the Year 2002.
Directions: Next to Cobh Heritage Centre.

offerings. Save room for the crème brûlée with blue Curacao ice cream. Reasonably priced wines represent both the Old and New World.

Cork Co Cork ⭐

Café Paradiso
City centre vegetarian restaurant

16 Lancaster Quay, Cork
Tel. +353(0)21 4277939
Email. info@cafeparadiso.ie
www.cafeparadiso.ie

Denis Cotter and Bridget Healy's ground-breaking vegetarian restaurant, five minutes from the centre of Cork, blows out of the water all notions that meatless cooking is stodgy, brown and lentil-laden. The wildly imaginative menu sparkles with seasonality, and ingredients are listed with a proud clarity that makes for an absorbing read. The dishes which emerge from Cotter's kitchen are no less compelling, with each individual taste both freshly distinct from and integral to the whole dish. Start, perhaps, with water-melon, feta and macadamia salad with lime, mint and green peppercorns and pumpkin-seed oil followed by carrot, cabbage and fennel springroll with chilli-coconut dip and sesame rice noodle salad. Desserts such as iced rhubarb soufflé with chilled rhubarb soup and orange shortbread biscuits, or dark chocolate silk cake with caramel sauce

Prices: Lunch main course from €12. Dinner main course from €21. House wine from €20.
Food Served: 12.00-15.00 and 18.30-22.30 Tue-Sat.
Closed: Sundays and Mondays and one week over Christmas.
Cuisine: Modern seasonal vegetarian.
Other Points: Children welcome. Winner-Restaurant of the Year 2004.
Directions: On Western Road, opposite Jury's Hotel.

and espresso ice cream are even better than they sound. The carefully sourced wine list has some interesting choices from Italy, New Zealand and beyond.

Cork City Co Cork ✕ ◗ ▽ ◉ ★

Farmgate Café & Restaurant
Daytime café and restaurant

Old English Market,
Princes Street, Cork
Tel. +353(0)21 4278134

The brainchild of sisters Kay Harte and
Maróg O'Brien (Kay runs this Cork
venture, Maróg the original Farmgate
Restaurant in Midleton, see entry),
Farmgate epitomises all that is authentic
about Irish cookery and hospitality.
Set above the English Market - Cork's
200-year-old food emporium - in a cosy
gallery space, the bustling surroundings and
country-kitchen decor make for an intimate,
round-the-kitchen-table atmosphere. The
market is the café's larder: fish comes
straight from the famous fish stalls; classic
meats such as tripe and drisheen from the
long-established butchers' shops; fresh produce from the greengrocers. They are transformed by the café into homely, delicious
creations - many based on recipes from
the Cork area - and simple, contemporary
dishes. Specials could include corned mutton with champ potato and spring onion;
baked organic salmon, or leek and Gubeen

Prices: Main course from €8.50.
House wine from €20 (€5 per glass).
Food served: 8.30-17.30 daily.
Closed: 1 Jan, Good Friday, 25-26
Dec.
Cuisine: Traditional Irish and Modern
European.
Other Points: Children welcome.
Winner - Café of the Year 2003.
Directions: In the Old English Market,
off Patrick Street in Cork City.

cheese tart. Desserts - seasonal crumble,
bread and butter pudding, chocolate and
orange cake - are all home-baked daily.

Farmgate Café & Restaurant, Cork

Cork City Co Cork

Fenns Quay Restaurant
City centre restaurant and café

No 5 Sheares Street, Cork
Tel. +353(0)21 4279527
Email. polary1@eircom.net
www.fennsquay.ie

This contemporary city-centre restaurant
is run by Pat and Eilish O'Leary. Inside,
funky modern art, sculptural light fittings
and wooden chairs with cherry red seats
create an upbeat atmosphere. The food
is similarly on the pulse, but grounded
by firmly-held principles that produce
should be local and carefully sourced. Chef
Linda Hickey produces a laudible range of
interesting vegetarian dishes - aubergine
Charlotte with mushroom and goat's
cheese custard, for example, or corn cake
with roast chilli vegetables. Elsewhere,
delicious meaty mains include roast lamb
chump with gratin of flageolet beans, and
organic Irish beef burger with house-cut
potato chips. Seafood choices feature chilli
crisp prawns with wasabi mayo and fish
fresh from the market. For dessert, there's
a mouthwatering raspberry and vanilla
pannacotta with mint cream (gluten-free),

Prices: Lunch main course from
€10.95. Dinner main course from
€16.95. House wine €17.50.
Food served: 10.00-22.00 Mon-Sat.
Closed: Sundays and Bank Holidays, 25
December.
Cuisine: Progressive Irish.
Other Points: Children welcome.
Directions: 2 minutes from Court-
house/city centre.

while the wine list has a global range and
well-informed notes. Service begins at
breakfast with eggs Benedict and freshly
baked muffins. Lunch brings soups, sandwiches and salads.

Cork City Co Cork

Franciscan Well Brew Pub
Brewery pub

North Mall, Cork
Tel. +353(0)21 4210130
Email. shane_long@hotmail.com

Built on the site of a Franciscan monastery
and well dating from 1219, this brewery
and brew-pub, founded in 1998, is the only
pub in the city which sells its own brews.
Stylishly decorated with giant copper kegs
behind the bar, it combines modern technology with age-old tradition in creating classic beer styles. Legend has it that the water
from the well has miraculous and curative
properties - certainly an asset in making
lager, ale, stout and wheat beer. All beers
are free of chemical additives and preserva-
tives. Among the brew-pub's offerings are
Blarney Blonde ale, brewed in the style of a
fruity German 'Grolsch' beer; robust Rebel
Red Ale, with a distinct caramel flavour
imparted by crystal malt; and Shandon
Stout, a creamy Cork-style dry stout with

Opening hours: 15.00-23.30 Mon-
Wed. 15.00-24.00 Thur. 15.00-00.30
Fri-Sat. 16.00-23.00 Sun.
Directions: Head straight down
North Main Street, cross over the
North Gate Bridge and then turn left.

roasted-malt overtones. Seasonal specialities include Bellringer Winter Warmer and
Purgatory Pale Ale. Don't miss the brewery
tours, or the brewery fests, which generally
include an all-day barbecue in the beer
garden.

Hayfield Manor Hotel, Cork

CHAPTER EL

whole village was suddenly des
of the as yet un-dreamed-of wh
from group to group, from h
graphic speed. Of course the
noon; the town would have
gory knife had been found
recognized by somebody
And it was said that a h
himself in the 'branch'
that Potter had at once
the washing, which w
town had been rans
the matter of siftin
could not be foun
direction, and th
night.

All the tow
vanished, and
thousand tin
countable s
wormed h
It seemed
his arm

Cork City Co Cork

Hayfield Manor Hotel
City centre hotel and restaurant

Perrott Avenue, College Road, Cork
Tel. +353(0)21 4845900
Email. enquiries@hayfieldmanor.ie
www.hayfieldmanor.ie

This luxury hotel - just 15 minutes from Cork airport - combines opulence with graceful home comforts in a tranquil setting. The large, redbrick manor house has been tastefully extended and renovated by owners Joe and Margaret Scully, and the mature gardens are meticulously maintained. Guests can enjoy an afternoon tea in the lovely drawing room, where deep-pile carpets and subtle lighting add to the sense of intimacy. Spacious bedrooms, all designed personally by Margaret and filled with fresh flowers and elegant furniture, are the perfect retreat. The Manor Room offers a classic French-inspired menu - roast pavé of brill with chorizo risotto and fennel provençal might be followed by warm fondant of Valrhona chocolate with praline cappuccino ice cream. More relaxed dining takes place in Perrotts, where the homemade burger comes with bacon and Gruyère cheese and handmade chips, and the rhubarb and strawberry crumble is made from organic local fruit.

Rooms: 88 ensuite. Double from €280. Single from €250.
Prices: Lunch main course from €15.50. Dinner main course from €15.50 House Wine from €6 per glass.

Food Served: 12.00-14.30 & 18.00-22.30 daily.
Cuisine: 2 restaurants: The Manor Room - Fine dining - French cuisine with an Irish heart, Perrotts - Bistro style modern Irish.
Other Points: Spa with leisure facilities. Library. Non-smoking bedrooms. Private gardens. Air conditioning. Children welcome. Car Park.
Directions: Leaving from outside the City Library at Grand Parade, continue straight through one set of traffic lights and at the next traffic lights, turn left on to Washington St. Continue straight for about a half mile. You will pass an Esso Service Station and come up to a set of traffic lights. The main gates to University College Cork will be in front of you. Turn left on to Donovans Road and continue straight up the hill. At the top of this road, turn right on to College Road and take the next immediate left, up Perrott Ave. The entrance to Hayfield Manor is directly in front of you.

Munchies Gourmet Coffee House, Fermoy

Isaacs, Cork

Cork City Co Cork

Isaacs Restaurant
City centre restaurant and café

48 MacCurtain Street, Cork
Tel. +353(0)21 4503805
Email. isaacs@iol.ie

Situated in a renovated Victorian warehouse with an inviting arched entrance, authentic bricked walls and high ceilings oozing with atmosphere, you immediately feel relaxed and full of high expectations at Michael Ryan's much talked about Bistro style restaurant. Happily, you are not disappointed as you browse through the menu. There is something for everyone; with a heart warming potato and chive cake with grilled Clonakilty black pudding, glazed apples and whole grain mustard sauce to crispy fried Ardsallagh goat's cheese with roast beetroot and chick pea salad or you can always opt for their reliable creamy seafood chowder. Similar to the wine list, the mains drew influence from all over the globe. You could be carried off in the direction of India with a mild madras lamb curry seved with popadoms, basmati rise and side dishes, or even to Thailand for their Thai red chicken curry served with fragrant rice and fresh

Prices: Lunch main course from €8.90-€12.90. Dinner main course from €14.80-€25.60. House wine from €17.50.
Food served: 10.00-14.30 and 18.00-22.00 Mon-Sat. 18.00-21.00 Sun.
Closed: One week at Christmas.
Cuisine: Modern Irish/Mediterranean.
Directions: Opposite the Gresham Metropole Hotel, on MacCurtain Street.

coriander. Or you can stay closer to home with a fine fillet or sirloin steak that never fails to please. A dessert of bread and butter pudding or for something with a less wintery-feel raspberry, champagne and mint jelly completes a successful meal. Vegetarians are catered for and dishes can be made up.

Cork City Co Cork

Les Gourmandises Restaurant
City centre French restaurant

17 Cook Street, Cork
Tel. +353(0)21 4251959
www.lesgourmandises.ie

The extremely committed and talented Patrick and Soizic Kiely's - he's Irish and she's French - three-year-old French restaurant, just off the South Mall, has the look and feel of a family-run establishment in France. Its long, narrow interior, with comfy armchairs and low tables for pre-dinner drinks, cream-toned walls, a plush red banquette, small fireplace, white linen-covered tables, and colourful paintings, offers a charming setting for a moderately-priced lunch of, say, roasted duck leg confit with red onions, black olive and balsamic dressing; or a gourmet open sandwich on homemade bread, followed by blackcurrant parfait with ginger bread & chocolate sauce. Dinner is slightly more formal: Specialties include terrine of braised ham, foie gras and sweetbread with celeriac puree and hazelnut salad; braised pork belly with rosemary, ginger and onion

Prices: Main course lunch from €17.50. Main course dinner from €23.50. House Wine from €22.00
Food Served: Dinner: 18.00-22.00 Tue-Sat. Lunch 12.00-14.00 (Friday only).
Closed: Sundays & Mondays, 2 weeks Easter, 2 weeks August.
Cuisine: French.
Other Points: Children over 6yrs welcome.
Directions: Cook Street, Off South Mall, City Centre.

marmalade; and lemon custard with red wine granite and almond biscuit. The wine list is well-chosen, as are the classic French cheeses.

Cork City Co Cork

Lotamore House
Georgian guesthouse

Tivoli, Cork
Tel. +353(0)21 4822344
Email. lotamore@iol.ie
www.lotamorehouse.com

This lovely Georgian house overlooks Cork Harbour on the main road to Cork City. It recently changed hands following a major refurbishment by the previous owner, but new proprietor Geri McElhinney looks set to continue the high standards which make staying here such a restful experience. The gracious rooms are decorated to a high standard, enhancing the many period details, such as a striking stained glass window visible from the entrance hall. Open fires burn in the reception rooms and the tranquil bedrooms are full of beautiful antique furniture, luxurious fabrics and the finest bedlinen. A full Irish breakfast is available, as well as homemade muesli, toasted granola, freshly baked brown bread and fresh orange juice, all served with impressive attention to detail. The bright, airy dining room overlooks four acres of

Rooms: 20 ensuite. Double from €120. Single from €75. Family from €150.
Other Points: Bedrooms non-smoking. Garden. Children welcome. Car park. Winner - Guesthouse of the Year 2004.
Directions: 5 minutes drive from the city centre off dual carriageway heading east out of the city.

peaceful, mature gardens. Cork airport is only 15 minutes away, and the city itself is within a few minute's drive.

The Symbols

🗝 Accommodation
✕ Restaurant
☕ Café
🍺 Pub/Bar
☀ Daytime opening only
🥪 Deli
🍷 Wine
🥖 Bakery
🍎 Gourmet/Farm Shop
🜂 Leisure Centre/Spa
CS Craft Shop
VC Visitor Centre

Les Routiers Awards

⭐ 2002 Award Winner
⭐ 2003 Award Winner
⭐ 2004 Award Winner
★ 2005 Award Winner

Cork City Co Cork

Nash 19 Restaurant
City centre restaurant and café

19 Princes Street, Cork
Tel. +353(0)21 4270880
Email. info@nash19.com
www.nash19.com

Situated in the heart of Cork's business district, just a stone's throw from the renowned English Market, this lively café has been serving excellent modern Irish food for over 15 years. Aromas of freshly baked scones, traditional pastries and hot coffee fill the air from the early morning hours, when scores of breakfasters stop in en route to work. Owner Claire Nash is committed to using the best regional produce, and a myriad of local suppliers deliver on a daily basis. All fish, meat and poultry is supplied by the English Market. Seasonal menus change regularly. Choose from such wholesome lunch specialties as tomato and basil soup; calamari and cod pasta tagliatelle; Mexican chicken and warm salad with salsa, guacamole and tortilla crisps; and Irish blue cheese, broccoli and cherry tomato tart. Desserts include rhubarb and blackberry crumble. The service is efficient and friendly, and there's a small selection of wines, bubbly and beer.

Prices: Main course from €11.90. House wine from €19.50
Food Served: 7.30-16.30. 7.30-16.00 Sat.
Closed: Sundays, Bank Holidays and 25 Dec to 2 Jan.
Cuisine: Modern Irish with European influences.
Other Points: Children welcome.
Directions: Located on Princes Street Lower between Patrick Street and South Mall, close to the Old English Market.

Nash 19 Restaurant

Douglas Co Cork   ✕ 𝖸

Nakon Thai Restaurant
Thai restaurant

Tramway House, Douglas Village,
Co Cork
Tel. +353(0)21 4369900
www.nakonthai.com

Quality produce with lots of fresh herbs and aromatics adds that essential dimension to the cooking in Nakon Thai Restaurant in Douglas Village. This small but friendly restaurant owned by David and Sineerat McGreal provides the diner with attentive and efficient service as well as freshly cooked, authentic Thai meals. You can order the old favourite, spicy soups Tum Yam Gai with the chicken or Tum Yam Gung with black tiger prawns both flavoured with lemon grass, lime juice, kaffir lime leaves, galangal root and Thai herbs. Or you could go for a different sort of appetiser like the Angel Wings - deep fried boneless chicken wings stuffed with pork, vermicelli and coriander. The menu is very easy to follow, even for those not that familiar with Thai cooking, with mains split into sections eg. duck, chicken, pork, local beef, vegetarian and a very comprehensive seafood section. For those who are familiar, there are the reliable Phad Thai noodles, red and green cur-

Prices: Main course from €13.95. House wine from €14.95
Food served: 17.30-23.00 Mon-Sat. 17.00-22.00 Sun.
Closed: 24-27 December and Good Friday.
Cuisine: Thai.
Other Points: Children welcome. Air-conditioning. Convenient Parking.
Directions: In Douglas Village, opposite the Rugby Club.

ries or you can branch out with their mixed seafood which includes squid, prawns, crab-claws and mussels served with onion, chillies, mushrooms and spring onions in oyster sauce served on a sizzling platter. With a fine selection of modestly priced wines and bottles of the delicious Singha beer on the menu, this restaurant really is great value for money!

Nearest Golf Courses
Cork Golf Club *Tel. + 353 (0)21 4353451*
Fota Island Golf Club *Tel. + 353 (0)21 4883710*
Old Head Golf Links *Tel. + 353 (0)477 844*
Youghal Golf Club *Tel. + 353 (0)24 92787*

$ Million Dollar World Greyhound Championship
In Cork's Curraheen Park, Greyhound Stadium in summer 2006. Tel. + 353 (0)21 4543095.

Durrus Co Cork

Carbery Cottage Guest Lodge
Coastal bed and breakfast

Durrus, Co Cork
Tel.+353(0)27 61368
Email.www.carberycottage@eircom.net
www.carbery-cottage-guest-lodge.net

"Our house is your house," says Julia Bird and Mike Hegarty, of their bright, cheerful, dormered 3-bedroom B&B, which, set on 2 acres of grounds, just outside Durrus village, overlooks Dunmanus Bay and the beautiful, unspoiled Sheep's Head Peninsula. If you're a nature lover, there are marvellous walks on the Sheep's Head Way and other routes, several golf courses nearby, and the stunning Carraig Abhainn and Kilravock Gardens to visit. The cottage's sitting room has satellite TV; bedrooms are large, fresh, tidy and comfortable, with superb views. Bathrooms (two are ensuite) are very clean and bright, with quality linens. Full Irish breakfasts of local organic and free-range ingredients are served in a homely dining room with a long communal table. Tasty snacks and meals are available, as well as freshly caught seafood and lobsters, courtesy of Mike, a fisherman. In business since 2001, Mike and Julia's heartfelt hospitality extends to dogs, who are welcome.

Rooms: 3(2 ensuite). Double from €70. Single from €35. Family from €100.
Prices: Standard supper menu from €15. Set dinner from €40. (Residents only)
Cuisine: Local organic produce, specialising in fresh seafood.
Other Points: Garden. Dogs welcome. Smoking areas. Credit cards not accepted.
Directions: When you reach Durrus village the road forks, take the right hand fork which is sign posted Ahakista, Kilcrohane and the Sheepshead Peninsula. Follow this road for exactly 2.4 miles. You will pass a lay-by on the right and then see a turn on the right (sign posted The Sheeps Head Cycle route). Turn right up this road for about 0.2 of a mile the road turns to the left then 50 yds later there is a turn to the right going up the hill between two farms. We are about 300 yds on the left.

Fermoy Co Cork

Munchies Gourmet Coffee House
Daytime coffee shop and restaurant

Lower Patrick Street, Fermoy, Co Cork
Tel. +353(0)25 33653
Email. munchiesfermoy@eircom.net

Since its opening in 2002, Jason and Fiona Hogan's bright, clean coffee house has established a reputation for its exceptionally warm and friendly atmosphere. The hardworking pair have clearly passed on this sunny outlook to their well-presented staff, who deal with customers with smiling efficiency. The interior is simple and clean, with pine tables, a dresser bearing pastas and sauces and a chalkboard displaying the daily menu. All food is fresh, with fruit and veg from the Hogans' organic plot, and made on the premises daily - for breakfast, there's French toast, pancakes with maple syrup and a huge choice of speciality teas alongside the excellent Segafredo coffee. Lunch might bring homemade soup - nicely presented on white china with a swirl of

Prices: Main course lunch from €9.20.
Food served: 9.00-17.00 Mon-Sat.
Closed: Sundays, Christmas week, Public Holidays.
Cuisine: Traditional Irish
Other Points: Gluten-free bread and cakes available. Children welcome. Car park.
Directions: On Tallow Road, next to the Mart car park.

cream and freshly baked soda bread - and dishes such as Wicklow wild venison sausages or, more outlandishly, kangaroo fillets, all served with roast vegetables, bacon mash and salad. There's a small selection of wines by the glass.

Goleen Co Cork

The Heron's Cove
Waterside restaurant and bed & breakfast

The Harbour, Goleen, Co Cork
Tel. +353(0)28 35225
Email. suehill@eircom.net
www.heroncove.ie

Sue Hill's lovely bed and breakfast is beautifully situated by a private cove, just a few hundred metres from the village of Goleen, whose name derives from "goilin," meaning "little inlet." It's a charming, romantic and peaceful spot on the Mizen Peninsula, where dolphins, whales and basking sharks can often be spotted alongside seals and kittiwakes. Three of the five cosy bedrooms have private balconies with magnificent views of the harbour. The experience of staying here is made all the more magical by the marvellous food, most of it local and organic: lobster, prawns, scallops and wild salmon straight from the sea; lamb, duck and steaks from nearby producers. During high season, surf 'n turf (lobster with fillet steak) is very popular. Starters include warm West Cork duckling salad, followed

Rooms: 5 ensuite. Double from €80. Single from €40. Family from €100 (3 adults or 2 adults & 2 children). **Prices:** Dinner main course from €20. House wine from €19.75 (litre). **Food served:** Daily from 19.00 - by reservation only Oct-Apr. **Closed:** 24 Dec-1 Feb. **Cuisine:** Irish. **Other Points:** Garden. Car park. **Directions:** Turn off the N71 and follow the R592 to Goleen. Turn left down to the harbour.

by collops and scallops (scallops in creamy bacon sauce and Goleen lamb chops). There are also delicious vegetarian choices and desserts, and an interesting wine list.

Kinsale Co Cork

Blue Haven Hotel
Coastal hotel and restaurant

3/4 Pearse Street, Kinsale, Co Cork
Tel.+353(0)21 4772209
Email.info@bluehavenkinsale.com
www.bluehavenkinsale.com

This charming small hotel stands on the site of the original Kinsale fish market, at the centre of this atmospheric harbour town. It changed hands in 2004 and has undergone extensive renovations under the expert leadership of Ciaran Fitzgerald. The cream and blue exterior - with tables outside Café Blue in clement weather - provides a sunny welcome to visitors, who come to enjoy shellfish from Oysterhaven and freshly caught lobster in the restaurant, bar and conservatory - all attractive public areas with their own distinctive charm. The restaurant, with its smart livery of oatmeal-striped wallpaper, upholstered chairs and sculptural blooms, opens on to a walled garden at the rear. Mille feuille of Clonakilty black pudding with rosemary apples and whiskey cream might be among the starters here, while Café Blue offers a relaxed menu including Kinsale beer battered haddock and fries, and Blue Haven's 'infamous' seafood pancake.

Rooms: 17 ensuite. Double from €120. Single from €120. **Prices:** Lunch main course from €13.50. Dinner main course from €22.50. Bar snack from €6.50. House Wine from €20. **Opening Hours(Bar):** 10.30-23.30 Mon-Sat 12.30-23.00 Sundays. **Food Served:** 12.00-22.00 daily. **Cuisine:** Modern Irish with emphasis on seafood. **Other Points:** Garden. Children welcome.Bedrooms non-smoking. **Directions:** Follow signs for Cork Airport, continue to Five Mile Bridge and take R600. Drive through Riverstick, Belgooly and arrive in Kinsale.

Seventeen ensuite bedrooms have luxurious bedspreads, crisp white sheets and superbly comfortable beds.

Lotamore House, Cork

Blue Haven Hotel, Kinsale

Kinsale Co Cork ★

Old Bank House
Georgian townhouse

Pearse Street, Kinsale, Co Cork
Tel. +353(0)21 4774075
Email. oldbank@indigo.ie
www.oldbankhousekinsale.com

Prepare to sleep and dine well in the harbour town of Kinsale, considered to be one of Ireland's "hospitality capitals." The Old Bank House is no exception; owners Michael and Marie Riese are veteran hoteliers, whose 17-room Georgian residence exudes charm. There's a sunny sitting room with overstuffed sofas, cushions, a high ceiling and a stone fireplace, while the individually decorated guest rooms and suites all offer supremely comfortable beds, original art and bathrooms stocked with fine toiletries and Egyptian cotton towels and bathrobes. Most rooms have lovely views of the town. Michael is a Euro-Toque chef, whose heavenly breakfasts feature the freshest farm eggs and omelettes, home-baked breads, fresh fruit compôtes, local bacon, sausage and black pudding, and scrumptious French toast with maple syrup. Kinsale is a lovely

Rooms: 17 ensuite. Double from €170. Single from €170. Family from €245.
Other points: Winner - Guesthouse of the Year 2005.
Directions: On the right hand side at the start of Kinsale town, next to the Post Office.

spot for strolling among its many galleries, or for venturing further afield for golf at the spectacular Old Head Golf Links.

Midleton Co Cork

Farmgate Restaurant & Country Store
Restaurant and country store

Coolbawn, Midleton, Co Cork
Tel. +353(0)21 4632771

Maróg O'Brien's food store and restaurant - in the picturesque town of Midleton - has been a popular spot for food lovers for over 20 years. At the front is the shop, where farm-fresh produce, organic fruit and vegetables, cheeses and home-baked treats are sold. At the back is the homely restaurant, where the lunchtime menu takes in sandwiches, salads and cheese plates, as well as hot dishes such as traditional Irish stew or catch of the day. On Thursday, Friday and Saturday nights, dishes become a little more elaborate - but always firmly anchored around local produce - with starters bringing warm salad of lamb's kidney with mushrooms and pink peppercorns. Main courses might include Farmgate free-range duck with sage and onion stuffing, with a sumptuous double chocolate mousse gateau for dessert. A well-considered wine list has a strong showing from France. This is a sister restaurant to the Farmgate Café in Cork (see entry).

Prices: Lunch main course from €10.95 Dinner main course from €16. House wine from €20.
Hours: 9.00-21.30.
Food served: Lunch 12.00-16.00 Mon-Sat. Dinner 19.00-21.30 Thurs-Sat.
Closed: Sundays, Bank Holidays, 10 days over Christmas and Good Friday.
Cuisine: Traditional Irish and Modern European.
Other Points: Children welcome. Garden.
Directions: Follow the signs for the Irish Distillery off the Waterford to Cork Road. Farmgate is located in the town centre.

Youghal Co Cork   ✏️ ✖️ 🍸 📙   ★

Aherne's
Townhouse and seafood restaurant

163 North Main Street, Youghal,
Co Cork.
Tel. +353(0)24 92424
Email. ahernes@eircom.net
www.ahernes.com

The Fitzgibbon family are the third generation to own this small luxury townhouse and restaurant in the historic walled port of Youghal. Aherne's is known for its seafood, which is, naturally, straight off the boat and as fresh as you'll find anywhere. David Fitzgibbons' skilful cooking brings this freshness to the fore in starters such as hot buttered shrimp; prawn and crab risotto with avocado salsa, and crab claws with rosemary beurre blanc. Main courses, including grilled turbot with fennel compôte, sweet chilli jam and beetroot salsa, combine subtle tastes and textures with perfectly complementary flavours. Dishes such as chargrilled lamb cutlets with peperonata and fresh mint sauce make use of locally reared meat, while bread is freshly baked. Oysters, mussels, smoked salmon, steaks and open sandwiches can be enjoyed in the cosy bars with their open turf fires. Thirteen bedrooms provide

Rooms: 13 ensuite. Double from €160. Single from €115. Family room - rates on request.
Prices: Dinner main course from €25. Bar snack from €7.50. House wine from €18.50.
Food served: Bar food 12.00-22.00. Dinner 18.30-21.30 daily.
Closed: 6 days over Christmas.
Cuisine: Seafood a specialty.
Other Points: Children welcome. Car park. Non-smoking house. Winner - Guesthouse and Restaurant of the Year 2005.
Directions: Located in the town centre.

comfortable accommodation with large beds, antique furniture and spotless modern bathrooms.

Local Farmers' Markets

Cork City, English Market
Open Every Day
Midleton Farmers Market
Saturdays 10am-2pm
Clonakilty *Thursdays & Saturday's 10am-2pm*
Cobh, Seafront *Fridays 10am-1pm*
Dingle *Fridays, 10am-4pm*
Tralee *Fridays 9am-5pm*
Killarney Country Market *Fridays 11.30am-1.30pm*
Killorglin *CYMS Hall, Fridays 11am-1pm*

Cobh, The Queenstown Story | *Place to visit*

Cobh Heritage Centre, Cobh, Co Cork
Tel. +353(0)21 4813591
Fax. +353(0)21 4813595
Email. info@cobhheritage.com
www.cobhheritage.com

The story of Cobh's unique origins , its history and legacy are dramatically recalled at The Queenstown Story - a multimedia exhibition at Cobh's restored Victorian Railway Station. Explore the conditions on board the early emigrant vessels , including the dreaded 'Coffin Ship'. Learn about an 'Irish Wake' - the special farewell for emigrating sons and daughters - many of whom never returned to Ireland. Experience life on board a convict ship leaving Cove for Australia in 1801. Discover Queenstown's special connections with the ill-fated Titanic, which sank on her maiden voyage in 1912. Relive the horror of World War 1 and the sinking of the Lusitania off Cork Harbour with the loss of 1,198 lives. Learn about Annie Moore and her two brothers who left Cobh for a new life in America and how she was the first emigrant ever to be processed in Ellis Island.

Other Points
Genealogy Record Finder Service, Self Guided Exhibition, French Speaking Guide available, Restaurant, Full Wheelchair Access, and Hourly train service from Cork Station to Cobh Heritage Centre.

Hours
May 1 to Oct 31 daily 9.30-18.00
Nov 1 to Apr 30 daily 9.30-17.00
Last admissions 1 hour before closing
Closed from Dec 22 to Jan 2

Directions
Cobh is situated 15km east of Cork City, just off the N25 take the Cobh Road and turn right at the bridge as you cross on to Cobh Island.

Fota House & Gardens | *Place to visit*

Fota Island, Carrigtwohill, Co Cork
Tel. +353(0) 21 4815543
Fax. +353(0) 21 4815541
Email. info@fotahouse.com
www.fotahouse.com

Fota House is Ireland's finest example of Regency period architecture with superb magnificent neoclassical interiors. Formerly owned by the Smith Barry family, Fota House began life as a humble hunting lodge. Expanded and redesigned by Sir Richard Morrison the lodge was transformed to a superb Regency residence. Within the house are some of the finest neo-classical interiors to be found in Ireland. Fota House was designed to form the centrepiece of a great ornamental estate. The gardens contain a large number of exotic plant species from around the world, which flourish due to the benign climate of the South West Coast.

Other Points
Tours of the house are self-guided. The property is wheelchair accessible. There is also a small shop and of course a Tea Room serving light lunches, snacks, teas and coffees (home baked). Car Park on site (€2.00 fee applies)

Admission Charged
Free entry to Fota Gardens and Arboretum.

Hours
Jan 01st - 31st Mar   11.00 - 16.00
Apr 01st - 30th Sept   10.00 - 17.00
Oct 01st - 31st Dec   11.00 - 16.00
(IMPORTANT NOTE: Fota House can on occasions be closed due to the holding of private functions. People or groups intending to visit the house should ring ahead to check opening times on the day of their proposed visit.)

Directions
Fota House is Located about 12 Kilometres east of Cork City, just off the main Cork - Waterford Road (N25). Take exit for Cobh and continue for about 1.6 kilometres. The entrance to Fota is shared with Fota Wildlife Park. Access also available by train (Cork Cobh line).

Mizen Head Signal Station | *Place to visit*

Mizen Head, Goleen, West Cork
Tel. +353(0) 28 35115/35225
Fax. +353(0) 28 35422
Email. info@mizenhead.ie
www.mizenhead.ie
www.mizenhead.com

Mizen Head Signal Station, the must-see award-winning Visitors Centre at Ireland's most Southwesterly Point. If you miss the Mizen you haven't done Ireland. Experience the Irish Lights Signal Station, the 99 Steps, Spectacular views of the south and west coasts, Navigational Aids Simulator, the Fastnet Lighthouse Model, the famous Bridge with seals below. Mizen Head is spellbinding in any weather.

Other Points
Guided tour of the Signal Station, Audiovisual DVD '*Mizen Head Carn ui Neid*', Gift/Souvenir Shop specialising in Maritime and West Cork themes, Café, Car Park.

Hours
Jun to Sep daily 10.00 - 18.00
Mid Mar to May & Oct
daily 10.30 - 17.00
Nov to mid Mar
Weekends 11.00 - 16.00

Directions
From Killarney follow N71 to Bantry, outside Bantry turn right to follow signs to Crookhaven on R591, go through Goleen, then follow signs for Mizen Head Drive. From Cork follow N71 to Ballydehob then follow signs to Mizen Head R592 through Schull to Goleen.

Skibbereen Heritage Centre | *Place to visit*

Old Gasworks Building
Upper Bridge Street
Skibbereen, West Cork
Tel. +353 (0) 28 40900
Fax. +353 (0) 28 40957
Email. info@skibbheritage.com
www.skibbheritage.com

Enjoy a visit to the Skibbereen Heritage Centre, located in the award winning, beautifully restored Old Gasworks building. **The Great Famine Exhibition** - learn about this period of Irish history using the latest in multimedia technology. Skibbereen was one of the worst affected areas in Ireland, as testified by the mass graves at Abbeystrewery, where almost 10,000 are buried. **The Lough Hyne Visitor Centre** reveals the unique nature of this marine lake, Ireland's first Marine Nature Reserve. Find out about the history, folklore and formation of this renowned natural phenomenon. **Genealogy information** is also available including the 1901/1911 censuses for Skibbereen and district.

Other Points
Archaeology information, gift shop, salt-water aquarium, multi language audiovisuals and twice weekly guided historical walks of Skibb town. Wheelchair friendly and car park adjacent.

Hours
Mid Mar - mid May
10.00 - 18.00 Tue - Sat
Mid May - mid Sept 10.00 - 18.00 Daily
Mid Sept - 31st Oct
10.00 - 18.00 Tue - Sat
Feb & Nov 10.00 - 18.00 Mon - Fri

Directions
Skibbereen Heritage Centre is centrally located in Skibbereen, one of West Cork's picturesque towns. From Cork City: Take the N71 road through Bandon and Clonakilty, approximately 50 miles. From Killarney: Take the N71 road via Kenmare and Bantry. Follow the road signs to Skibbereen, approximately 50 miles.

Moynihans
Poultry
BUTTERED
EGGS

TRAY
PACKS
2 DOZ.
€2·60 EACH

Ballybunion Co Kerry

Íragh Tí Connor
Guesthouse, restaurant and bar

Main Street, Ballybunion, Co Kerry
Tel. +353(0)68 27112
Email. iraghticonnor@eircom.net
www.golfballybunion.com

The name of this lovely 19th-century country house, which translates as 'the inheritance of O'Connor' says volumes about the care which owners John and Joan O'Connor have lavished upon it. Set in its own walled gardens, but close to Ballybunion's world-famous golf links and the bustle of the town itself, the house has 17 spacious bedrooms furnished with antiques to complement the convenience of satellite television, large bathrooms and direct-dial phones. Downstairs, the public rooms are also inviting, with open fireplaces and period furniture. The restaurant, with its crisp white and rose-coloured linens and baby grand piano, is the perfect backdrop for the elegant menu, which includes grilled seabass on a potato cake with smoked salmon and leek sauce, or roast rack of Kerry lamb with braised red cabbage, root vegetables and a port wine reduction.

Rooms: 17 ensuite. Double from €195. Single from €150.
Prices: Dinner main course from €19.95. House wine from €18.
Food served: 17.30-21.30. 13.00-21.30 on Sunday.
Closed: Closed Dec and Jan.
Cuisine: Modern Irish.
Other Points: Children welcome. Garden. Car park. Commended - Guesthouse with Restaurant 2003.
Directions: On the N69 north coastal route from Limerick to Tralee, at the top of Main Street.

Breads and preserves are homemade, and the wine list is a treat for connoisseurs and novices alike.

Cahirciveen Co Kerry

QC's Seafood Bar & Restaurant
Restaurant and bar

3 Main Street, Cahirciveen,
Ring of Kerry, Co Kerry
Tel. +353(0)66 9472244
Email. info@qcbar.com
www.qcbar.com

Kate and Andrew Cooke are the enthusiastic owners behind this Basque-inspired seafood restaurant, now in its sixth year. All fish is supplied straight from the boats by the family business, and guests can enjoy a spot of fishing on Andrew's yacht before returning for dinner. The eighteenth-century building has been renovated with tasteful attention to detail - driftwood from local beaches and other nautical memorabilia adorn the interior, and the red Basque tablecloths make a pretty contrast with the dark blue walls. Kate has used her experience working in a Basque restaurant to shape the menu, bringing dishes such as pan-fried brill with toasted garlic and chilli salsa, and a terrific tapas menu including deep-fried squid with chilli jam, chorizo in cider, fresh crab claws and sizzling prawns.

Prices: Bar snack from €4.50. Lunch main course from €7.50. Dinner main course from €17.50. House wine from €17.50.
Food Served: Lunch 12.30-14.30 Tue-Sat. Dinner 18.00-21.30 Tue-Sun. Apr-Oct. Open 7 days July & August. Dinner 18.00-21.30 Fri-Sun. Nov-Mar.
Closed: Closed 7th Jan to mid Feb.
Cuisine: Modern Irish with Spanish influences.
Other Points: Garden. Car park. Patio/courtyard.
Directions: In the centre of town. On the right hand side as if coming into town from Waterville.

Other, non-fishy options include chargrilled fillet steak with scallion mash. A beautifully maintained garden and a covered patio - with heaters - are a bonus in fine weather.

Dingle Co Kerry

Doyle's
Seafood restaurant and townhouse

John Street, Dingle, Co Kerry
Tel. +353(0)66 9151174
Email. cdoyle@iol.ie
www.doylesofdingle.com

Doyle's has been a fixture in Dingle since 1974, establishing for itself a widespread and well-deserved reputation for its fabulous seafood, which comes straight off the boats in Dingle harbour. Charlotte Cluskey continues the tradition of enhancing these super-fresh flavours with a simple, skilfully cooked menu based around supply. Inside the distinctive red-and-white building the decor remains attractively low-key, with flagstone floors and country kitchen furniture. Next door, a recently refurbished townhouse provides high quality accommodation including a Victorian drawing room and eight bedrooms with luxury marble bathrooms and antique furniture. Lobster, chosen from the tank, is the house specialty; other superb starters include oysters baked in Guinness, and home-cured salmon flavoured with orange and cardamom. The house fish pie is a classic treat, while meat dishes - roast veal chop with ravioli and

Rooms: 8 ensuite. Double from €100. Single from €95.
Prices: Dinner main course from €22. House wine from €19.50.
Food served: Dinner 18.00-22.00 Mon-Sat.
Closed: 22 Nov to mid Dec. Open one week over Christmas then closed to mid Feb. Restaurant closed Sundays.
Cuisine: Modern Irish with oriental themes.
Directions: On approaching Dingle town take the third left off the roundabout into the Mall. At the junction turn left into John Street. Doyle's is on the left.

sage butter, confit of lamb fillet in Parmesan crumb - are appealing enough to tempt even committed fish fanciers.

Dingle Co Kerry

 ★★

Heatons House
Waterfront guesthouse

The Wood, Dingle, Co Kerry
Tel. +353(0)66 9152288
Email. heatons@iol.ie
www.heatonsdingle.com

Cameron and Nuala Heaton and their daughter, Jackie, work hard to make this beautifully situated guesthouse, just across the road from Dingle Bay, a welcoming home-from-home. The town centre and marina are just a short walk away and there are magnificent views to be had from many of the 16 comfortable bedrooms. All have spacious bathrooms and the newest additions are decorated in tranquil creams and blues with good-looking, contemporary furniture. Jackie is the breakfast chef, and her fabulous morning menu has put Heaton's House on the map. The extensive choice ranges from hot porridge with Drambuie, brown sugar and cream, to fresh fish of the day, local smoked salmon with scrambled egg and Dingle kippers. Naturally, there's a full Irish breakfast, which includes home-made sausages and local black pudding. In

Rooms: 16 ensuite. Double from €90 - €144. Single from €60-€99. Family €115-€170.
Closed: 24-26 Dec and 2 weeks in Jan.
Other Points: Non-smoking house. Children welcome over 8 years old. Garden. Car park. Winner - Guesthouse of the Year 2002. Commended - Guesthouse of the Year 2003.
Directions: Take the harbour road out of Dingle and Heatons House is 500 yards past the marina at the front of Dingle town.

addition, there's a good selection of cereals, fresh fruit, cold meat and Irish cheeses. Scones and bread are all homemade.

Dingle Peninsula Co Kerry

Gorman's Clifftop House & Restaurant
Seaview guesthouse and restaurant

Glaise Bheag, Ballydavid,
Dingle Peninsula, Co Kerry
Tel. +353(0)66 9155162
Email. info@gormans-clifftophouse.com
www.gormans-clifftophouse.com

Watching the sun sink into the Atlantic from Gorman's spectacular west-facing dining room is an unforgettable experience. Vincent and Sile Gorman's exceptionally comfortable house on the Slea Head scenic drive offers beautiful views, plenty of lounging areas with open fires, and wonderfully warm hospitality. The owners are a goldmine of information about nearby walks, and the scenery in this Gaeltacht (Irish-speaking) area is unparalleled. There are nine, spacious en-suite bedrooms, decorated in pine with hand-thrown pottery lamps and tapestry wall-hangings. Superior rooms have king-sized beds. Alongside a hearty cooked breakfast, there's a groaning buffet of fresh fruit salads, juices and yoghurt with honey, as well as cashew nut and sunflower seed paté, smoked wild salmon

Rooms: 9 ensuite. Double from €100. Single from €75. Family from €150.
Prices: Dinner (set menu) €38. House wine from €18.50.
Food served: 18.30-20.30 Mon-Sat. By reservation only Nov-Mar.
Closed: Restaurant closed Sundays.
Cuisine: Seafood & modern Irish.
Other Points: Garden. Children welcome. Car park. Bicycle hire. Situated on Dingle way walking route. Winner - Little Gem Award 2001.
Directions: Straight across roundabout west of Dingle signposted "An Fheothanach" 8 miles, veer to left but do not turn left.

and poached smoked herring. Vincent Gorman makes inspired use of locally caught seafood in dishes such as trio of monkfish, dill and prawns with carrot and dill cream sauce. The wine list is French-accented, straightforward and reasonably priced.

Kenmare Co Kerry

The Lime Tree Restaurant
Town centre restaurant

Shelburne Street, Kenmare, Co Kerry
Tel. +353(0)64 41225
Email. benchmark@iol.ie
www.limetreerestaurant.com

This popular restaurant - now in its twenty-first year - is housed in an attractive, early nineteenth century stone schoolhouse framed, in season, by an abundance of fuchsia and foliage. Inside, features such as open fireplaces and exposed stone contribute to the mellow, relaxed atmosphere, with waiting staff managing just the right balance of friendliness and discretion. The menu is contemporary, but pleasingly straightforward and dishes are artistically presented with just the right amount of flourish. Start, perhaps, with warm tartlet of fresh salmon and leeks, or perennially popular ovenroasted chicken wings. Local ingredients are showcased in main courses such as roast Kerry lamb with honey thyme jus, or Kenmare seafood potpourri en papillote. Finish with a classic crème brûlée, or

Prices: Dinner main course from €14.95. House wine from €18.95.
Food Served: 18.30-21.30 daily.
Closed: From end of Oct to end of Mar.
Cuisine: Modern Irish & seafood.
Other Points: Car park. Winner - Restaurant of the Year 2005.
Directions: At the top of town, next to The Park Hotel.

chocolate lasagne - an intriguing layering of dark, milk and white chocolate mousses. The wine list, helpfully, places bottles in distinct flavour categories. The adjoining art gallery is a great place for a post-prandial stroll.

Killarney Co Kerry

Killarney Royal Hotel
Town centre hotel and restaurant

College Street, Killarney, Co Kerry
Tel. +353 (0)64 31853
Email. royalhot@iol.ie
www.killarneyroyal.ie

Built in 1900 and located in the heart of
Killarney town, this luxurious and
welcoming family run hotel prides itself on
personal service for its clients. The professional, helpful and friendly staff, along with
the large, open fire and fresh flowers, put
you immediately at your ease; confident
that your stay with them will be a success
whether it is for business or pleasure.
Situated in the town itself, it is never too far
away from the best of outdoors activities!
With such spectacular locations like the
National Park, it's three lakes and magnificent mountain ranges, The Gap of Dunloe
and Killarney Golf & Fishing Club, as well
as some of the finest Golf courses in the
Southwest there is something for everyone!
The hotel consists of 24 superior guest-
rooms and 5 junior suites, which are all
individually decorated with fine antiques by
the owners, Margaret and Joe Scally. Each
unique room is spacious and comfortable,
not to mention, luxurious, down to the
linen, fluffy towels and of course the chocolate! For dining, there are two options, the
café bar, which has a contemporary feel
serving well-presented, fresh food. For a

Rooms: 29 ensuite. Double from
€130-€250. Single from €120-€205.
Family from €250.
Prices: Lunch main course from €9.
Dinner main course from €14.95
Bar Snack from €4.50. (bar snacks
served all day). House wine from
€18.50.
Food served: 12.30-21.00 daily.
Closed: 24-27 Dec.
Cuisine: Modern Irish.
Other Points: Children welcome.
Dogs welcome.
Directions: Just off the N22 on
College Street.

more formal approach, the hotel restaurant
with its linen clothes and napkins is the
perfect spot. Sourcing its produce locally
where possible, you could go for the Kenmare Bay Fresh Oysters, the Tender Roast
Rack of Kerry Lamb or (when in season)
the Fresh Dingle Bay Lobster.

Nearest Golf Courses

Ballybunion Golf Club Tel. + 353 (0)68 27146

Dunloe Golf Club Tel. + 353 (0)64 44578

Killarney Golf Club Tel. + 353 (0)64 31034

Killorglin Golf Club Tel. + 353 (0)66 9761979

Ring of Kerry Golf & Country Club
Tel. + 353 (0)64 420000

Tralee Golf Club Tel. + 353 (0)66 7136379

Killarney Co Kerry

Loch Lein Country House
Lakeside hotel and restaurant

Old Golf Course Road, Fossa, Killarney,
Co Kerry
Tel. +353(0)64 31260
Email. stay@lochlein.com
www.lochlein.com

Taking its name from the location, this pleasing, secluded, modern country house hotel is located on the shores of Loch Lein which is the gateway to the Ring of Kerry. Along with the views of the lake, its relaxing, bright and airy residents' lounge boasts spectacular views of the Macgillicuddy Reeks. There are 25 generous ensuite rooms with equally generous beds and once again some breathtaking views. Owned by Paul and Annette Corridan, the hotel also takes pride in its elegant home cooking with starters like roast quail with a red wine reduction or tian of crab with grapefruit. Modestly priced, their dinner menu offers the diner such choices as tender breast of duck with a mushroom and wine sauce or roast collops of Monkfish on a bacon and leek mash. There are a selection of three red and white house wines.

Rooms: 25 ensuite. Double from €100. Single from €75. Family from €120.
Prices: Dinner main course from €18. House wine from €18.50.
Food Served: Dinner 18.30-21.00 daily.
Closed: 5 Nov to 17 Mar.
Cuisine: Modern Irish/Mediterranean.
Directions: From Killarney take N72 through Fossa Village, take sharp left 50m after the church, the hotel is 100m on the right.

Breakfast can be traditional in style or you can opt for warm waffles with blueberry and maple syrup or even their buffet, which includes cheeses, salamis and juices.

Killarney Co Kerry

Mentons at the Plaza
Town centre bistro

Killarney Plaza Hotel, Killarney, Co Kerry
Tel. +353(0)64 21150
Email. info@mentons.com
www.mentons.com

Chef Gary Fitzgerald's chic and buzzy two-level bistro in the swank Killarney Plaza Hotel, in downtown Killarney, has an unusual vaulted ceiling with an intriguing mural, polished wooden floors, arched windows, and a variety of plush contemporary seating arrangements. Service is top-notch, and you will be hard-pressed to choose from a lunch menu of delectable designer sandwiches: hot panini filled with chicken and basil pesto and Mozzarella cheese, or toasted Italian ciabatta stuffed with grilled bacon, sliced vine tomatoes, and melted cheddar cheese, among others. Dinner choices are even more difficult, featuring starters of steamed Cromane mussels Provencal style, or Vietnamese pork patties with Thai dipping sauce, followed by perhaps pan-fried breast and confit leg of Guinea fowl with scallion champ or fillet of

Prices: Dinner main course from €12.95. House wine from €18.
Food served: 12.30-21.00 daily.
Cuisine: Modern and European.
Directions: Located in The Killarney Plaza Hotel in the town centre.

fresh sea trout with a green pea and fennel seed risotto. Desserts are equally stellar.

Loch Lein Country House, Killarney

Caragh Lodge, Killorglin

Ballygarry House Hotel, Tralee

Killarney Co Kerry   ✗ ◆ ♀ ◉ CS VC

The Garden Restaurant at Muckross House
National Park daytime restaurant and coffee shop

Muckross, Killarney, Co Kerry
Tel. +353(0)64 314440
Email. restaurant@muckross-house.ie
www. muckross-house.ie

The Garden Restaurant can be found on the site of Muckross House. This historic building, with its gardens, craft shop and traditional farms, is one of the most popular heritage sites in the country and enjoys a stunning lakeside setting at the heart of Killarney National Park. Originally owned by Henry Arthur Herbert, MP, the house passed to the Guinness family, then to the Bourn Vincents, before being presented to the Irish nation in 1933. Previous eminent visitors include Queen Victoria, who was entertained here in 1861. Chef Colin Baker ensures all produce is sourced locally, and breads, scones and pastries are baked on the premises. The varied menu includes Dingle Bay sole fillets stuffed with seafood mousse on a brandy-flavoured bisque, and

Prices: Lunch main course from €9.50. Wine from €3.95.
Food served: 9.00-17.00 daily.
Closed: 23 Dec - 2 Jan.
Cuisine: Modern Irish.
Other Points: Garden. Children welcome. Free car parking. Available for private/corporate events.
Directions: 6km from Killarney on N71 to Kenmare.

apple and spiced baked cod in a light curry cream sauce. Meat options might bring traditional roast beef with bordelaise sauce and horseradish cream, or oriental chicken breast with orange and rosemary sauce and pilaf rice.

Killarney Co Kerry   ▌ ✗ ♀

The Laurels Pub & Restaurant
Restaurant, pub and wine bar

Main Street, Killarney, Co Kerry
Tel. +353(0)64 31149
Email. info@thelaurelspub.com
www.thelaurelspub.com

A fixture on Main Street for just under a century, Con and Kate O'Leary's self-styled restaurant and 'singing pub', with its tiled floors, beamed ceilings, dusky alcoves and log fires, is a charming throw-back to another time. There's plenty of colourful history associated with this place: back in 1930 the family-owned Kilbrean Boy greyhound travelled to Wimbledon to triumph in the first-ever Laurels greyhound meeting. Despite all this history, the Laurels is right on the button with its food. The menu is predominantly traditional - bacon and cabbage is served every Monday - and sourced from the best local and seasonal ingredients. Other specials from the daily changing menu might include rich home-made chicken liver pâté, chicken and field mushroom pastry pie, smoked fishcakes, or grilled fillet of seabass with aromatic ginger

Prices: Lunch main course from €8.95. Bar snack from €6. Dinner main course from €13.95. House wine from €17.
Hours: Bar: 10.30-23.30, until 00.30 Fri-Sat. 12.30-23.00 Sunday.
Food served: Lunch: 12.00-15.00. Bar Snack: 15.30-17.30 (summer). Dinner: 18.00-21.45 Mon-Sat.
Closed: Restaurant closed Nov to Apr. Call ahead for seasonal changes.
Cuisine: Traditional Irish and International.
Other Points: Children welcome.
Directions: Centre of Killarney Town.

rice. Don't miss the house champ and the homemade desserts. There are soups, sandwiches, stone-baked pizzas, and a global, reasonably priced wine list.

Killorglin Co Kerry

Caragh Lodge
Lakeside country house and restaurant

Caragh Lake, Killorglin, Co Kerry
Tel. +353(0)66 9769115
Email. caraghl@iol.ie
www.caraghlodge.com

Mary and Graham Gaunt's Victorian fishing lodge, on Caragh Lake by the Mc-Gillicuddy Reeks is less than a mile from the Ring of Kerry, yet, surrounded by lush gardens filled with rhododendrons, magnolias, azaleas and other sub-tropical plants, it feels like a peaceful retreat. The house is beautifully furnished with antique furniture, plump sofas, log fires, and profusions of fresh flowers. Its 15 ensuite rooms are charming and luxurious, with spectacular views of the lake and mountains from the garden rooms. Chef Elizabeth Nieman, under Mary Gaunt's supervision, offers truly excellent Irish cuisine. Dinner might begin with Caragh Lodge Caesar salad with smokey bacon, croûtons, Parmesan and anchovy dressing, followed by roast cannon of Kerry lamb with pea and mint purée. Desserts include sticky toffee pudding with butterscotch sauce and vanilla ice cream, or lemon parfait with berry compôte. There's an impressive wine list, featuring both Old and New World selections.

Rooms: 15 ensuite. Double from €195. Single from €140.
Prices: Dinner main course from €20.50. House wine from €24.
Food served: Dinner 19.00-20.30 daily.
Closed: Mid-Oct to end of Apr.
Cuisine: Modern Irish.
Other Points: Garden. Children welcome over 12 years old. Car park. Trout fishing. Winner - Guesthouse with Restaurant 2003.
Directions: From Killorglin on N70 towards Glenbeigh. After approx. 3 miles turn left at blue sign for Caragh Lodge, at lake turn left. The Lodge is on your right.

Molls Gap Co Kerry

Avoca Café
Daytime café and shop

Molls Gap, On the Ring of Kerry, Co Kerry
Tel. +353(0)64 34720
Email. info@avoca.ie
www.avoca.ie

This outpost of the County Wicklow handcrafts company is situated high up at Moll's Gap on the Ring of Kerry, overlooking Carrauntoohill (Ireland's highest mountain), the Gap of Dunloe and the famous lakes of Killarney. The Gap is named after Moll Kissane, who reputedly ran a shebeen (a hostelry of dubious reputation) in this area in the 1800s. As in all the Pratt family's Avoca stores, this one features the company's own clothing range for men, women and children, using soft wools and other natural fibres, as well as tasteful accessories and handcrafts. The attractive, self-service café serves up wholesome, home-cooked foods including roasted carrot, courgette and almond soup; shepherd's pie; selection

Prices: Main course from: €9.50.
Food Served: 9.30-17.00.
Closed: 8 Nov - 10 Mar.
Cuisine: Traditional and modern Irish.
Other Points: Children welcome. Craft shop.
Directions: Located in Molls Gap on the Ring of Kerry.

of quiches and freshly made salads; and chicken and mushroom pie. Choose from such tempting desserts as double chocolate cheesecake, mascarpone cheesecake, lemon curd cake, strawberry meringue roulade, berry crumble, and blue cheese tart. Wine includes a selection of quarter bottles.

Tralee Co Kerry

Ballygarry House Hotel
Country manor hotel and restaurant

Killarney Road, Tralee, Co Kerry
Tel. +353(0)66 7123322
Email. info@ballygarryhouse.com
www.ballygarryhouse.com

Situated on the main road from Tralee to Killarney, and set amid six acres of mature gardens, this pleasant 18th-century private house was converted into a hotel in 1958, and recently refurbished by owner Padraig McGillycuddy. "Character, courtesy, calm and charm" are its watchwords, as well as another "c-word" - comfort. The welcoming public rooms are tastefully decorated with rich, warm colours, fine antiques, oriental rugs, and a blazing fireplace. The 46 spacious guest rooms are furnished to a high standard; bathrooms feature fluffy white bathrobes and luxury toiletries. Leebrook Lounge is a lively informal bar, where you can enjoy a quick coffee, or lunch, early dinner or a cocktail. Brooks restaurant offers excellent service and well-prepared modern Irish classics including char-grilled Irish Angus beef, or medallions of pork tenderloin with soy and ginger sauce. Local activities include hill walking, and golf at the renowned Ballybunion, Mahoney's Point and Tralee golf courses.

Rooms: 46 ensuite. Double from €150. Single from €100. Family from €185.
Prices: Main course lunch from €9.25. Set Sunday lunch €25. Dinner main course from €20. Bar snack main course from €12.50. House wine from €20.
Food served: Bar -12.30-21.30 daily. Restaurant 18.30-21.30 daily.
Closed: 20-26 December.
Cuisine: Traditional with a contemporary twist.
Other Points: Garden. Children welcome. Car park. Library. Licence for Civil Weddings. Winner - Hotel of the Year 2005.
Directions: Situated on the main Tralee to Killarney road, 5 minutes from Tralee town centre and 10 minutes from Kerry International Airport.

Tralee Co Kerry

Restaurant David Norris
Town centre restaurant

Ivy House, Ivy Terrace, Tralee, Co Kerry
Tel. +353(0)66 7185654
Email. restaurantdavidnorris@eircom.net

With its inviting sunflower-yellow walls, white linen-covered tables, and wooden Charles Rennie Macintosh-style chairs, this six-year-old fine-dining establishment epitomises clean, modern chic. David Norris is a member of Euro-Toques, and he uses organic ingredients whenever possible, never sacrificing quality and flavour for over-complicated presentation. The menu is simple, vibrant and reasonably priced: crisp-fried calamari with a spicy tomato/chilli sauce, or cassoulet of venison sausage with chorizo and a brioche and herb crust are representative starters. Main courses range from rainbow trout to pan-fried duck breast to grilled prime sirloin steak to fettuccine of wild mushrooms, all prepared simply but imaginatively. Desserts include hot sticky toffee pudding with vanilla mascarpone, and meringue nest with lemon

Prices: Dinner main course from €16.50-€21.95. House wine from €19.95
Food Served: 17.00-22.00 Tue-Fri. 18.30-22.00 Sat.
Closed: Sun and Mon. One week in Jan, one week in Feb.
Cuisine: Modern Irish.
Directions: Facing Siamsa Tíre in Tralee Town.

curd, whipped cream and passionfruit sauce. An intelligent wine list of global offerings nicely complements the menu. The extra-value Early Bird menu (5 - 7 p.m., Tuesday -Friday, and 5 - 6:30 p.m. Saturday) at €24.95 is worth a detour.

Tralee Co Kerry

The Tankard Bar & Restaurant
Coastal bar and restaurant

Kilfenora, Fenit, Tralee, Co Kerry
Tel. +353(0)66 7136164/7136349
Email. tankard@eircom.net

A long established and well-respected family run pub and restaurant, perfectly situated on Tralee Bay, with fantastic food and wine menus, sounds hard to beat and this one definitely comes up trumps! The Tankard, which claims to be the oldest pub in the area, has been in the family for a few hundred years and is owned by Jerry and Mary O'Sullivan. With a choice between a bar menu for those in a casual mood, which has a range of salads, sandwiches, pastas, burgers, steaks and fish dishes, as well as a children's menu, or if you would like something a bit more upscale, the à la carte restaurant menu equally caters for the seafood or meat lover or indeed the vegetarian! Favouring local and organic produce where possible, the seafood lover could go for oysters from the oyster bed just in front of the pub, followed by the house "speciality" The Seafood Symphony (for 2) which consists of half lobster, scallops, prawns,

Prices: Lunch main course from €11.75. Dinner main course from €13.75. Bar snack from €3.50. House wine from €17.
Food served: 12.00-22.00 daily.
Cuisine: Modern Irish.
Other Points: Children welcome. Car park. Garden. Open Christmas Day.
Directions: 7km on the bayside of Tralee, a bright yellow building.

mussels, grilled oysters, crab claws, salmon and plaice. For those who would rather not go in that direction, there is a boule of Mozzarella served with black and white Clonakilty pudding, apple compôte and crisp leaves or perhaps for mains the rosemary encrusted lamb rack, ovenbaked and served with a honey and rosemary sauce. They have a comprehensive wine list with a very good half bottle selection for the more modest consumer!

Valentia Island Co Kerry

Glanleam House
Island country house

Glanleam Estate, Valentia Island, Co. Kerry
Tel. +353(0)66 9476176
Email. info@glanleam.com
www.glanleam.com

Meta and Jessica Kreissig have owned this eighteenth-century manor house since 1975. Originally a linen factory, it was turned into a private residence in the nineteenth century. The house is hidden away down a winding drive and surrounded by forty acres of painstakingly restored subtropical gardens. The lighthouse on the grounds marks Europe's most westerly point, and there are spectacular views of sea and gardens all around. The sense of space at Glanleam is constantly arresting; a vast hall with a stunning chandelier leads into an equally grand drawing room with floor-to-ceiling bookcases, while a sweeping staircase takes you up to six comfortable bedrooms filled with antiques, each with a sizeable bathroom. Dinner, in keeping with guests' preferences is homecooked and locally sourced, could bring Portmagee crab

Rooms: 6 ensuite rooms. Double from €140-€300.
Prices: Set dinner from €40-€50. House Wine from €12.
Food served: Dinner served at 20.00 approx. (residents only).
Closed: November to March
Cuisine: International, based on organic and local produce.
Other Points: Non-smoking bedrooms. Garden. Children welcome under supervision. Car Park.
Directions: By car ferry after Caherciveen or leave N70 towards Portmagee and take road bridge. On Island follow signs.

claws or roasted zucchini soup with red onion flatbread, followed by baked monkfish with rosemary and garden vegetables.

Muckross House, Gardens & Traditional Farms | *Place to visit*

The National Park, Killarney, Co. Kerry
Tel. +353(0)64 31440
Fax. +353(0)64 33926
Email. muckrosshouse@duchas.ie
www.muckross-house.ie

Situated close to the shores of Muckross Lake, amidst the beautiful scenery of Killarney National Park, the house is the focal point within the Park and is the ideal base from which to explore it's terrain. The elegantly furnished rooms portray the lifestyles of the landed gentry, while downstairs in the basement, experience the working conditions of the servants employed in the house. From April to July Muckross Gardens are spectacularly adorned with the red and pink flowers of mature Rhododendrons. Take a stroll down memory lane at Muckross Traditional Farms, which recreate and portray the traditional farming methods and way of life, of a typical local, rural community of the 1930's.

Other Points
Multi-lingual Guided Tours, Walled Garden Centre, Mucros Craft Shop and Workshops including Mucros Weaving and Mucros Pottery and Garden Restaurant.

Hours
Open daily all year round (except the Christmas period).
Muckross House:
Daily Jul to Aug 9.00 - 19.00
Daily Sep to Jun 9.00 - 18.00
Traditional Farms:
Weekends & bank holidays
Mar 20 to Apr 29
Daily May to Oct

Admission charged to House and Traditional Farms. Gardens Free.

Killimer-Tarbert Car Ferry | *Local amenity*

Shannon Ferry Group Limited
Killimer, Kilrush, Co Clare
Tel. +353 (0)65 905 3124
Fax. +353 (0)65 905 3125
Email. enquiries@shannonferries.com
www.shannonferries.com

Killimer-Tarbert Car Ferry, "Bridging the Best of Ireland's West", links the main tourist routes of the West of Ireland from Killimer, Co. Clare to Tarbert, Co. Kerry as part of the N67. With scheduled sailings every day, this pleasant twenty minute journey across the Shannon Estuary will save 85 miles /137 km from ferry terminal to ferry terminal providing a staging point for the many attractions of Clare, Kerry and adjoining counties. Take some time to enjoy our visitor centre, which stocks an extensive range of books, souvenirs, music, tea, coffee, sweets and ice-creams.

Timetable
Service every day of the year except Christmas Day (weather permitting)

1st April to 30th September

	Departure	Mon-Sat	Sun
1st Ferry	Killimer every hour on the hour	7.00 - 21.00	9.00 - 21.00
	Tarbert every hour on the 1/2 hour	7.30 - 21.30	9.30 - 21.30
Mid May - end Septmber (Additional Sailings)			
2nd Ferry	Killimer every hour on the 1/2 hour.	10.30 - 17.30	
	Tarbert every hour on the hour.	11.00 - 18.00	

1st October to 31st March

	Departure	Mon-Sat	Sun
1st Ferry	Killimer every hour on the hour	7.00 - 19.00	9.00 - 19.00
	Tarbert every hour on the 1/2 hour	7.30 - 19.30	9.30 - 19.30

MORE THAN A LOAD OF OLD COCOA

Real chocolate, as distinct from confectionary, is no laughing matter.

Charlotte Coleman-Smith seeks out the few really serious players scattered about the country.

Charlotte Coleman-Smith is a freelance writer specialising in food

Country Choice
DELICATESSEN & COFFEE BAR

Delicious
Sesame & Poppy
Seed Biscuits

Country Choice
POPPY & SESAME SEED
BISCUITS
150 g

Country Choice
POPPY & SESAME SEED
BISCUITS
150 g

Country Choice
POPPY & SESAME SEED
BISCUITS
150 g

cocoabean

Cocoa Coasters
Delicious delicate discs of
dark chocolate in eight stunning flavours.

Hot
ulge!
Vanilla,
Cinnamon.

cocoabean

cocoabean
cocoa coasters

cocoabean
cocoa coasters

BABLAMA
FIGS

In recent years, thanks to a dedicated band of small, artisan businesses, there's been a revolution in our attitude to chocolate. Content, for decades, to munch on waxy, vegetable-fat-laden bars - but happy to shell out on fine wine and lavish restaurants - we're now waking up to the notion that really good chocolate is a substance apart, something which, when produced with care and the best raw ingredients, has as many complex and subtle flavours as vintage wine, good olive oil or coffee.

Cocoa Bean Handmade Chocolates

Sisters Sarah Hehir and Emily Sandford of Cocoa Bean in Limerick see themselves at the cutting edge of this chocolate revolution. Their passion is for dark chocolate and their funky, brightly packaged pieces in bold flavours like lime zest and black pepper, or tamarind with star anise and ginger, break the gold-and-brown mould of so many 'classic' chocolates. That such mind-bending flavour combinations should be used successfully with chocolate is part of the excitement. One of their 'hottest' flavours is a chilli chocolate, made with pink peppercorns, essence of oak and chilli flakes. 'It's incredible', says Sarah. 'It's fragrant at first, then a tickle of heat hits the back of the tongue.'

Four years ago, unable to find the kind of good quality dark chocolate they craved, Sarah and Emily began by experimenting in Sarah's kitchen. Regular, positive feedback from customers at Limerick market gave them the impetus and capital to expand, without compromising their ethos that all ingredients, where possible, should be ethically traded and grown to organic principles. Now, they source from the best growers around the world. Their cocoa beans are traceable to single estates where, they say, 'standards go beyond organic', and they diligently seek out the freshest produce they can, with seasonal ingredients such as crab apple often finding their way into the truffles. At Cocoa Bean's Limerick workshop, ingredients are zested, roasted, crushed by hand, and all chocolates are carefully handwrapped. 'It's so exciting', says Sarah, 'because the potential for different combinations is huge. You really have to open your mind. Chocolate can cross between sweet and savoury, it can take on exotic spices, even fresh herbs'.

It's so exciting', says Sarah, 'because the potential for different combinations is huge. You really have to open your mind'.

The Skelligs Chocolate Company

Eleven years ago, the kitchen table was also the starting point for Skelligs, Michael and Amanda McGabhann's distinct brand of artisan chocolates. Now owned by businessman Colm Healy, Skelligs chocolates are produced on the Iveragh peninsula in West Kerry. This remote setting is an intimate part of the Skelligs identity; the collectable boxes are handpainted with evocative images of the Kerry landscape, as if sea and sky have permeated the flavours themselves. 'There's a romance to being here', says Colm. 'We're at the foot of the glen, among sheep and cows, and we're the most westerly chocolate factory in Europe. We're not hassled by the same pressures as other businesses and we can afford to take time.'

Milk and dark chocolate truffles such as rum and black cherry, champagne and raspberry are handmade by traditional methods, and have proved a huge hit. The company has expanded into the corporate market and maintains a steady retail trade. But the essence of Skelligs is the location; visitors to the open-plan factory are, says Colm, overwhelmed by the glorious aroma of chocolates and seduced by the gorgeous surroundings. Hardly any leave empty-handed.

And what of the growing number of competing small businesses? 'It's not exactly competition', says Colm. 'After all, no two recipes are the same. It's like if two cooks make a casserole, the end result is always different. And if it gives people more choice, then, that's great.'

Gallwey's Chocolates

When Ciara Power first tasted a Gallwey's royal praline, she liked it so much she bought the company. 'I was so impressed by the whole package – the wonderful purity of taste, the exquisite box, the sense of history. I didn't want to change a thing.' But she knew her youth and energy could bring something special to the business. When Ciara took over, Grichie Gallwey, now in her seventies, was more or less doing everything herself, and the chocolates were still being made in the kitchen of the Gallwey family house in Waterford, where Grichie had started making them twelve years earlier, initially for dinner party guests. 'I realised I could really get out on the road and spread the word,' says Ciara. 'The other day, we loaded up the car and drove to France to fulfil an order'. With the business, Ciara took on the guardianship of the family whiskey recipe - the first time it had been revealed to an outsider since Henry Gallwey founded his whiskey blending business in 1835. The company now operates from new premises, but Power, helped by her parents, employs the same five skilled staff. There are three handmade truffles in the range -Irish whiskey, royal praline and Irish coffee - and this tight focus, combined with locally sourced ingredients, ensures that standards remain high. The look is sleek, luxurious and timeless - and Power insists things will stay that way. ∎

Cocoa Bean Handmade Chocolates

Unit 3b, Limerick Food Kitchen, The Crossagalla Industrial estate, Bally, Co. Limerick.
Tel. +353 61 44 6615. Fax. +353 6144 6615. Mail order. Available from all good delicatessens nationwide and Limerick Market. www.cocoabeanchocolates.com

The Skelligs Chocolate Co.

St Finian's Bay, Ballinskelligs, Co Kerry.
Tel. +353 66 947 9119. From good delicatessens, mail order. Factory open all year round from 10am-5pm Mon-Fri (until 4pm winter); 12-5pm Sat and Sun. www.skelligschocolate.com

Gallwey's of Waterford

Abbeylands Business Park, Ferrybank, Waterford.
Tel. +353 51 830 860.
For superb handmade Irish whisky truffles

Try also

Aine's for luxury handmade chocolates.
Ann Rudden, Raffin, Castletown, Navan, Co Meath, Ireland. Tel. +353 49 8542769. Fax. +353 46 9052914.

Blake's for fine imported Swiss 100% organic chocolate. Denise Gleeson, Tuam, Co Galway.
Tel. +353 46 9557077.

O'Conaill Chocolatiers for handmade, diabetic and couverture chocolate; The Rock, Church Rd, Carrigaline, Co Cork. Tel. +353 21 437 3407.
www.oconaillchocolate.com

Wilde's Irish Handmade Chocolates for crafted designs based on cultural and literary themes. Patricia Farrell, Unit 6, Enterprise Centre, Tuamgraney, Co Clare, Ireland. Tel. +353 61 922080. Fax. +353 61 922080.

Key Events

Festival St Patrick's Day Festivals	Throughout Region March 13 - 17	
Music Fleadh Nua	Ennis May 23 - 30	
Festival Lisdoonvarna Matchmaking Festival	Lisdoonvarna Sept 1 - Oct	

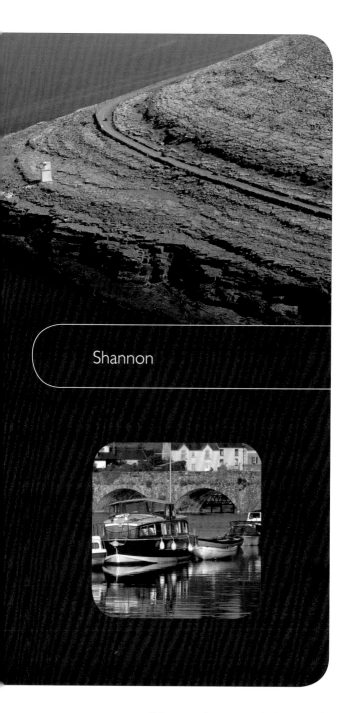

Shannon

| **Ballyvaughan** Co Clare | |

Rusheen Lodge
Guesthouse

Ballyvaughan, Co Clare
Tel. +353(0)65 7077092
Email. rusheen@iol.ie
www.rusheenlodge.com

This 9-room, family-owned guesthouse is the perfect base from which to explore the magnificent the Burren, the cliffs of Moher, the Aran Islands, and the lively village of Ballyvaughan. Karen McGann is in charge, having taken over from her parents, John and Rita McGann, and she runs the house with warmth and efficiency. Large, bright, comfortable bedrooms with generous-sized beds and pleasant bathrooms overlook a stunning garden, whose colourful plantings are echoed in the abundance of fresh flower arrangements around the house. The guest lounge provides a relaxing spot to read or watch TV. Breakfast is served in a mint green-themed dining room, overlooking the spectacular Burren mountains. Its choices might include local smoked salmon and scrambled eggs, local smoked ham, or a

Rooms: 9 ensuite. Double from €76. Single from €68. Family from €90.
Closed: Mid Nov - mid Feb.
Other Points: Non-smoking house. Garden. Children welcome. Car park.
Directions: Situated 0.75km outside the village of Ballyvaughan on the N67 Lisdoonvarna road.

traditional Irish or continental breakfast. Evening meals are available at a number of pubs and restaurants in the village, and for golfers, the excellent Lahinch and Galway Bay courses are nearby.

| **Ballyvaughan** Co Clare | VC |

The Farmshop at Aillwee Cave
Farmshop and cheese makers

Ballyvaughan, Co Clare
Tel. +353(0)65 7077036
Email. barbara@aillweecave.ie
www.aillweecave.ie

Visitors to the two-million-year-old cave at Aillwee, in the spectacular limestone landscape of the Burren, should make time for the splendid farm shop alongside. Ben Johnson, cheesemaker and apiarist, is responsible for the production of award-winning Burren Gold, a Gouda-type cheese which you can watch being made before tasting. If inspiration strikes, you can sign up to one of Ben's cheesemaking courses. A wide range of other local cheeses - Poulcoin goat's cheese, Cratloe sheep's cheese - as well as pickles, homemade jams, pestos, oil and spiced vinegars fill the shelves. Ben dons his beekeeping hat to produce honeycombs and wildflower honey. The shop also stocks up to 20 varieties of homemade fudge, ranging from triple

Hours: Open daily.
10.00-18.30 April-September.
10.00-17.00 October-March.
Other Points: Car Park. Children welcome. Cheese making.
Directions: Located 5km south of Ballyvaughan on the R480.

chocolate to maraschino cherry. There's a potato bar, with attractive stone seating and outsize images of local wildflowers, as well as a tea room for freshly made soups, sandwiches, quiches and ginger bread, and a kiosk selling hot dogs and muffins in peak season only.

Lahinch Co Clare

Barrtra Seafood Restaurant
Coastal restaurant

Lahinch, Co Clare
Tel.+353(0)65 7081280
Email. barrtra@hotmail.com
www.barrtra.com

This intimate restaurant feels like a real find, set as it is down a small country lane just outside Lahinch. The white modern-style cottage overlooks Liscannor Bay, and there are splendid views from the restaurant and conservatory. Paul O'Brien serves drinks and takes orders in the cosy bar, while his wife, Theresa is in charge of the kitchen. Her menu is always stylishly simple, with seafood the main focus. Starters such as mussels in wine and garlic, and oysters on the half shell showcase the freshest produce, while main courses, including cod with orange and ginger sauce, and lemon sole stuffed with crab, leave diners spoilt for choice. There are plenty of non-fishy dishes, too: lamb shank with red wine sauce, for example, while vegetarian options include St Tola goats' cheese in filo pastry with aubergine. There's homemade ice cream to finish, and a well balanced wine list includes half bottles and dessert wines.

Prices: Dinner main course from €18. Set Sunday lunch €28. House wine from €17.
Food Served: 13.00-21.00 Sun. 17.00-22.00 Mon-Sat.
Closed: Jan & Feb.
Cuisine: Modern Irish.
Other Points: Garden. Car park. Children welcome. Commended - Restaurant of the Year 2003.
Directions: From Lahinch follow the signposts to Miltown Malbay road, the N67. About one and a half miles along this road take a right hand turn down a small road to Barrtra Restaurant.

Local Farmers' Markets

Ballyvaughan Thursdays 10am-2pm
Birr, The Full Moon Market
Every 3rd Saturday
Ennis Farmers Market Fridays 8am-2pm
Killaloe Sundays 11am–3pm
Kilrush Saturdays 8am-2pm
Limerick Market Saturdays 8am-2pm

Lisdoonvarna Co Clare   ● ◉ CS VC

The Burren Smokehouse
Smoked fish/gourmet store & craft shop

Lisdoonvarna, Co Clare
Tel. +353(0)65 7074432
Email. info@burrensmokehouse.ie
www.burrensmokehouse.ie

Will it be a side of oak-smoked Irish Atlantic salmon for a large family gathering, or a selection of smoked trout, mackerel and eel for a house gift, or a luxurious Aran Basket, laden with smoked salmon, smoked Gouda cheese, Butlers Irish chocolate, and a 75cl bottle of ruby port, for a sumptuous picnic? Birgitta and Peter Curtin started their business in 1989, and since then its products have earned a prestigious Gold medal at the U.K.-based "Great Taste" awards, and other accolades. Tour the old-fashioned stone smokehouse for a look at the fish-smoking process from filleting to dispatch; view its replica working kiln, and learn about ancient Irish techniques for smoking salmon. Between the shop's fine selection of gourmet products - smoked fish, Irish cheeses, patés, chutneys, chocolates, honey, traditional Irish porter and whisky cakes and utensils, maps, crafts,

Opening hours: 9.00-17.00 & 9.00-18.00 Jun & Aug and weekends. 10.00-16.00 Jan to Mar.
Closed: Good Friday. 25, 26 Dec.
Other Points: Video presentation on smoking of fish. Craft shop. Children welcome. Car park.
Directions: Eight kilometres from the Cliffs of Moher. Five hundred metres from the square in Lisdoonvarna on the Doolin side of the town. Two hundred metres from The Roadside Tavern.

music and books, there is something for everyone at this Burren landmark.

Lisdoonvarna Co Clare   P ✗ Y

The Roadside Tavern
Traditional pub and restaurant

Lisdoonvarna, Co Clare
Tel. +353(0)65 7074084
Email. info@burrensmokehouse.ie
www.burrensmokehouse.ie

The Roadside Tavern, just 8km from the cliffs of Moher, is renowned as one of the oldest pubs in Clare. It has been run by the Curtin family, who also run The Burren Smokehouse, for over 100 years and has a deserved reputation for its relaxed atmosphere and live music - seven nights a week during the summer. It has become a meeting point for musicians of the North Clare area, as well as a focus for visitors. Enjoy a pint of creamy stout with a nicely concise menu of unfussy, traditional dishes, featuring smoked salmon, trout and eel from the smokehouse, with meat and organic salad leaves from local producers. There are homemade chowders, boiled bacon and cabbage, freshly baked apple pie, and irresistible fishy dishes such as pickled herring with warm buttered baby potatoes and natural yogurt dressing, and baked 'hot smoked salmon' on colcannon. Vegetarian

Prices: Main course from €9. Bar snack from €3.50. House wine from €15.
Opening hours: 10.00-23.30
Food served: 12.00-21.00 May-Sept. 12.00-15.00 rest of year.
Closed: Good Friday & 25 Dec.
Cuisine: Modern Irish and traditional.
Other Points: Car park. Traditional Irish music nightly during the summer months and Friday & Saturday nights rest of year.
Directions: Eight kilometres from the Cliffs of Moher. Two hundred metres down from the square of Lisdoonvarna on the Doolin road.

and coeliac-friendly options are helpfully marked up.

Bunratty Medieval Castle Banquet

Newmarket-on-Fergus Co Clare

Carrygerry Country House
Country house and restaurant

Newmarket-on-Fergus, Co Clare
Tel. +353(0)61 360500
Email. info@carrygerryhouse.com
www.carrygerryhouse.com.

Gillian and Niall Ennis' beautiful country house is set in seven acres of mature woodlands with lovely views over the Shannon estuary, just three miles from Shannon airport. Built in 1793, it was carefully restored in the late 'eighties. The restaurant is a handsome space in shades of warm plum with chairs upholstered in matching fabric. The same colours predominate in the drawing room, where period furniture adds gracious charm. Niall's modern Irish menu - using organic fruit and vegetables, home-grown herbs and the best local meat and seafood - includes classics such as deep-fried Brie with raspberry coulis, and a house Caesar salad with smoked chicken breast. Main courses bring satisfying dishes such as supreme of guinea fowl stuffed with dill cream cheese, red onion mash and red wine sauce. To finish, there are delicious homemade cheesecakes, ice creams, tarts and a 'light' banoffi pie. Twelve ensuite

Rooms: 12 ensuite. Double from €110. Single from €55. Family from €145.
Prices: Set dinner (5-course) €35. House wine from €18.50.
Food Served: 18.30-21.30 Tue-Fri. 18.30-22.00 Sat.
Closed: 25, 26 December.
Cuisine: Modern and traditional Irish.
Other Points: Children welcome. Car park. Non-smoking house.
Directions: Take slip road for airport, then take first exit for airport at next roundabout, take fourth exit for Newmarket, next roundabout take second exit, continue for two miles to T-junction, turn right, Carrygerry House quarter mile on the right.

bedrooms are luxuriously furnished, some with four-posters.

New Quay Co Clare

Linnanes Lobster Bar
Coastal bar and restaurant

New Quay, Burrin, Co Clare
Tel. +353(0)65 7078120
Email.linnaneslobsterbar@hotmail.com

Linnane's is just the sort of simple, "real Irish" seafood place that is becoming increasingly rare. Situated just 500 metres off the main Galway road, with its back doors opening on to beautiful Galway Bay, the traditional, yellow-painted cottage boasts a cosy bar, where pints of Guinness and lots of friendly banter are the norm. The tempting and affordable menu includes ocean-fresh seafood chowder with brown bread, open smoked salmon sandwich, open crab sandwich, crab cakes, clams and pasta, steamed fresh mussels, salmon steak, scallops New Quay, seafood platter and, of course, lobster. Sirloin steak and vegetarian dishes are available, too. The fish is all supplied by the Ocean West Fishery, from the pier opposite, and the nearby Kinvara smokery. A limited wine list offers bottles by the full, half- and quarter-bottle. There

Prices: Lunch main course from €9. Dinner main course from €10. House wine from €16.
Food Served: 12.30-21.00 high season & weekends only in off season. Check in advance.
Closed: Good Friday. 25 Dec.
Cuisine: Traditional Irish. Seafood a speciality.
Other Points: Children welcome. Car park.
Directions: Off the main Kinvara Ballyvaughan road on journey from Galway to Lisdoonvarna.

are a few homely desserts, or round off the meal with a smooth and warming Irish coffee.

Quin Co Clare

The Gallery Restaurant
Village restaurant

Main Street, Quin, Co Clare
Tel. +353(0)65 6825789
Email. marian@thegalleryquin.com
www.thegalleryquin.com

Gerry and Marian Walsh's Gallery Restaurant, situated in the small, historic village of Quin opposite the abbey and a short distance from Knappogue castle, was tastefully refurbished in 2005. The attractive stone exterior is softened by window boxes overflowing with flowers and two smart, potted bay trees. Gerry is in charge of the kitchens, and his menu is an appetising list of familiar dishes which make good use of seasonal produce. For Sunday lunch, there are soups, roasts and fish of the day, as well as toasted sandwiches and deep-fried plaice with salad and chips. Dinner brings signature dishes such as rack of Burren lamb with rosemary and garlic sauce and timewarp favourites such as prawn cocktail Marie Rose. Elsewhere, there's fillet of brill with a chive and butter sauce, tagliatelle

Prices: Set Sunday lunch €20. Dinner main course from €17.50. House wine from €19.50.
Food served: Lunch 12.00-16.00 Sun only. Dinner 18.00-22.00 daily.
Cuisine: Traditional Irish.
Other Points: Children welcome.
Directions: Located in Quin village, seven miles from Ennis on the R469 and two miles from Knappogue Castle.

with parmesan, broccoli and basil cream, and honeycomb ice cream with butterscotch sauce. The concise wine list includes an organic French sauvignon.

Admiralty Lodge, Spanish Point

Spanish Point Co Clare

Admiralty Lodge
Seaside country house & restaurant

Spanish Point, Milltown Malbay,
Co Clare
Tel. +353 (0)65 7085007
Email.info@admiralty.ie
www.admiralty.ie

This country house stands in a peaceful setting overlooking the beautiful beach at Spanish Point, forty minutes from Shannon airport. It's ideally situated for golfing guests, with the Spanish Point Links course just minutes away, and the Doonbeg and Lahinch championship courses a short drive. Inside, pretty wallpaper in shades of dark pink, plenty of comfortable, brown leather armchairs, antique prints and ornate ceilings lend an elegant, feel to the interior. Twelve spacious, individually designed bedrooms with four-poster beds, marble en-suites and flat screen tvs, provide guests with comforts both traditional and modern. The smart restaurant, complete with grand piano and white, wood-panelled walls, offers sophisticated country house cooking. Baked roulade of Inagh goat's cheese with red pepper and ginger chutney and hazelnut tapenade is a typical starter, while mains might include pan-roasted cod with

Rooms: 12 ensuite. Double from €160. Single from €125. Family from €200.
Prices: Lunch main course from €15 Dinner main course from €20. Bar Snack from €6. House Wine from €24.
Food served: Afternoon tea & Lounge menu served daily. Dinner served from 18.30-21.30 daily.
Closed: Closed mid-week in Jan & Feb.
Cuisine: (European) Contemporary Mediterranean.
Other Points: Non-smoking bedrooms. Garden. Car Park. Helipad. Children over 3 years welcome.
Directions: On the main Galway/ Kerry coastal Road. 10 minutes drive from Lahinch.

braised baby gems and velouté of haricots blanc. Finish with a selection of delicious homemade ice-creams.

Nearest Golf Courses
Birr Golf Club *Tel. + 353 (0)509 20082*
Doonbeg Golf Club *Tel. + 353 (0)65 9055600*
Ennis Golf Club *Tel. + 353 (0)65 6824074*
Nenagh Golf Club *Tel. + 353 (0)67 31476*
Lahinch Championship Links *Tel. + 353 (0)65 7081003*
Limerick Golf Club *Tel. + 353 (0)61 415146*
Spanish Point Links Course *Tel. + 353 (0)65 7084219*

Nearest Racecourses
Limerick Racecourse *Tel. + 353 (0)61 320000*
Thurles Racecourse *Tel. + 353 (0)504 22253*

Brian Boru Heritage Centre | *Place to visit*

Killaloe, Co Clare
Tel. +353(0)61 360788
Fax. +353(0)61 361020
Email. reservations@shannondev.ie
www.shannonheritage.com

The lake town of Killaloe is picturesquely situated at the southwest tip of Lough Derg. The 11th. century High King of Ireland, Brian Boru who was one of the most influential and colourful figures in Irish history was born here.
The heritage centre, which is located within the Tourist Information Centre, reveals the story of Brian Boru through a series of colourful exhibits, graphic illustrations and an interactive audio-visual presentation

Other Points
Gift/souvenir shop, parking.

Admission charged

Hours
May to Sept: daily 10.00 - 18.00
(last admission to exhibition 17.30)
Times may be subject to change.

Directions
Situated off the N7 between Limerick and Nenagh - take the R 494 route to Killaloe & Ballina.

Bunratty Folk Park Traditional Irish Night | *Place to visit*

The Corn Barn, Bunratty Folk Park, Bunratty, Co Clare
Tel. +353(0)61 360788
Fax. +353(0)61 361020
Email. reservations@shannondev.ie
www.shannonheritage.com

Experience the magic of Irish music, song and dance. The Corn Barn is the perfect setting for a celebration of the best traditions of Ireland today. You are invited to enjoy the company of the finest singers, dancers and musicians of the local villages and experience the homeliness, friendship and warmth of a true traditional Irish evening. This evening has something to offer everyone: stories of life in Ireland in bygone days, traditional and contemporary dancing and Irish music that will have your feet tapping and your hands clapping. Dine on home cooked food and excellent wine while enjoying lively entertainment.

Hours
Apr to Oct: Nightly at 19.00
(reservations necessary).

Admission charged

Directions
Located just off the N18 between Limerick City and Ennis, 7.4 miles from Shannon Airport and 8 miles from Limerick City.

Bunratty Castle & Folk Park | *Place to visit*

Bunratty, Co Clare
Tel. +353(0)61 360788
Fax. +353(0)61 361020
Email. reservations@shannondev.ie
www.shannonheritage.com

At Ireland's premier visitor attraction, enjoy two wonderful experiences - the acclaimed 15th century Bunratty Castle and 19th century Folk Park. The Castle is the most complete and authentic medieval fortress in Ireland thanks to its splendid restoration. At night time it is the impressive setting for medieval banquets which are held year round. Bunratty Folk Park is where 19th century Irish life is recreated, in a 'living' village and rural setting. Meet the "Bean an Ti" and street characters including the Policeman and the Schoolteacher who give the site its sparkle. Enjoy the tastes, scents, sights and sounds of this enchanting place.

Other Points
Gift/souvenir shop, parking, toilets, picnic area, wheelchair access.

Admission charged

Hours
Open year round
Jan, Feb, Mar, Nov. & Dec 9.30-17.30
(Last Admission to Folk Park 16.15)
Apr, May, Sept & Oct - 9.00-17.30
(Last Admission to Folk Park 16.15)
June, July & Aug - 9.00 - 18.00
(Last Admission to Folk Park 17.15)
Last Admission to the Castle - 16.00
Year round.
Closed Good Friday & Dec 24th, 25th, 26th.
Times may be subject to change

Directions
Located just off the N18 between Limerick City and Ennis, 7.4 miles from Shannon Airport and 8 miles from Limerick City.

Bunratty Medieval Castle Banquet | *Place to visit*

Bunratty, Co Clare
Tel. +353(0)61 360788
Fax. +353(0)61 361020
Email. reservations@shannondev.ie
www.shannonheritage.com

Join the Earl of Thomond for a glorious banquet at this majestic 15th century castle. The Earl's Butler welcomes guests from the four corners of the world toasting an era of great Irish taste with excellent food, fine wine and honey mead. You will be entertained by the world famous Bunratty Singers with enchanting melodies to harp and violin accompaniment. For over 40 years the Ladies of the Castle along with the Earl's Butler have entertained guests in time honoured tradition. The Castle Entertainers have toured extensively, appeared on top television shows and entertained many well known dignitaries and celebrities.

Hours
Twice nightly, year round (reservations necessary) at 17.30 and 20.45.

Admission charged

Directions
Located just off the N18 between Limerick City and Ennis, 7.4 miles from Shannon Airport and 8 miles from Limerick City.

Cliffs of Moher & O'Brien's Tower | *Place to visit*

Near Liscannor, Co Clare
Tel. +353(0)61 360788
Fax. +353(0)61 361020
Email. reservations@shannondev.ie
www.shannonheritage.com

A must on any itinerary to Ireland is the Cliffs of Moher and O'Brien's Tower. The Cliffs are 8kms long and 214m high, it is here that you can most easily get a feel for the wildness of the terrain over which the Celts wandered. O'Brien's Tower was built by Cornelius O'Brien, a descendant of Brian Boru, the High King of Ireland, as an observation point for tourists visiting the Cliffs. From here one can easily view the Aran Islands, Galway Bay, the Twelve Pins and the Maum Turk mountains to the North in Connemara and Loop Head to the South.

Visitor Centre
Open all year. Closed from week before Christmas until December 27th.

Directions
From Ennis, take the N85 to Ennistymon and then travel to Lahinch (via N67). Take the R478 via Liscannor to the Cliffs of Moher. From Galway travel the N18 to Kilcolgan and turn right on to the N67 and travel via Lisdoonvarna and then on to the R478 which leads to the Cliffs of Moher.

Other Points
Gift/souvenir shop, tearoom/restaurant, parking, toilets, picnic area.

Hours
O'Brien's Tower
Mar to Oct: daily 9.30 - 17.30 (weather permitting).

Craggaunowen - The Living Past | *Place to visit*

Near Kilmurry, Co Clare
Tel. +353(0)61 360788
Fax. +353(0)61 361020
Email. reservations@shannondev.ie
www.shannonheritage.com

Craggaunowen - the Living Past Experience is Ireland's original award winning Pre-historic Park. Situated on 50 acres of wooded grounds, it features a stunning recreation of some of the homesteads, animals and artefacts, which existed in Ireland over 1,000 years ago. Explore the Crannog, the Ring Fort, and the 'Brendan Boat' - a leather hulled boat used to re-enact the Atlantic voyage of St. Brendan and the early Christian monks reputed to have discovered America centuries before Columbus. Enjoy the fresh air and lake walks in a most enjoyable rural setting. Savour the wonderful home made fare in the charming farmhouse tearoom.

Hours
Mid Apr to Sept: daily 10.00 - 18.00 (Last admission 17.00)
Opening times may be subject to change.

Other Points
Gift/souvenir shop, tearoom, parking, toilets, picnic area, wheelchair access.

Admission charged

Directions
Situated off the N18 - from Limerick take the R462 from Cratloe and after Kilmurry take the R469. From Ennis take the R469.

Knappogue Medieval Castle Banquet | *Place to visit*

Knappogue Castle, Quin, Co Clare
Tel. +353(0)61 360788
Fax. +353(0)61 361020
Email. reservations@shannondev.ie
www.shannonheritage.com

Enjoy a night of musical splendour and entertainment at historic Knappogue Castle. Once the splendid home of Sean MacNamara, a medieval Lord, it is now the imposing venue for a memorable evening of the feast of kings. Here the ladies of the Castle welcome guests with a programme of music, song and dance taking you on a musical journey from medieval times to the present day. This colourful and vivid show will enthral and delight from the moment of arrival through an entire evening of good food and wines, as the Earl's Butler ensures that everything proceeds in time-honoured tradition.

Hours
Apr to Oct: 18.30.
(Reservations necessary).

Admission charged

Directions
Located off the N18 outside the village of Quin. From Limerick, take the R462 from Cratloe until you arrive at Kilmurry and then take the R469 towards Quin. From Ennis take the R469.

Knappogue Castle & Walled Gardens | *Place to visit*

Quin, Co Clare
Tel. +353(0)61 360788
Fax. +353(0)61 361020
Email. reservations@shannondev.ie
www.shannonheritage.com

Don't miss this truly magnificent medieval Castle in the unspoilt landscape of idyllic Quin, Co Clare. Knappogue Castle was built in 1467 by Sean MacNamara, son of Sioda (who built Bunratty Castle) and has a long and varied history. It has been host to two Irish Presidents as well as other heads of state including General de Gaulle. Visit the magical setting of the recently restored Walled Garden - a romantic oasis to sit and muse or just escape the 'madding crowd'. The castle also plays host to the famous medieval banquet and is available for hire as an exclusive wedding venue.

Other Points
Gift/souvenir shop, parking, toilets.

Admission charged

Hours
May to Mid Sept: 9.30 - 17.00
(last admission 16.15)
Times may be subject to change.

Directions
Located off the N18 outside the village of Quin. From Limerick, take the R462 from Cratloe until you arrive at Kilmurry and then take the R469 towards Quin. From Ennis take the R469.

The Burren Perfumery | *Place to visit*

Perfumery, Floral Centre and Tearooms
Carron, Co Clare
Tel. +353 (0)65 7089102
Email. burrenperfumery@eircom.net
www.burrenperfumery.com

A visit to the Burren Perfumery is a pleasure for all the senses. Perfumes, floral waters, soaps and other plant-based products are prepared by hand on the premises all year round. There is an excellent free slideshow on the flora of the region, which is complemented by the organic herb garden, in which visitors can examine samples of the plants and herbs used by the Perfumery. Relax in the rose covered Tea rooms, which serve a mouth watering selection of organic cakes, scones and pies. Homemade soups with freshly baked bread and selections of local cheeses and salads are all made with organic vegetables from local suppliers. Enjoy fresh herbal teas from the garden and coffees from around the world. An oasis of tranquility in the heart of the Burren - rest in the quietness far from crowds and traffic, broken only by birdsong.

Hours
Open daily all year round.
May - Aug 9.00 - 19.00
Sept - Apr 9.00 - 17.00

Tearooms: 9.00 - 17.00 daily Apr to Sept, weekends only Oct - Dec.

Other Points
Floral Centre and perfumery. Tearooms (organic local produce). Free audiovisual show, distillation, soap making, herb garden and shop. Children welcome.

Admission Free

Directions
Twenty minutes drive from Corofin, Ballyvaughan, or Kinvara. 2 km from Carron village. Signposted.

Killimer-Tarbert Car Ferry | *Local amenity*

Shannon Ferry Group Limited
Killimer, Kilrush, Co Clare
Tel. +353 (0)65 905 3124
Fax. +353 (0)65 905 3125
Email. enquiries@shannonferries.com
www.shannonferries.com

Killimer-Tarbert Car Ferry, "Bridging the Best of Ireland's West", links the main tourist routes of the West of Ireland from Killimer, Co. Clare to Tarbert, Co. Kerry as part of the N67. With scheduled sailings every day, this pleasant twenty minute journey across the Shannon Estuary will save 85 miles /137 km from ferry terminal to ferry terminal providing a staging point for the many attractions of Clare, Kerry and adjoining counties. Take some time to enjoy our visitor centre, which stocks an extensive range of books, souvenirs, music, tea, coffee, sweets and ice-creams.

Timetable
Service every day of the year except Christmas Day (weather permitting)

1st April to 30th September

	Departure	Mon-Sat	Sun
1st Ferry	Killimer every hour on the hour	7.00 - 21.00	9.00 - 21.00
	Tarbert every hour on the 1/2 hour	7.30 - 21.30	9.30 - 21.30

Mid May - end Septmber (Additional Sailings)

2nd Ferry	Killimer every hour on the 1/2 hour.	10.30 - 17.30	
	Tarbert every hour on the hour.	11.00 - 18.00	

1st October to 31st March

	Departure	Mon-Sat	Sun
1st Ferry	Killimer every hour on the hour	7.00 - 19.00	9.00 - 19.00
	Tarbert every hour on the 1/2 hour	7.30 - 19.30	9.30 - 19.30

Adare Co Limerick

Lloyd's of Adare
Restaurant, coffee shop, deli and wine bar

Main Street, Adare, Co Limerick
Tel. +353 (0)61 395796
Email. anncaline@yahoo.co.uk

Anne Fitzgerald has owned this restaurant, deli and wine bar in the picturesque village of Adare for the past three years. She is committed to using the finest produce - organic and local wherever possible - and sources from local butchers and fishmongers, with all game coming from a private shoot in Cork, and vegetables and fruit locally grown. All meals are freshly prepared daily on the premises, and the straightforward menu offers some delicious, traditional dishes such as Irish stew, alongside bistro favourites such as chicken liver paté, salmon fishcakes, gratin of crab, lasagne and quiche lorraine. Vegetarian diners, and anyone who enjoys good homebaking, will love the roast pepper and goat's cheese tart. Soups are seasonally driven, with a delicate lettuce and mint a particular summer treat, and carrot and ginger with coriander offering a subtle blend of earthy

Prices: Breakfast from €6.95. Lunch main course from €9.50. Dinner main course from €18.50. House wine from €15.95.
Food served: 9.00-18.00 Sat-Wed. 9.00-21.00 Thu & Fri.
Closed: 25 Dec for one week.
Cuisine: Modern Irish with Mediterranean influences.
Other Points: Children welcome. Outside catering service.
Directions: From Limerick - after the roundabout on the right fork of road. From Kerry - left at fork of road.

flavours. There's a selection of homemade desserts and ice creams to finish.

Glin Co Limerick

Glin Castle
Historic country house

Glin, Co Limerick
Tel. +353(0)68 34173
Email. knight@iol.ie
www.glincastle.com

This magnificent gothic castle - our 2004 Country House of the Year - was built in the eighteenth century to succeed the medieval ruin in the village of Glin. It stands in splendid grounds on the banks of the river Shannon, and is owned and lived in by the 29th Knight of Glin. It's also an impressive country house, full of the family's original paintings and antiques, which bring warmth to the baronial splendour of the surroundings. Particularly elegant is the airy drawing room, with its Adam ceiling and views over the croquet lawn. Fine country cooking uses fresh produce from the walled garden to make fabulously simple, seasonal dishes. Start, perhaps with a tossed green garden salad with honey lemon vinaigrette and follow with pan-fried cornfed chicken breast with apple tart and a Robert sauce, or steamed fillet of cod with Mediterranean vegetables and a parsley sauce. To finish, what else but a warm apple crumble?

Rooms: 15 ensuite. Double from €280.
Prices: Set dinner from €48 (residents only.) House wine from €23.
Food served: 19.00-21.30.
Closed: November to March.
Cuisine: Country house.
Other Points: Non-smoking. Garden. Car park. Tennis. Croquet. Winner - Country House of the Year 2004.
Directions: On the N69 between Foynes and Tarbert. From Shannon follow the signs for Cork and Tralee and the N69 for 32 miles. Turn left off the main road in Glin village and right at the top of the square.

Glin Castle, Limerick

Foynes Flying Boat Museum | *Place to visit*

Foynes, Co Limerick
Tel. +353(0)69 65416
Fax. +353(0)69 65600
Email. famm@eircom.net
www.flyingboatmuseum.com

Re-live the pioneering aviation era. From 1939 to 1945 Foynes, Co Limerick was the centre of the aviation world. The famous flying boats were frequent visitors, carrying a diverse range of passengers, from celebrities to refugees. The Foynes Museum recalls this era with exhibits and graphic illustrations. You can travel back in time in the museum's authentic 1940s-style cinema, while watching the award-winning film 'Atlantic Conquest', which has been compiled from original footage shot in the days of the flying boats. The museum is situated in the original terminal building with its Radio and Weather Room. The exhibits feature an introduction to the first transatlantic passenger service and Foynes during the war years. Irish Coffee was invented in Foynes by Chef Joe Sheridan.

Other Points
Coffee Shop and Souvenir & Gift Shop, Picnic Area and Free Car & Coach Parking.

Hours
Mar 31 to Oct 31: daily 10.00 - 18.00
Last Admission 17.00.

Admission Charged

Directions
Located on the N69 Coastal Route from Limerick to Kerry, 23 miles from Limerick City.

King John's Castle | *Place to visit*

Kings Island, Limerick City
Tel. +353(0)61 360788
Fax. +353(0)61 361020
Email. reservations@shannondev.ie
www.shannonheritage.com

King John's Castle is a 13th century Castle on 'King's Island' in the heart of medieval Limerick City overlooking the majestic river Shannon. Explore 800 years of history brought to life in the imaginative historical exhibition, excavated pre-Norman houses, fortifications, siege mines and the battlement walks. King John, as "Lord of Ireland" minted his own coins at this very location. The sights, scenes and sounds of the Castle and its environs all combine to recreate the atmosphere of the era.

Hours
Open Year round
Jan, Feb, Nov, Dec - 10 - 16.30
last admission 15.30
Mar, Apr & Oct - 9.30 -17.00
last admission 16.00
May - Sept - 9.30 -17.30
last admission 16.30
Closed Good Friday & Dec 24th, 25th,26th.
Times may be subject to change.

Other Points
Gift/souvenir shop, parking, toilets, picnic area, wheelchair access.
Car park open May - Sept.

Directions
Located in Limerick City. Travel on N18 from Shannon.

Admission charged

Lough Gur Visitor Centre | *Place to visit*

Near Bruff, Co Limerick
Tel. +353(0)61 360788
Fax. +353(0)61 361020
Email. reservations@shannondev.ie
www.shannonheritage.com

The story is told of the pre-Celtic settlers of Ireland who farmed and lived in this peaceful valley. Over time, the lake, which dominated the everyday lives of the people, became sacred and valuable offerings were made to the gods of the lake. The Visitor Centre houses an audio-visual show, exhibition of artefacts and display panels which interpret the story of man from the Stone Age. This story stretches back over 5,000 years and continues in the people who still farm and dwell in the valley. You will be captivated by the beauty, charm and tranquillity of this ancient place.

Other Points
Gift/souvenir shop, parking, toilets, picnic area.

Admission charged

Hours
May to Mid Sept: daily 10.00 - 18.00
Last admission 17.30
Opening times may be subject to change.

Directions
Leave Limerick taking the Tipperary roundabout. Drive to Ballyneety, Grange, and Holycross turning left at Holycross on R514 and arrive at Lough Gur.

Birr Co Offaly

Emma's Café Deli
Town centre café, restaurant, deli & wine bar

31 Main Street, Birr, Co Offaly
Tel. +353(0)509 25678
Email. emmascafedeli@eircom.net

This newly opened café in the heart of the Georgian town of Birr is a great place to stop for lunch if you're visiting the beautiful castle gardens - as, indeed, TV gardener Diarmuid Gavin found on a recent visit. Owner Emma Ward is a genuine foodie and produces, with fellow chef Helen Grogan, some fine examples of homecooking on her contemporary Irish menu. The daily changing soup is made from local organic vegetables - there's a child's portion, too- and Emma's Salad deli plate comes with homemade bread, relish and cheese. Breakfast treats include homemade muffins, cherry scones, muesli with organic yogurt and fairtrade coffees. A deli counter offers a wide range of Irish cheeses, fresh pesto and good quality hams. Brightly painted walls surround a

Prices: Main course lunch from €6. House wine from €4 per glass.
Food served: 9.30-18.00 Mon-Sat, 13.00-17.30 Sundays. Wine Bar open 20.00-23.00 Fri & Sat May-Sept.
Closed: Bank Holidays.
Cuisine: Modern Irish.
Other Points: Children welcome. Credit Cards not accepted. Live music occasionally during wine bar opening hours. Piano in shop so feel free to play if the mood takes you!
Directions: In the centre of town. On the left hand side half way down the Main Street.

large wooden table with soft leather seating in the separate dining area.

Birr Co Offaly

The Thatch Bar & Restaurant
Country pub and restaurant

Crinkill, Birr, Co Offaly
Tel. +353(0)509 20682
Email. thethatchcrinkill@eircom.net
www.thethatchcrinkill.com

Des Connole's attractive thatched pub has been in the same family for over 200 years. The traditional whitewashed exterior is beautifully maintained, with cobblestones and tubs of flowers making up a nostalgic snapshot. Tiny windows shed a soft light on the nooks and crannies in the neat bar area, which displays memorabilia from its two centuries of history. The restaurant at the rear, simply decorated with kitchen-style furniture, offers a diverse menu of traditional and contemporary dishes. Starters might bring salmon and prawn potato cake with chive and tarragon cream and main courses range from baked breast of chicken with sage and onion stuffing to smoked haddock with parsley and spring onion sauce. There are pasta and vegetarian dishes, a joint of the day, and wickedly indulgent desserts such as hot toffee and pecan pie. Traditional roasts and children's dishes make Sunday lunch

Prices: Lunch main course from €9-€10. Set Sunday Lunch €22. Dinner main course from €20. Bar snack from €7. House wine from €20.
Food served: Lunch 12.30-14.30. Early Bird 17.00-19.30 Mon-Sat. Dinner 18.30-21.00 Tue-Sat.
Closed: Good Friday and 25 Dec.
Cuisine: Traditional/modern Irish and international dishes.
Other Points: Children welcome. Car park. Winner - Food Pub of the Year 2005.
Directions: The Thatch is located one mile from Birr on the Roscrea side.

a family affair, and there's a well-priced early-bird menu.

Birr Castle Demesne

Birr, Co Offaly
Tel. +353 509 20336
Fax. +353 509 21583
Email. mail@birrcastle.com
www.birrcastle.com

Birr Castle Demesne with unique and
fascinating 120 acres of gardens and
parkland providing a lovely backdrop
for an afternoon stroll amongst its
formal gardens; wildflower meadows;
river walks and fernery. A visit in spring
or summer is rewarded with splashes
of colour and heady scents from the
different flowers. The grounds, which
are open to the public, are also home
to the Great Telescope, which for 70
years held the title of the world's largest
telescope. There are other interesting
features on display in the Science Centre,
which takes the story from the terrestrial
problems of constructing the telescope to
the celestial rewards of all it revealed in
the heavens. Birr Castle Demesne offers
an excellent way to spend an afternoon
in relaxing surroundings, as well as learn
of the important scientific achievements
of the Irish in the 18th century.

Hours
Mid Mar to Oct 31 daily 9.00-18.00
Nov 1 to Mid Mar daily 10.00-16.00

Admission Charged

Directions
Birr Town is in the centre of Ireland
and can be easily reached from the N6
via Tullamore, or the N7 via Roscrea.
In Birr Town Centre Square, take the
exit beside Bank of Ireland and after
200m take left at high castle wall. The
entrance is on right, car parking 50m
further on left.

Peter Ward, Country Choice, Nenagh

Nenagh Co Tipperary 🍴 🫖 ☕ ● ◉ ★

Country Choice
Coffee shop, deli and gallery

25 Kenyon Street, Nenagh,
Co Tipperary
Tel. +353(0)67 32596
Email. peter@countrychoice.com

A veritable landmark for foodies from all over Ireland, Peter and Mary Ward's unique delicatessen/café reflects its owners' passion for the finest regional farm produce, artisanal food products and wholesome home-cooked meals. Painted a festive wine colour, with pots of magenta petunias adding a cheery touch to its exterior, the shop is chock-a-block with farmhouse cheeses; sausages, pates, eggs and meats; seasonal vegetables; home-baked breads; preserves and honeys; wines, teas, coffees and chocolate. Regulars usually head straight for the homely café at the rear of the shop first, where a typical menu might feature braised chicken and ham pie served with creamed colcannon potato; black olive, roast aubergine, spinach and Abbey Brie savoury tart; and homemade lasagne. Desserts include homemade bread and butter pudding; mixed berry compôte; and

Prices: Lunch main course from €9.
Food served: 9.00-18.00 Mon-Sat.
Closed: Sunday, Good Friday & 25 Dec.
Cuisine: Modern Irish.
Other Points: Art Gallery. Winner - Special Award 2004.
Directions: Leave N7 for Nenagh. Go to traffic lights, turn left at Bank of Ireland. Country Choice is half-way down the street on right hand side.

chocolate cake. Don't leave here empty-handed; the cheeses are particularly notable, and the Christmas puddings are so good that ordering in advance is essential.

Thurles Co Tipperary 🗇 🍴 🍸 🍷

Inch House
Country house and restaurant

Thurles, Co Tipperary
Tel. +353(0)504 51348/51261
Email. inch-hse@iol.ie
www.inchhouse.ie

This handsome Georgian house was built in 1720 by landed Catholic gentleman, John Ryan. The house remained in the Ryan family until 1985, when it was sold to John and Nora Egan. The Egans now farm the surrounding land, and undertook the painstaking restoration that has made Inch such a gracious country house. Some of the original features include the Ryan family coat of arms set in the window of a mid-staircase landing; and the magnificent plasterwork ceiling in one of the William Morris-style drawing rooms. Large log fires light up the reception rooms and restaurant, where guests can enjoy a classic menu with Irish influences, using fresh vegetables and herbs supplied by the farm. A five-course dinner might begin with fruit sorbet or soup followed by, say, smoked salmon tagliatelle. Main courses include veal steak with sundried tomato and wholegrain mustard mash and redcurrant

Rooms: 5 ensuite. Double from €110. Single from €65.
Prices: Set dinner from €45-€47. House wine from €17.
Food served: 19.00-21.30 Tue-Sat.
Closed: One week at Christmas.
Cuisine: Modern Irish.
Other Points: Garden. Car park. Children welcome.
Directions: From Thurles take Nenagh road, travel for 4 miles, pass the (Ragg) and Inch House is on the left 200 yards further on.

sauce, and seabass baked with almonds, served with ratatouille.

FROM FARM TO PLATE
IN ONE EASY STEP

Farmers' markets are growing all over Ireland. Local, seasonal and fresh produce sold without resorting to middle men. Elizabeth Field gets her fix.

Farmers' markets are among the brightest stars on the Irish food scene. There are now over 90 markets nationwide, concentrated on the East Coast, with some 3 to 4 new ones opening each month.

For consumers, they offer extended choice - more and varied food items straight from the producer; a guarantee of locally raised products; education about the production and origin of products; the excitement of sampling new foods, particularly ethnic specialties, and the enjoyable experience of interacting within a social market environment.

For farmers, relationships with consumers generate a new income stream. (Some farmers can develop an average turnover, depending on product category, of €400 per day). The marketplace itself offers an ideal place for sourcing new customers; obtaining feedback on products and ideas, and developing mutually beneficial contacts with other growers.

As for the community and environment at large, farmers' markets keep "food miles" low; encourage sustainable farming techniques; attract tourism, and encourage local regeneration. According to Bord Bia, when a farmers' market takes place in a town on a given day, it increases activity for other businesses in the town by between 18 percent and 30 percent.

"We're in the midst of a massive food revolution brought on by instant affluence and awareness, and travel to foreign countries," says Sean McArdle, organiser of commercial, i.e. for-profit, markets, including 5 weekly ones in Dublin and 2 in Northern Ireland. His newest one, on the pier in Howth, features a large selection of gourmet food, organic cheese and - the real draw - fresh fish and seafood including live lobsters and crayfish.

He plans to stay abreast of the nation's general obsession with shopping by establishing a new farmers' market at the Liffey Valley Shopping Centre. "We're targeting a broader market," he says. "It's the way forward."

Maggie Bowen provides websites and information for community-based food producers. (These include the rapidly expanding network of farmers' markets nationwide that are organised by a committee of local residents, food producers and town councils, who do not profit from the enterprise.) "We're getting much more support from local chambers of commerce and town councils recently," she says. "They are seeing that the stores near farmers' markets benefit 30 to 50 percent."

So what's on offer around Ireland?

The Midleton (Co. Cork) farmers' market, held Saturdays, has a true "market town" feeling, with stall-holders including Darina Allen hawking her own range as well as Ballymaloe Cookery School's offerings; Tim and Fiona York's fruit, vegetables, baskets and salsa; Arbutus artisan breads, and Clodagh McKenna's patés, chutneys and marmalades. The Dunhill (Co. Waterford) farmers' market, held on the last Sunday of the month in the parish hall, is a small endeavour offering local cheeses, free-range eggs, artisan breads, and home-baked goods and jams. Shoppers come straight from Mass.

For enormous selection, the Friday market at the Leopardstown Racecourse (Dublin) features 3,000 square feet of indoor shopping with excellent organic meat, fish and game; organic produce from Denis Healy; artisan oils, olives, chutneys, pasta and chocolates; and much more. There are also Irish, Spanish, Indian, French, Mexican and vegetarian food stalls, selling ethnic specialties to eat in or take away.

FORTUNES
FARM
FRESH·VEG

The "mother" of all markets is the Temple Bar market, a venerable Saturday institution in Meeting House Square in Dublin. As much an "event" as a market, it has a lively buzz,

as well as John McInerney's Atlantic oysters; cheeses from Sheridan's, Frank Hederman's smoked fish, and the Gallic Kitchen's savoury potato pancakes, quiches, and chocolate brownies. ∎

The following websites provide a geographic listing of markets, as well as other useful information.

Irish Farmers Markets *www.irishfarmersmarkets.ie*
Ireland Markets *www.irelandmarkets.com*
Bord Bia *www.bordbia.ie*

Irish Farmers
MARKETS

Contact Sean McArdle . Tel. +353 (0) 87 6115016

Fridays
Leopardstown Race Course
10am to 3pm

Saturdays
Malahide - GAA Facilities
Centre of Malahide. 10am -3pm

Sundays
Howth Market
at the Harbour 10am to 3pm
Ranelagh Market
at Multidenominational School
Ranelagh Road, Ranelagh.
10am to 3pm

10% Discount
to all Les Routiers
customers on
presentation of this guide
at any of the above
markets

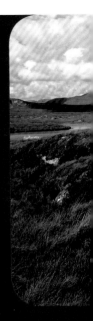

Key Events

Festival	Throughout Region	
St Patrick's Day Festivals	March 13 - 17	
Festival	Ballycastle	
Ould Lammas Fair	Aug 29 - 30	
Music	Galway	
Galway Early Music Festival	May 18 - 21	
Film	Galway	
18th Galway Film Fleadh	July 11 - 16	
Arts	Galway	
Galway International Arts Festival	July 17 - 30	
Equestrian	Galway	
Galway Festival	July 31 -Aug 6	
Food	Galway	
Galway Oyster Festival	Sept 28 -Oct 01	

West

Barna Co Galway

O'Grady's On the Pier
Oyster and seafood restaurant

Seapoint, Barna, Co Galway
Tel. +353(0)91 592223
Email. ogradysonthepier@hotmail.com
www.ogradysonthepier.com

This fine oyster and seafood restaurant is scenically situated at the end of a pier overlooking Galway Bay. Owner Michael O'Grady has made spanking fresh seafood the raison d'etre of this place and the opportunities afforded by its seaside location are not squandered. Chef Martin Sheriff delivers the classics - grilled Dover Sole on the bone with sauce vierge; crab claws in garlic butter - with consummate ease. More unusually, specials such as grilled blue shark with herbed potato cake in a sweet chilli beurre blanc sauce, are focused around deep-sea varieties of fish, which represent an alternative to overfished species such as cod, haddock and so on. Various meat dishes - traditional roast breast of duckling with sweet apricot glaze, for example - are also on offer, but rather than being sidelined, are prepared with equal care and consideration. Desserts include crowd-pleasing chocolate

Prices: Set Sunday lunch from €23. Dinner main course from €18.50. House wine from €19.
Food Served: Lunch 12.30-14.45 (Sunday only). Dinner 18.00-22.00 daily (times may vary in Winter).
Closed: One week over Christmas.
Cuisine: Irish seafood.
Other Points: Children welcome.
Directions: Take Spiddal Road west out of Galway, turn left at traffic lights in Barna Village to end of pier.

brownies with chocolate sauce; profiteroles; banoffi pie and a palate-cleansing fresh fruit salad with raspberry sorbet.

Clifden Co Galway

Abbeyglen Castle
Seaview hotel

Sky Road, Clifden, Co Galway
Tel. +353(0)95 21201
Email. info@abbeyglen.ie
www.abbeyglen.ie

Set just off the famous Sky Road, amid beautiful gardens overlooking Clifden Bay and against the backdrop of the Twelve Bens, this 19th century castle is impossibly romantic. It was rescued from dereliction by the Hughes family in 1969 and has been on the upswing ever since. Gracious touches include afternoon tea in the spacious drawing room or before an open peat fire in the relaxing, pubby bar; charming, individually decorated bedrooms with fine views, and seven suites. Paul and Brian Hughes are generous hosts, which often results in late nights around the piano. Chef Kevin Conroy delivers French-International cuisine, with all fish and shellfish caught locally. A typical dinner - served by diligent, attentive staff - might start with Cleggan Bay seafood chowder, or Connemara smoked salmon stuffed with chive and potato salad, followed by Beef Wellington, or pan-fried halibut with a sun-dried tomato

Rooms: 38 ensuite. Double from €198. Single from €129 (rates include dinner bed and breakfast). 12.5% service charge will apply.
Prices: Lunch main course from €10 (served in the bar). Dinner main course from: €23. Set Dinner €49. House wine from €22.50.
Food Served: Bar lunch 12.30-14.00 daily. Restaurant dinner 19.15-21.00 daily.
Closed: 4 Jan to 1 Feb.
Cuisine: French, International.
Other Points: Garden. Children welcome over 12 years old. Car park.
Directions: N59 west, 50 miles from Galway.

sauce. The wine list is divided by style, delivering a good international overview.

Clifden Co Galway ✕ ♣ ♟ ♪ ☀ CS VC

Kylemore Abbey & Garden
Daytime coffee shop and restaurant

Kylemore, Connemara, Co Galway
Tel. +353(0)95 41146
Email. info@kylemoreabbey.com

Kylemore Abbey, a baronial-style castle built in 1868, sits in breathtaking surroundings by the shores of a lake in the heart of Connemara. Parts of the house, a gothic church and a Victorian walled garden are open to the public, but the remainder of the abbey is still home to the Benedictine nuns and pupils of the International Girls' Boarding School. Next to an excellent craft shop stands the Abbey's renowned self-service restaurant - a large, light, modern space, which offers a daily-changing, traditional menu of locally-sourced, freshly cooked dishes. These could include homemade, gluten-free soups such as cream cheese and broccoli, hot dishes such as Irish stew and chicken in white wine and bacon sauce, four vegetarian options and baked potatoes with a choice of fillings. Afternoon tea brings homemade fruit scones with excellent jams,

Prices: Main course from €8.
Food Served: 9.30-17.30.
Closed: Good Friday and 25 Dec.
Cuisine: Homemade traditional Irish.
Other Points: Garden. Children welcome. Car park. Complimentary shuttle bus to/from the garden. Visitor centre. Craft shop.
Directions: On the N59 in north Connemara, two and half miles north east of Letterfrack.

made by the nuns and available by the jar, chocolate coconut biscuits and a selection of homemade cakes.

Nearest Racecourses
Galway Race Course
Festival Meet
Last week in July. Tel. 091 753870

Nearest Golf Courses
Connemara Golf Club
Tel. + 353 (0)95 23502
Galway Bay Golf Resort
Tel. + 353 (0)91 790503
Roscommon Golf Club *Tel. + 353 (0)906 625998*
Westport Golf Club *Tel. + 353 (0)91 632244*

Connemara/Renvyle Co Galway

Renvyle House Hotel
Coastal hotel and restaurant

Renvyle, Connemara, Co Galway
Tel. +353(0)95 43511
Email. info@renvyle.com
www.renvyle.com

Romantic, restful and spectacularly situated on 200 acres, between the Twelve Bens mountains and the Atlantic Ocean, this consummately comfortable, 68-room country house epitomises Irish hospitality. One of the earliest Irish country house hotels - Mrs. Caroline Blake first opened it in 1883 - its fascinating past includes ownership by a Gaelic chieftain and Oliver St. John Gogarty, visits from W.B. Yeats and Lady Gregory, and numerous tear-downs and renovations. A wonderful, plant-filled conservatory, with commanding views of the unspoilt Connemara landscape, and a cosy Long Lounge, decorated in rich claret colours with lots of mellow woodwork and an open turf fire, are perfect for reading, relaxing or afternoon tea. Spacious bedrooms are tastefully furnished. Head chef Tim O'Sullivan's lovely meals feature locally sourced lamb, seafood, produce and game. Facilities include a heated pool, 9-hole golf course, trout fishing, and tennis, while the nearby beaches and countryside are unrivalled for hill walking and touring.

Rooms: 68 ensuite. Double from €60. Single from €30. Family (2 adults & 2 children) from €110.
Prices: Lunch main course from €15. 5-Course dinner from €40. Bar snack from €5. House wine from €19.

Food Served: Breakfast 8.30-11.00. Bar Food/Afternoon Tea 12.00-17.30. Dinner from 19.00. Last orders 21.00 daily.
Cuisine: Modern Irish, International. Specialising in fresh seafood and Connemara lamb.
Other Points: Non-smoking bedrooms. Garden. Children welcome. Dogs welcome. Car Park. 9-hole golf course. Lake for boating and fly fishing. Tennis courts. Lawn Bowls. Croquet. Outdoor swimming pool (summer months). Clay pigeon shooting. Childrens' playground.
Directions: From Galway take the N59 towards Clifden. Go straight through the towns of Moycullen, Oughterard and Maam Cross. At Recess (one mile past Joyce's Craft Shop) take a right (signposted) and drive through the Inagh Valley. At the end of the Inagh Valley take a left towards Kylemore. Pass Kylemore Abbey and when you reach the crossroads at Letterfrack take a right. Go through the village of Tully Cross (veer left at the church) and through Tully and you will arrive at the gates of Renvyle House. Entire journey is approx 55 miles.

The Symbols

Accommodation

Restaurant

Café

Pub/Bar

Daytime opening only

Deli

Wine

Bakery

Gourmet/Farm Shop

Leisure Centre/Spa

CS Craft Shop

VC Visitor Centre

Les Routiers Awards

2002 Award Winner

2003 Award Winner

2004 Award Winner

2005 Award Winner

Galway City Co Galway

Goyas
City centre café and bakery

2/3 Kirwan's Lane, Galway
Tel. +353(0)91 567010
Email. info@goyas.ie
www.goyas.ie

Situated on a corner site on cobbled
Kirwan's Lane in the heart of Galway, this
enticing bakery and cafe has floor-to-ceiling
windows, with an attractive exterior painted
midnight blue, with gold lettering. Within,
there are seductive aromas, delightful staff,
and the excited buzz of satisfied customers.
Emer Murray is arguably one of the country's best bakers and her list of homemade
treats is long: 3-layer chocolate gateau,
tiramisu, cranberry and almond tart, lemon
meringue pie, baked cheesecake with
fruit, orange Madeira cake, raspberry and
apple Jonathan, apple and pear crumble,
triple-decker shortbread, and many more.
Freshly ground coffee, cappuccino or hot
chocolate are the perfect accompaniments.
If it's lunchtime, there are homemade
soups, toasted sandwiches, pates, quiches
and daily specials. Emer sells whole cakes,
too, and makes fabulous wedding cakes

Prices: Main course from €7.95
Food Served: 9.30-18.00 Mon-Sat.
Lunch served 12.30-15.00.
Closed: Sundays.
Cuisine: Modern Irish.
Other Points: Children welcome.
Directions: On the corner of
Kirwan's Lane, off Quay Street.

to order. A mail-order service despatches
Irish specialties such as plum pudding,
Christmas cake, Dundee and Porter cakes,
and cranberry-almond tart countrywide.

Galway City Co Galway

Kirwan's Lane Restaurant
City centre restaurant

Kirwan's Lane, Galway
Tel. +353(0)91 568266

Chef Mark Hopkins cooks up an eclectic
menu at this well-loved city centre
restaurant. The dining room is a calm space
of neutral colours, with tables covered in
smart white linen - the perfect backdrop
for dishes combining a vibrant mix of
global influences. This said, many are
focused around Irish ingredients - dinner
might begin with fresh Carna Bay prawns,
horseradish and tomato mayo with zest of
lime and quail egg, followed by roast breast
of Silver Hill duck with parmesan-baked
celeriac and a cassis reduction. Banana and
ginger tarte tatin with honey ice cream is a
clever variation on a classic and, together
with a good Irish cheeseboard, makes an
elegant finish. Lunch brings crowd-pleasers
such as Cumberland sausage, champ and
onion gravy, and interesting vegetarian options such as nutty bean burgers with broad
bean mash and mango relish. The global
wine list provides useful tasting notes, and
some interesting French examples.

Prices: Lunch main course from
€11.95. Dinner main course from
€17.95. House wine from €19.50.
Food Served: Lunch 12.30-14.30.
Mon-Sat. Dinner 18.00-22.00 daily.
Closed: 24-29 December.
Cuisine: Modern Irish.
Other Points: Children welcome.
Outdoor seating in summer.
Directions: City centre location, just
off Quay Street.

Galway City Co Galway ✗ ▼

McDonagh's Seafood House
Seafood restaurant and fish and chip bar

22 Quay Street, Galway
Tel. +353(0)91 565001
Email. fish@mcdonaghs.net
www.mcdonaghs.net

This landmark Galway restaurant, inge-niously divided in two, with a fabulous take-away fish and chip shop on one side, and a traditional table-service seafood restaurant on the other, exudes old-fash-ioned hospitality. The chips are superior - they are cut on the premises - and the menu, illustrated with tantalising fish and seafood, is straightforward and unpreten-tious. Choose from such classic dishes as Clarenbridge oysters with brown bread, homemade fish soup, oak-smoked salmon, wild mussels and trout, cod, haddock, brill, lemon sole, John Dory, hake and other freshly caught fish either grilled with dill sauce, or poached in white wine and cream. Diners traditionally buy a pint from the pub next door, and bring it in to drink in McDonagh's. Established in 1902, the restaurant has evolved under PJ and Mary

Prices: Dinner main course from €8.50-€22. House wine from €16.
Food Served: Restaurant 17.00-22.00. 17.00-23.00 Sun. Fish and chips available 12.00-24.00.
Closed: Sundays Nov-May. 25, 26 Dec & 1 Jan.
Cuisine: Traditional Irish seafood.
Other Points: Children welcome.
Directions: At the bottom of Quay Street.

McDonagh's efforts to change with the times. Don't leave Galway without a visit.

Leenane Co Galway ✗ ☕ ▼

Blackberry Café
Waterside café & restaurant

Leenane, Co Galway
Tel. +353(0)95 42240

Sean and Mary Hamilton's small café and restaurant in the pretty village of Leenane is a real find. It's poised on the edge of Killary harbour, Irelands' only genuine fjord, and a stunning sight for the first-time visitor. For over a decade, it has offered a deliciously simple, seafood-dominated menu - available in high season from midday until 9pm - to walkers, tourists and locals. Dinner might begin with half a dozen oysters, or a plate of Connemara smoked salmon, followed by plump fishcakes served with a crisp salad or hot smoked trout. Meat options include traditional Irish stew or homemade burgers with a choice of sauce. Open sandwiches, panini and wraps can be had at lunchtime, as well as salads of local seafood, fresh crab or salmon. A concise list of French and New World wines offers two house wines by the half bottle and a minicellar of wines by the generous glass. Service is friendly and prompt.

Prices: Snack from €9.95-€12.50. Dinner main course from €12-€25. House wine from €19.
Food Served: 12.00-16.30 and 18.00-21.00 Wed-Mon. Open daily July/August.
Closed: 30 September-Good Friday.
Cuisine: European.
Directions: 40 miles from Galway. 20 from Westport, 20 from Clifden. Situated on Killary Harbour.

Leenane Co Galway

Delphi Lodge
Lakeside country house

Leenane, Co Galway
Tel. +353(0)95 42222
Email. info@delphilodge.ie
www.delphilodge.ie

Nestled lakeside in a quiet, unspoilt valley and surrounded by Connacht's highest mountains, Delphi Lodge boasts unparalleled natural beauty. The early 19th-century house, built by the Marquis of Sligo, has 12 exceptionally comfortable, individually decorated bedrooms, each with a lake or mountain view. Cosy amenities include a well-stocked library, a spacious drawing room and a billiard room. Owner Peter Mantle is a consummate host, and dinners held around a large oak table, with lots of good food, wine and conversation, evoke a house party. A typical meal might start with warm rare wild duck and woodcock paté, followed by steamed asparagus with poached duck eggs and butter sauce; roast rib of beef with roasted vegetables; and rhubarb tartlets with vanilla cream sauce. Coffee and homemade chocolates are served in the Piano Room. A paradise for anglers, hill walkers or those seeking a

Rooms: 12 ensuite. Double from €150. Single from €105.
Prices: Set dinner €49. House wine from €22.
Food served: Dinner 20.00 daily (residents only).
Closed: 20 Dec-10 Jan.
Cuisine: Combination of traditional and new wave.
Other Points: Flyfishing. Non-smoking. Garden. Car park. Snooker. Library. Food and Wine weekends offered in autumn and winter. Winner - Country House of the Year 2005.
Directions: 8 miles northwest of Leenane on the Louisburgh road.

restful hideaway, Delphi Lodge is a classic Irish destination.

"Connemara is a savage beauty"

Oscar Wilde

Delphi Lodge

Moycullen Co Galway ★

Killeen House
Country house bed and breakfast

Killeen, Bushypark, Galway
Tel. +353(0)91 524179
Email. killeenhouse@ireland.com
www.killeenhousegalway.com

Owner Catherine Doyle has lavished thoughtful attention to detail on this lovely nineteenth century country house on the shores of Lough Corrib, just four miles from Galway. It is set in some 25 acres of immaculately maintained private grounds, and the scenic walk to the water's edge through the pretty garden makes a perfect pre-breakfast stroll. There are countless elegant touches which combine to make Killeen a haven of tranquillity; on arrival, guests are served afternoon tea on a silver tray with fresh linen; there are vases filled with cut flowers in all the rooms, and breakfast, which includes homemade soda bread, scones and preserves, is served with silver cutlery and fine china. Each of the ensuite bedrooms follows a Victorian, Edwardian, Regency or Art Nouveau theme, and the overall impression is one of exquisite good

Rooms: 6 ensuite. Double from €140-€180. Single from €100-€140. Family from €160-€195.
Other Points: Garden. Children welcome over 12 years old. Car park. Winner - Guesthouse of the Year 2003.
Directions: On the N59, the main Clifden road. Killeen House is 4 miles from Galway city centre and half way between Galway city and Moycullen village.

taste and style. Antique furniture has been chosen with care to complement the luxurious furnishings and bedlinen.

Moycullen Co Galway

White Gables Restaurant
Cottage restaurant

Moycullen Village, Co Galway
Tel. +353(0)91 555744
Email. info@whitegables.com
www.whitegables.com

Kevin and Anne Dunne's well-loved restaurant has the intimate feel of a place apart, somewhere where you might come for a special occasion. At the crossroads in Moycullen village, just 8km from Galway, the restaurant is housed in a most attractive, nineteenth-century, whitewashed stone cottage with contrasting red window frames. Cooking is traditional and focused around seafood, with classics such as seafood cocktail Marie Rose and scallops thermidor served by professional, attentive staff. There are plenty of choices for meat lovers, too, most of them - such as homemade chicken liver paté, pork schnitzel, and a perennially popular duck à l'orange - equally timeless. Local produce is well used, in à la carte starters such as wafer-thin slices of Smoked Connemara lamb with mixed pickles, and deep-fried Blue Bell Falls goats cheese with honey and soya dressing. There are fresh flowers, even in the spotless bathrooms,

Prices: Set Sunday lunch €24.50. Dinner main course from €25. House wine from €19.
Food Served: Dinner 19.00-22.00 Tue-Sun. Lunch 12.30-15.00, Sunday.
Closed: Mondays (except early August). 23 Dec - 14 Feb.
Cuisine: Traditional, with seafood specialities.
Other Points: Children welcome. Car park. Bar waiting area for guests.
Directions: Situated at the crossroads in Moycullen Village. Located on the N59 8km from Galway City.

and candles are lit at dinner.

Dunguaire Castle | *Place to visit*

Kinvara, Co Galway
Tel. +353(0) 61 360788
Fax. +353(0)61 361020
Email. reservations@shannondev.ie
www.shannonheritage.com

Visit Ireland's most photographed and picturesque Castle in the idyllic location of Kinvara, Co. Galway. It has for hundreds of years stood proudly on the site of the 7th. century stronghold of Guaire, the King of Connaught, its majesty dominating the shore of Galway Bay. The Castle bridges almost 5 centuries of Irish history, from the skirmishes, battles and sieges that characterise its colourful past, through to the literary revival of the early 20th century. In 1924, Oliver St. John Gogarty, surgeon, poet, and author, a contemporary and friend of WB Yeats and Lady Gregory, acquired the Castle as a place of quiet retreat.

Other Points
Gift/Souvenir Shop, Parking, Toilets.

Admission charged

Hours
Mid Apr to Sept: 9.30 - 17.00
(Last admission 16.30)
Opening times may be subject to change.

Directions
Located near the village of Kinvara. From Ennis take the main Galway road (N18) through Gort. A short distance after Gort (about 2.5 miles) take a left for the road to Kinvara. From Galway take the Gort/Limerick road (N18) through Oranmore and Clarinbridge to Kilcolgan, turn right on to the N67 and continue to Kinvara.

Dunguaire Medieval Castle Banquet | *Place to visit*

Dunguaire Castle, Kinvara,
Co Galway
Tel. +353(0) 61 360788
Fax. +353(0)61 361020
Email. reservations@shannondev.ie
www.shannonheritage.com

Enjoy an enchanting evening at 500-year-old Dunguaire Castle, on the shores of Galway Bay - one of Ireland's most picturesque locations. Following the tradition of medieval 'King Guaire' who resided at Kinvara, we invite you to savour a delicious four-course dinner with wines - food to please the palate and entertainment to lift the soul. In a truly intimate setting, the castle's superb artists will inspire you with extracts chosen from works of great literary writers such as Synge, Yeats, Shaw and O'Casey, chosen to lighten the heart and performed by artists perfectly moulding themselves into their parts.

Admission charged

Hours
Apr to Oct: Twice nightly at 17.30 and 20.45 (reservations necessary)

Directions
Located near the village of Kinvara. From Ennis take the main Galway road (N18) through Gort. A short distance after Gort (about 2.5 miles) take a left for the road to Kinvara. From Galway take the Gort/Limerick road (N18) through Oranmore and Clarinbridge to Kilcolgan, turn right on to the N67 and continue to Kinvara.

Kylemore Abbey & Garden | *Place to visit*

Kylemore, Connemara, Co Galway
Tel. +353 (0)95 41146
Fax. +353 (0)95 41440
Email. info@kylemoreabbey.ie
www.kylemoreabbey.com

Set in the Connemara Mountains is Kylemore Abbey, a beautiful neo-Gothic Castle (under restoration). Built by the English industrialist Mitchell Henry in 1868, visitors to the three reception rooms in the Abbey are touched by its history steeped in romance and tragedy. Kylemore Castle was sold to Benedictine nuns fleeing war-torn Belgium in 1920, and the Castle became an Abbey. The Community of Nuns re-opened their International Boarding School for girls here, and also established a day school for local girls. Mitchell Henry built the Neo-Gothic Church (under restoration) between 1877 and 1881 as a memorial to his wife following her untimely death. The Church, a 'cathedral in miniature', is a centre of reflection and prayer for many visitors. A short walk from here takes visitors to the Mausoleum where the original owners are buried. Complimentary shuttle buses take visitors to the recently re-opened, 6-acre Victorian Walled Garden (under restoration). The Garden was originally laid out by the head gardener, James Garnier, and the glasshouses were designed by Cranstons of Birmingham. In the early 1900s, the Garden went into decline, in time becoming a wilderness with the glasshouses collapsing, leaving only their brick bases. Following extensive restoration, which is still on-going, the Garden was re-opened by the Nuns in 1998 and won the prestigious Europa Nostra Award in 2000.

At the end of your visit, why not take the opportunity to view our unique Kylemore Abbey Pottery as it is produced in our Pottery Studio adjacent to our Craft Shop. The Kylemore Abbey Craft Shop is open all year round stocking products unique to Kylemore, such as Kylemore Abbey Pottery and Jams, knitwear and fashions, glassware and handmade Irish jewellery. Home-cooked food is served in our Restaurant, which is open all-year-round, and is renowned for our home-made jams and scones!

Other Points

Generally self-guided tours, but guided tours can be organised by prior arrangement, Audio Visual Presentation (3 languages), Craft Shop, Pottery making can be seen from viewing area in the Craft Shop, Restaurant, Complimentary Shuttle Bus Service take visitors to and from the Garden.

Hours

Abbey, Gothic Church, Mausoleum, Shop, Restaurant
Mar to Nov: daily 9.30 - 17.30
Nov to Mar: daily 10.30 - 16.30
Garden
Easter to Oct: daily 10.30 - 16.30

Directions

Situated on the N59 in North Connemara, 3 miles North East of Letterfrack.

Knock Co Mayo

Knock House Hotel
Hotel and restaurant

Ballyhaunis Road, Knock, Co Mayo
Tel. +353(0)94 9388088
Email. info@knockhousehotel.ie
www.knockhousehotel.ie

This striking, purpose-built hotel - the local limestone of its walls blending harmoniously with the peaceful countryside around - provides pilgrims and guests with the perfect setting for restful contemplation. It was constructed in 1999 to stand alongside the famous pilgrimage site of Knock shrine and Basilica. The building's curves, which mirror the natural lines of the hill on which the Shrine stands, house 68 simply decorated, but comfortable en-suite rooms with lovely views. Six of these are specially designed for wheelchair users, and there are facilities and staff available for guests with certain medical needs. The interior is tranquil and minimalist, and an airy foyer, again with limestone walls, overlooks rolling countryside through dramatic floor-to-ceiling windows. The Four Seasons restaurant blends local and international influences with dishes such as spicy chicken quesadillas and roast leg of Mayo lamb with herb stuffing. The wine list offers a good mix of European and New World bottles.

Rooms: 68 ensuite. Double from €106. Single from €63.
Prices: Lunch main course from €9.50. Dinner main course from €18. Bar snack from €5. House wine from €19.50.
Food Served: 12.30-17.00 & 18.00-22.00.
Cuisine: Traditional and modern.
Other Points: Non-smoking. Garden. Children welcome. Car park.
Directions: 1 hour from Galway city, 1 hour from Sligo on N17 road.

Westport Co Mayo

Quay Cottage
Waterside restaurant

The Harbour, Westport, Co Mayo
Tel. +353 (0)98 26412
Email. quaycottage@eircom.net
www.quaycottage.com

Kirstin and Peter McDonagh's small whitewashed cottage with gleaming, bright red front door is the picturesque home of this atmospheric seafood restaurant. The cottage, at the gate of Westport House, overlooks beautiful Clew Bay and is within sight of the magnificent slopes of Croke Patrick. Inside, the space opens up to a sizeable three-roomed establishment with seating possible for private parties up to 80 guests. The nautical theme is hard to miss; there's seafaring memorabilia - ships, shells, crustaceans and compasses - from floor to ceiling, but the effect is cheerful and busy. Specials include lobster fresh from the tank and mussels steamed in a white wine and basil vinaigrette. Main courses might bring grilled fillets of brill with sun-dried tomatoes in truffle oil, or tandoori monkfish. Elsewhere, choose from chargrilled steak with a Gaelic Irish whiskey sauce, baked chicken breast and a Thai vegetarian stir-fry. The winelist is usefully annotated with suggestions for suitable dishes for each bottle.

Prices: Dinner main course from €17.90. House wine from €17.50.
Food Served: from 18.00-22.00.
Closed: 3 days at Christmas. January, also Sun & Mon during the winter season.
Cuisine: Modern Irish
Other Points: All children welcome.
Directions: On Westport Harbour at the entrance gates to Westport House.

Quay Cottage, Westport

Killeen House, Moycullen

Roscommon Town Co Roscommon ★

Gleeson's Townhouse & Restaurant
Townhouse, restaurant and café

Market Square, Roscommon
Tel. +353(0)90 6626954
Email. info@gleesonstownhouse.com
www.gleesonstownhouse.com

Eamonn and Mary Gleeson have done a fine job of restoring this nineteenth-century townhouse. Overlooking Roscommon's historic main square, it's attractively finished with Blue Bangor Quarry slates and ashlared stonework. Nineteen bedrooms provide comfortable accommodation, while food is served seven days a week in the Manse restaurant and the café, open for breakfast from 8am for the full Irish. Lunch - including homemade lasagne, steaks, sandwiches and baked potatoes - can be taken in the pretty front courtyard, along with coffee, tea and delicious homemade cakes, breads and scones. The restaurant has a sturdy, 'modern Irish' menu, combining tried-and-trusted dishes with innovative twists. A typical meal could bring Gleeson's seafood chowder, local rack of lamb with rosemary and redcurrant, or baked halibut steak with Asian vegetables, cucumber and tomato beurre blanc. Finish with a moreish French apple tart with ginger caramel and vanilla ice cream, or sticky toffee pudding with toffee sauce.

Rooms: 19 ensuite. Double from €120. Single from €60. Family from €130.
Prices: Lunch main course from €8.50-€10.95. Dinner main course from €11.95-€24.95. House wine from €15.50.
Food served: Café 8.00-21.00 daily. Restaurant 18.30-21.00 Sun-Thur. 18.30-22.00 Fri-Sat.
Closed: 25, 26 Dec.
Cuisine: Modern Irish/European.
Other Points: Garden. Children welcome. Car park. Dogs welcome. Winner - Host of the Year 2004.
Directions: From Dublin take N6 to Athlone, then take the N61 to Roscommon. From Sligo, N4 to Boyle, then the N61. Located in Roscommon Town Centre, next door to tourist office.

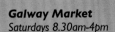

Local Farmers' Markets

Galway Market
Saturdays 8.30am-4pm

Cruising *in Co. Roscommon.*

Must See
Visit one of the seven islands off Ireland's West Coast – the three Aran Islands, Innismore, Inismaan and Inisheer and further north Inishbofin, Inishturk, Clare Island and Achill Island.

Fishing
County Roscommon is surrounded by prime coarse fishing rivers and lakes. These catchments have consistently produced good bags of exceptional size fish and being sparsely populated and removed from areas of populations it boasts a clear, unspoilt environment.

National Museum of Ireland - Country Life | *Place to visit*

Turlough Park, Castlebar, Co Mayo
Tel. +353 (0) 94 90 31755
Fax. +353 (0) 94 90 31628
Email. tpark@museum.ie
www.museum.ie

This award-winning Museum, a branch of the National Museum of Ireland, is set in the spectacular grounds of Turlough Park. It brings to life the traditions of rural life throughout Ireland from 1850–1950 through the innovative combination of artefacts and displays, archival video footage and interactive screens. Fascinating artefacts deal with domestic life, agriculture, fishing and hunting, clothing and textiles, furniture and fittings, trades and crafts, transport, sports and leisure and religion. Over four floors, the Museum treats visitors to a taste of how our ancestors lived their daily lives, in both difficult and joyful times. This is history truly come to life. Admission to the Museum is free.

Other Points
Free car and coach parking, Museum shop and café, Family Programme and events for all ages, wheelchair accessible, Audio-visual presentation, garden walks and daily guided tours. Groups must book guided tours in advance.

Hours
Open all Year. Tue -Sat 10.00 -17.00.
Sun 14.00 -17.00
Closed Mondays (incl. Bank Holiday Mondays).
Closed Good Friday & Christmas Day.

Directions
Access is from Turlough Village, which is situated off the N5, 8 kms east of Castlebar, Co. Mayo.

Key Events

Festival St Patrick's Day Festivals	Throughout Region March 13 - 17	
Music Fleadh Cheoil na héireann	Letterkenny Aug 26 - 28	

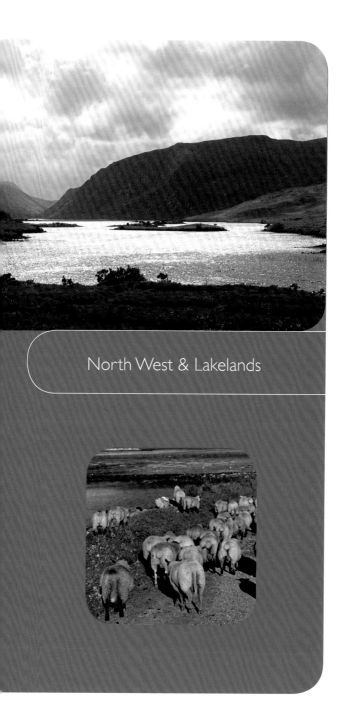

North West & Lakelands

Dunkineely Co Donegal

Castle Murray House Hotel
Clifftop hotel and restaurant

St John's Point, Dunkineely, Co Donegal
Tel. +353(0)74 9737022
Email. info@castlemurray.com
www.castlemurray.com

The magnificent location of Marguerite and Martin Howley's ten-roomed hotel and restaurant - set against the Donegal mountains and overlooking McSwyne's bay - makes dining here a special experience. Chef Rémy Dupuis menu makes the most of fresh, local fish and seafood in simply conceived, imaginative dishes. McSwyne's bay blue lobster - from the tank - with spicy lobster cream is a particular highlight on the dinner menu. Either side of this, there are fresh or grilled oysters with beurre blanc sauce and a satisfyingly indulgent warm chocolate cake with white chocolate ice cream. Sunday lunch might begin with tartar of trout with balsamic vinegar and chive on blinis and proceed with roast leg of spring lamb stuffed with sage. Desserts such as honey crème brûlée or strawberry soufflé are elegantly simple. The extensive wine list is dominated by

Rooms: 10 ensuite. Double from €120. Single from €80. Family from €120.
Prices: Set Sunday lunch €26. Bar snack from €5-€8.50. Dinner main course from €20. House wine from €19.
Food Served: Bar snacks 12.00-15.00 Mon-Sat(high season only). Sunday lunch 13.30-15.30. Dinner 18.30-21.30 daily.
Closed: Mid Jan to mid Feb. Mon & Tue during low season.
Cuisine: Modern Irish & French.
Other Points: Non-smoking. Children welcome. Garden. Car park. Small dogs welcome.
Directions: Fifteen minutes from Donegal town in Killybegs direction. One mile off the main road for St John's Point.

French examples, with a good choice of half bottles. All rooms are ensuite with seaviews.

Inishowen Penninsula Co Donegal

McGrorys of Culdaff
Guesthouse, pub and restaurant

Culdaff, Inishowen, Co Donegal
Tel. +353(0)74 9379104
Email. info@mcgrorys.ie
www.mcgrorys.ie

This family-run inn, established in 1924, has just undergone a major refurbishment, with seven bedrooms added to the existing ten, all ensuite and offering a good level of comfort. All the more reason to use McGrory's as your base for touring the stunning Inishowen Peninsula. In fact, this friendly place will serve as far more than just a base; apart from the renowned music sessions, which are terrific fun and well worth catching, there is food served throughout the day in the atmospheric bar - don't miss the signature chicken liver paté with fresh herbs and cognac. There's also a fuller menu of imaginative seafood, meat and vegetarian dishes with starters such as Inishowen oysters with chilli raspberry vinaigrette, and wild mushroom tagliatelle. Main courses include several ways with steak, lamb, chicken and fish dishes such as roast fillet of monkfish

Rooms: 17 ensuite. Double from €110. Single from €60.
Prices: Lunch main course from €8. Dinner main course from €16. Bar snack from €6. House wine from €15.
Food served: Bar 12.30-20.00.daily. Restaurant 18.30-21.30 Tue-Sat. 18.30-20.00 Sun.
Closed: 23-27 December.
Cuisine: Modern Irish.
Other Points: Car park. Children welcome.
Directions: On the R238 between Moville and Malin Head.

with fennel and smoked bacon. The wine list has well-informed notes and an interesting global range.

Laghey Co Donegal

Coxtown Manor
Country house and restaurant

Laghey, Co Donegal
Tel. +353(0)74 9734575
Email. coxtownmanor@oddpost.com
www.coxtownmanor.com

This lovely, ivy clad Georgian house is set in mature countryside, six miles from Donegal town. Owned by Belgian Eduard Dewael, it has a fine restaurant and 9 comfortable bedrooms spread between the main building (150 years old) and the coach house (350 years old), with most enjoying glorious views over the surrounding countryside. The elegant dining room is the main focus and guests will find a menu diplaying an impressive range of local produce: Donegal Bay scallops and lobster, Lissadell mussels and clams, for example. Starters might include Donegal Bay lobster and prawn salad, while main courses bring Breast of organic Thornhill duck, or pan fried Turbot with a champagne sauce. Homemade desserts include Strawberry shortcake and Belgian chocolate mousse made with real Belgian chocolate and served with Crème Anglaise. The clear succinct wine list is predominantly French.

Rooms: 9 ensuite. Double from €150-€220. Single from €90-€115. Family from €165-195.
Prices: Dinner main course from €23.90. House wine from €21.50.
Food Served: 19.30-20.30 Tue-Sat. By reservation only.
Closed: 1 Nov-10 Feb.
Cuisine: Traditional Belgian.
Other Points: Non-smoking house. Garden. Children welcome. Car park.
Directions: Off the N15 between Ballyshannon and Donegal town, on the old Laghey-Ballintra road. 6 miles from Donegal town.

Local Farmers' Markets

Letterkenny Market
1st & 3rd Saturday of each month, 9am-3pm
Donegal Town Market
Diamond, Saturdays monthly

Nearest Golf Courses

Ballyliffin Golf Club
Tel. + 353 (0)74 9376119
Donegal Golf Club
Tel. + 353 (0)74 9734054
Dunfanaghy Golf Club
Tel. + 353 (0)74 36335
North West Golf Club
Tel. + 353 (0)74 9361715
Rosapenna Golf Club
Tel. + 353 (0)74 9155301

Rathmullan Co Donegal ★ ★

Rathmullan House
Country house hotel and restaurant

Rathmullan, Co Donegal
Tel. +353(0)74 9158188
Email. info@rathmullanhouse.com
www.rathmullanhouse.com

This renowned country house hotel was originally the holiday home of the Batt family, founders of the Belfast bank, now the Irish National Bank. It was bought by Bob and Robin Wheeler in 1962 and is now run by their sons, William and Mark, and daughter-in-law Mary. It's an attractive, white-painted nineteenth-century building, set above Lough Swilly, and with lovely gardens that stretch down to a deserted sandy beach. When not taking in the stunning scenery, guests can relax in three grand drawing rooms with open log fireplaces, or enjoy a splash in the indoor swimming pool. Chef Peter Chessman cooks up a stylish country house menu with the focus on seasonal produce. Dinner might bring Confit of Donegal bay wild salmon with vanilla butter and cauliflower panna cotta, roast loin of Rathmullan lamb with saffron ratatouille broad beans and, to finish, steamed sticky ginger and apple pudding. There's an impressive global wine list, and service is impeccable

Rooms: 32 ensuite. Double from €170. Single from €85. Family from €85 per adult with rates for children available on request.
Prices: Lunch main course from €15. Dinner main course from €30. Bar snack from €10. House wine from: €21.
Food served: 13.00-14.30 and 19.30-20.45 daily.
Closed: 19 - 27 Dec.
Cuisine: Modern Irish with emphasis on seasonality and produce from artisan suppliers.
Other Points: Garden. Children welcome. Swimming pool. Tennis courts. Dogs welcome by prior arrangement. Dog friendly bedroom available. Highly Commended - Hotel of the Year 2003. Winner - Hotel of the Year 2004.
Directions: From Letterkenny take the R245 to Ramelton, turn right at bridge to Rathmullan (R247), go north through village, gates on the right.

Sligo Town Co Sligo

Kate's Kitchen
Town centre gourmet food and wine shop

3 Castle Street, Sligo
Tel. +353(0)71 9143022
Email. info@kateskitchensligo.com
www.kateskitchensligo.com

Kate Pettit and Frank Hopper have owned this unusual "twin shop" in the centre of Sligo since 1982. On either side of a single entrance, Kate's Kitchen and Hopper and Pettit display their respective wares through large bay windows, top-notch toiletries, soaps and cosmetics on one side, and Kate's gourmet foods on the other. The old fashioned, black-painted frontage, with its red and gold lettering, sets the elegant tone. Inside and to the right, Kate's Kitchen is a treasure house of fine foods, with organic pasta, pasta sauces and marmalade. There are patés, tea bracks and carrot cakes made

Opening Hours: 9.00-18.30.
Closed: Sundays and bank holidays.
Directions: Town centre location.

to Kate's own recipes, and produce from local organic farms. Smart floor-to-ceiling wooden shelves are crammed with bottles, jars and tempting packages, including Gallwey's chocolates and fine teas and coffees. There's smoked Irish wild salmon from Woodcock's, Tipperary organic ice cream, a good range of wines and Irish and continental cheeses.

Rathmullan House

Coxtown Manor

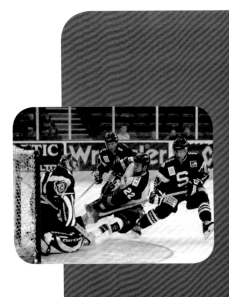

Key Events

Arts	Belfast
Cathedral Quarter Arts Festival	April 28 - May 8
Féile an Phobail	July 29 - Aug 7
Belfast Festival at Queen's	23 Oct - 5 Nov
Sport	Belfast
Belfast City Marathon	May 01
Agricultural	Belfast
Balmoral Show	May 11 - 13
Agricultural	Ballywalter
29th Game and Country Fair	April 29 & 30
Equestrian	Downpatrick
Downpatrick Festival	May 13
Equestrian	Lisburn
Down Royal - Festival of Racing	Nov 3 & 4
Festival	Enniskillen
Lady of the Lake Festival	July 14 - 21
Music	Omagh
Appalachian and Bluegrass Music Festival	Sept 2 - 04

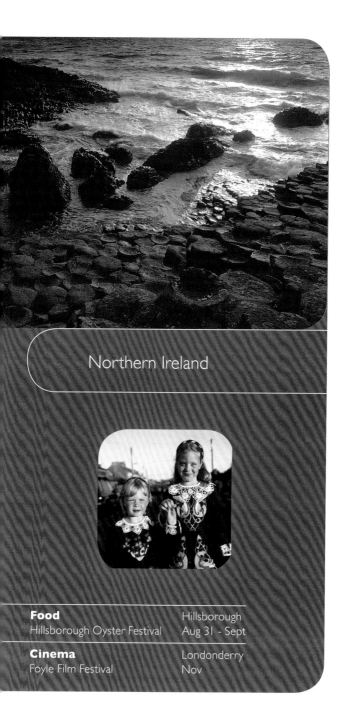

Northern Ireland

Food Hillsborough Oyster Festival	Hillsborough Aug 31 - Sept
Cinema Foyle Film Festival	Londonderry Nov

Ballymena Co Antrim ⭐

Marlagh Lodge
Country house and restaurant

71 Moorfields Road, Ballymena
Co Antrim BT42 3BU
Tel. +44(0)28 2563 1505
Email. info@marlaghlodge.com
www.marlaghlodge.com

Robert and Rachel Thompson have restored this listed nineteenth-century house with immense good taste. It was built for the rebellious heir to the now-destroyed Crebilly castle and his headless ghost is said to haunt the grounds. The light, well-proportioned rooms are full of original Victorian features, with open fireplaces, antique pianos and beautiful William Morris wallpaper. The Thompsons are keen musicians with eclectic tastes, which are reflected in the plentiful reading matter throughout the house. Evening meals are dinner-party style, with a typical summer menu taking in roasted pears with Cashel Blue cheese and walnut salad, monkfish en papillote with Thai fragranced butter, and fresh raspberry and blueberry jelly with mint cream. Breakfast brings a 'tummy warmer' of porridge with whiskey, cream and brown sugar. Bedrooms have luxurious sheets and antique dressers. Splendid bathrooms, two ensuite, come with roll-top baths and salvaged sinks.

Rooms: 3(2 ensuite). Double from £70. Single from £35.
Prices: Set dinner £25/£27.50 (residents/non residents respectively). House wine from £14.50.
Food Served: Dinner served daily for residents - book by noon. Non-residents must book 24 hours in advance.
Closed: Christmas & New Year.
Cuisine: Modern Irish.
Other Points: No-smoking area. Garden. Children welcome. Car park. Winner - Guesthouse & Restaurant of the Year 2004.
Directions: A26 to Ballymena. One mile after "Line Bridge" turn right to "Country Garage", cross two crossroads to Rankinstown Road, house at end on the right (gravel drive).

Belfast Co Antrim

Restaurant H20
Restaurant

Tel. + 44(0)28 9030 9000
Email. eat@restauranth2o.com
www. restauranth2o.com

H20 produces food that's far above the ordinary. Chef Raymond Murray uses the finest raw materials available: organic where possible, GM - and additive-free, and from local producers. Dishes are inventive, without being outlandish, and bring together international and Irish influences. Contrast, for example, a main course of Lebanese chicken with farika, braised fennel, cinnamon, rosemary and crème fraîche, with another based around Irish Charr, a rare fish from Lough Neagh, which comes baked with bacon, cabbage and peas. Simple delights such as a starter of fresh herb gnocchi with broad beans and blue cheese dressing or a stunning Baked Alaska, with lemon and almond filling, bring a nice balance to proceedings. A huge range of Irish, French and English cheeses, including

Prices: Dinner main course from £13.50 House wine from £9.95
Food Served: 17.00-22.00 Tue-Thur & 17.00-23.00 Fri 16.00-24.00 Sat.
Closed: Sunday and Mondays. 2 weeks in July. Good Friday and Easter Monday. 25 Dec & 1 Jan.
Cuisine: Grande Mère.
Other Points: Dining area is non-smoking and mobile phone free. Children welcome up to 19.00. Car park.
Directions: Please phone.

Ardagh vintage Irish cheddar, St Killian and Colston Bassett, rounds off a refreshingly original menu.

Belfast City Co Antrim ✗ ♉ ▮ ☕

Apartment
City centre cocktail bar, restaurant & coffee bar

2-4 Donegall Square West
Belfast, Co Antrim BT1 6JA
Tel. +44(0)28 9050 9777
Email. info@apartmentbelfast.com
www.apartmentbelfast.com

Centrally located opposite Belfast City Hall, Apartment is a stylish, casual eatery that provides all things - breakfast, lunch and dinner to a mixed crowd of shoppers, business people and young professionals. A sleek, modern ground-level bar utilises lots of dark wood panelling, oversize armchairs and quality leather sofas to create a funky-hip ambiance, while a sweeping staircase leads to a bright, cutting-edge contemporary first-floor dining area. Buttery croissants and more substantial fare are available for breakfast, and head chef Phil Rodgers showcases fresh, local ingredients in a reasonably priced lunch/dinner menu that includes homemade soups; warm salad of crispy squid, chorizo, and charred baby potatoes; and char-grilled steaks with peppercorn sauce and fries. The Apartment's

Prices: Lunch main course from £6.50. Dinner main course from £6.50. Bar snack from £5.95. House wine from £12.95.
Opening Hours: 8.00-01.00 Mon-Fri. 9.00-01.00 Sat. 12.00-00.00. Sun
Food Served: Coffee Bar 8.00-17.00 Mon-Sat (hot food until 15.00). Closed Sundays. Restaurant 12.00-21.00 Mon-Sat. 12.00-20.00 Sun.
Cuisine: Modern traditional.
Other Points: Children welcome. Euros accepted.
Directions: Located right in the city centre, overlooking the grounds of City Hall.

evolving list of cocktails - Mojitos, Cosmopolitans, apple martinis - is a favourite with celebrities Matthew McConaghy and Eddie Irvine when they are in town.

Belfast City Co Antrim ✗ ♉ ▮

Cayenne
City centre restaurant

7 Ascot House, Shaftesbury Square,
Belfast, Co Antrim BT2 7DB
Tel. +44 (0)28 9033 1532
Email. reservations@cayennerestaurant.com
www.rankingroup.co.uk

Paul and Jeanne Rankin's flagship restaurant has been a Belfast hotspot since it opened 18 years ago. Despite its longevity, it has a funky, fresh feel which is enhanced by the contemporary light installations and clean lines of the newly extended interior. The menu makes for an exciting read, and the theme is one of seasonality, Irishness and innovation, with plenty of inspiration from the East. From the carte, there's salt 'n' chilli squid, or Strangford lobster ravioli, followed by grilled dry aged Irish sirloin with asparagus and anchovy butter. Elsewhere, there are Korean spice lamb chops with kimchee, and roast monkfish with Chinese red braised oxtail. A full vegetarian menu is stuffed with enticing options, and desserts such as lemon thyme crème brûlée, or apricot clafoutis

Prices: Lunch main course from £10.50. Dinner main course from £10.50. House wine from £14.25.
Food served: 12.00-14.30 Mon-Fri. 18.00-22.15 Mon-Thu. 18.00-23.15 Fri-Sat. 17.00-21.00 Sun.
Closed: 25 Dec. 12 July.
Cuisine: Fusion.
Other Points: No-smoking area. Children welcome. Private dining room. Bar/lounge area. Conference Room.
Directions: Top of Great Victoria Street.

with lemon buttermilk sherbert are unmissable. A set dinner menu offers excellent value, and the wine list contains a section of fine bottles from Paul's cellar.

Cayenne, Belfast

Belfast City Co Antrim

Madisons Hotel
Hotel and restaurant

59-63 Botanic Avenue, Belfast,
Co Antrim BT7 IJL
Tel. +44(0)28 9050 9800
Email. info@madisonshotel.com
www.madisonshotel.com

Situated on tree-lined Botanic Avenue, five minutes from Queen's University, Madison's is a stylish, 35-room hotel, café, bistro and nightclub. The hotel has a Parisian art-deco feel, and a sense of drama heightened by the deep red of the lobby. Bedrooms, accessible by lift, are painted in soft, warm colours that recall the natural world; echoing this theme, there's a large photographic canvas above each bed depicting a soothing country scene. Crisp, white duvets, remote control TV, tea and coffee-making facilities and spacious bathrooms complete the sense of contemporary luxury. The extensive breakfast menu brings kippers; scrambled eggs with smoked salmon and eye-opening bloody Marys. The bistro, decked out in suede and velvet, mosaics and mirrors, offers a diverse choice, including crispy plum and

Rooms: 35 ensuite. Double from £70. Single from £60.
Prices: Lunch main course from £4.95. Dinner main course from £8.95. Bar snack from £2.50. House wine from £12.95.
Food served: Breakfast 7.00-11.00. Lunch 12.00-17.00 daily. Dinner 17.00-22.30 Mon-Sat. 17.00-21.30 Sun
Closed: 12 July.
Other Points: No-smoking area. Children welcome.
Directions: Situated on Botanic Avenue 5 mins from Queen's University and 10 mins from the city centre.

ginger marinated duck with spring rolls, and blackened fillet of plaice with crème fraîche and sweet chilli jam. New world wines are modestly priced, the bar is buzzy,

Belfast City Co Antrim

McHughs Bar & Restaurant
City centre pub and restaurant

29-31 Queen's Square, Belfast,
Co Antrim BTI 3FG
Tel.+44(0)28 9050 9999
Email. info@mchughsbar.com
www.mchughsbar.com

This bar and restaurant is located in the thriving dock area of Belfast in one of the city's oldest buildings. Dating from 1711, and Grade-A listed, it sits under the Albert clock behind a striking red facade. Bare brick walls from the original building, stone floors, old and new pine furniture blend successfully with modern art and funky light fittings. Downstairs, an authentic pub full of regulars offers a good choice of draught beers including Belfast Ale, with live music at weekends. The menu is predominantly modern Irish with some Asian twists. For lunch, there are spring rolls of shredded duck and noodles, or fresh Dundrum Bay mussels in a saffron cream to start, a choice of wok dishes, and puddings such as lemon buttermilk tart or warm barmbrack bread and butter pudding. Dinner brings a wider choice of seafood, steaks and

Prices: Lunch main course from £4.95. Dinner main course from £7.25. Bar snack from £2.50. House wine from £12.95.
Hours: 12.00-01.00 Mon-Sat. 12.00-24.00 Sun.
Food Served: Bar 12.00-17.00 daily. Restaurant 12.00-15.00 Thu-Fri and 17.00-22.30 Mon-Fri. 17.00-22.30 Sat. 12.00-17.00 Sunday Carvery. 17.00-21.00 Sun
Closed: 25 Dec. 1 Jan. 12 July.
Cuisine: Traditional Irish with a fresh twist.
Other Points: Children welcome.
Directions: Beside the Albert Clock and the new Custom House Square.

vegetarian dishes. Portions are generous, and service is keen and willing. The wine list leans towards France, with six half bottles.

Belfast City Co Antrim

Nicks Warehouse
City centre restaurant & wine bar

35-39 Hill Street, Belfast,
Co Antrim BT1 2LB
Tel. +44(0)28 9043 9690
Email. info@nickswarehouse.co.uk
www.nickswarehouse.co.uk

Nick's Warehouse opened up in Belfast's cathedral quarter a pioneering seventeen years ago, and is a lively focus for this developing area of the city. The bar, large-scale Anix restaurant and the more sedate first-floor dining area, provide ample choice for a steady stream of locals and visitors who, nevertheless, seem to cram the enormous space at busy times. The bar, with its red-brick walls, aluminium air pipes and chalkboards, buzzes with atmosphere and the amusingly written wine list offers some interesting bottles. There's a sturdy menu of appealing dishes, and Owen McMahon's pork sausages on mash with a Tasso mushroom sauce, or chicken breast on basmati rice with Thai coconut sauce, go down a storm with shirt-sleeved business lunchers. Else-

Prices: Lunch main course from £6. Dinner main course from £7.95. House wine from £12.50.
Food served: 12.00-15.00 Mon-Fri. Dinner 18.00-21.30 Tue-Thurs. 18.00-22.00 Fri-Sat.
Closed: Sundays. Easter Sun & Mon. 12 July, 25, 26 December.
Cuisine: Modern Irish.
Directions: Near St Anne's Cathedral, off Waring Street.

---

where, there are soups - butternut squash and ginger - sandwiches, and hearty salads. The airy restaurant offers slightly more elegant fare, including grilled fillet of halibut on Parmesan risotto with soft Italian herb dressing.

Local Farmers' Markets

St Georges Market
Fridays, Variety market 6am-1pm.
Saturdays, City Food & Garden Market 9am-3pm

Lisburn Market
Every Saturday

Portadown Market *Last Saturday of Every Month*

Templepatrick *4th Sunday 11am-6pm*

Belfast City Co Antrim

Rain City
Café and restaurant

33-35 Malone Road, Belfast,
Co Antrim BT9 6RU
Tel. +44(0)28 9068 2929
www.rankingroup.co.uk

Paul and Jeanne Rankin are the celebrity names behind this funky upbeat café/grill, just a 5-minute walk from Queen's University. The interior combines original Belfast red brick walls alternating with walls done in cream paint, wooden floors, pine tables and colourful artworks. Inspired by America's west coast, it specialises in affordably priced American diner staples: 8-ounce cheeseburgers with fries; Rain City chicken wings with slaw and blue cheese dip; and classic club sandwiches with grilled chicken, bacon, lettuce, tomato, and onion on a focaccia roll with fries. Desserts such as pecan pie continue the stateside theme. The dinner menu brings more elegant dishes including Vietnamese BBQ chicken with peppers, bok choy and rice noodles and char-grilled lamb "t-bones" with garlic rosemary potatoes. Cocktails such as

Prices: Lunch main course from £5.75. Dinner main course from £5.75. House wine from £14.50.
Food Served: Lunch 12.00-17.00 Mon-Fri. Dinner from 17.00. Brunch 10.00-16.00 Sat & Sun.
Closed: 25 December.
Cuisine: American/Modern Irish.
Other Points: No-smoking area. Children welcome. Private dining room.
Directions: Five minutes walk from Queen's University.

Mojitos and Long Island Iced Tea add to the festive atmosphere. A great spot for families, Rain City's Tex-Mex nights also draw a lively crowd.

Belfast City Co Antrim

Roscoff Brasserie
City centre restaurant

7-11 Linenhall Street, Belfast,
Co. Antrim BT2 8AA
Tel. +44(0)28 9031 1150
www.rankingroup.co.uk

Paul and Jeanne Rankin's one-year-old Roscoff Brasserie, located directly behind Belfast City Hall, embodies the style and panache associated with the couple's expanding local restaurant empire. Its clean, modern interior has a cool pearl and gun-metal-grey colour scheme, complemented by a blonde wood floor; charcoal-grey upholstered banquettes; large, well-spaced, white linen-covered tables, and artwork by Belfast/London artist Peter Anderson. There are attractively priced, set two- and three-course lunch and dinner menus at £27 and under. Chef Conor MacCann's classic and modern French specialties include chicken liver parfait with peach chutney and toasted brioche, followed by grilled halibut with fresh tagliatelle, peas, favas and lemon oil, and pear crumble with vanilla ice cream for dessert. An intelligent wine list comprising both Old

Prices: Lunch main course from £14. Dinner main course from £14. House Wine from £16.95.
Food served: Lunch 12.00-14.30. Mon-Fri. Dinner 18.00-22.15 Mon-Thurs. 18.00-23.15. Fri & Sat
Closed: Sundays. Lunch Saturdays. July 12. Dec 25, 26. Jan 1.
Cuisine: Modern & classic French.
Other Points: Children welcome.
Directions: Located directly behind City Hall.

and New World selections is also strong on ports, liqueurs, whiskies and premium vodkas.

Nick's Warehouse, Belfast

Belfast City Co Antrim

Tara Lodge
City centre bed and breakfast

36 Cromwell Road, Belfast,
Co Antrim BT7 1JW
Tel. +44(0)28 9059 0900
Email. info@taralodge.com
www.taralodge.com

This friendly bed and breakfast is well located in a lively area close to the Botanic Gardens and Queen's University, and less than one mile from the centre of Belfast. It takes its name from the seat of the High Kings of Tara, County Navan, the royal residence from the third to the sixth century. The eighteen bedrooms are simply decorated and fitted out with mod-cons such as trousers presses, tvs and telephones, while a special suite and lift caters for mobility impaired guests. Breakfast, taken in a dining area fronted by tall arched windows, presents a wide choice of healthy options and well as plenty of indulgent ones. Choose from homemade porridge with cream and sultanas, poached eggs with smoked salmon and warm pancakes with honey and hot lemon butter. For fans of the

Rooms: 18 ensuite. Double from £65. Single from £52.50. Family from £80.
Closed: 11-13 July & 24-27 December.
Other Points: Car park. Children welcome. Some non-smoking rooms.
Directions: M2 to exit roundabout, fifth exit towards Boucher Road, first left, exit next roundabout. At traffic lights take left, turn right six hundred yards after next left, next right, turn left into Botanic Cave, third right into Cromwell Road.

Ulster fry, there's also bacon, eggs and tomatoes served with soda bread. Private car parking is available for guests.

Belfast City Co Antrim

The Errigle Inn
Pub and restaurant

312/320 Ormeau Road, Belfast,
Co Antrim BT7 2GE
Tel. +44(0)28 9064 1410
Email. philip@errigle.co.uk
www.errigle.com

The Errigle Inn first opened in 1935, and the art-deco glasswork in the Oak Lounge - one of five bars under one roof - dates from that time, a detail which adds to the retro atmosphere of this oak-panelled, low-lit space. In the other bars, there's an 'infamous' Monday night quiz, interactive sports and live music to rival anywhere in the city. The express lunch menu is perfect for a quick bite, with dishes such as homemade vegetable broth with wheaten bread, hot roast beef on ciabatta, salads and soda tops - half a grilled soda with, say, black pudding - hit the spot. A hearty Errigle fry takes star billing on a favourites menu, which also includes scampi and chips, Caesar salad and hot spicy buffalo wings. Desserts such as apple and raspberry nut crumble are appealing variations on classic puds.

Prices: Lunch main course from £5.25. Dinner main course from £8. House wine from £9.45. Bar snack from £3.50.
Hours: 11.30-01.00 Mon-Sat. 12.30-24.00 Sun.
Food served: 11.30-15.00 and 17.00-21.00 Mon-Thur. 11.30-22.00 Fri-Sat. 12.30-20.00 Sun.
Closed: 25 December.
Cuisine: Modern/traditional Irish
Other Points: Children welcome. Live music venue. Roof garden.
Directions: From M2 (north) follow signs for Newcastle. Turn roundabout at top of Ravenhill, follow Ormeau Road towards the city centre.

The wine list includes a choice of Chardonnays from around the world.

Belfast City Co Antrim

The King's Head
City centre pub and restaurant

829 Lisburn Road, Belfast,
Co Antrim BT9 7QY
Tel. +44(0)28 9050 9950
Email. info@kingsheadbelfast.com
www.kingsheadbelfast.com

This newly renovated pub has established itself as one of the best entertainment venues in Northern Ireland. There are a range of events and live music, including jazz, throughout the week, as well as Sunday lunch and brunch, good bar food, and a restaurant serving dinner six days a week. The new extension blends seamlessly with the older part - details such as wooden floors, attractive artwork, books, statues and a wine display running from ground to first floor, combine to create an established air. Richard Crozier's menu is a contemporary blend of Irish, British and international influences. A well-flavoured Irish Caesar salad comes with Gubeen shavings, and Asian-inspired dishes such as crab and sweetcorn spring rolls and lemongrass tiger prawns sit alongside meat dishes such as rib-eye of county

Prices: Lunch main course from £4.95. Dinner main course from £7.95. Bar snack from £1.95. House wine from £11.95.
Opening Hours: 11.30-01.00 Mon-Sat. 12.00-24.00 Sun
Food Served: Bar 12.00-20.00 Mon-Sat. 12.00-17.00 Sun. Restaurant 17.00-21.30 Mon-Sat. 12.00-21.00 Sun.
Closed: 25 Dec. 12 July.
Cuisine: Traditional with a modern twist using fresh local produce.
Other Points: Children welcome. Car Park. Extensive beer garden.
Directions: Directly opposite the King's Hall at Balmoral.

Down beef, and seared loin of lamb with roasted aubergine. The wine list makes entertaining reading, with a bias towards wines from Down Under

The Symbols

🏠 Accommodation
✖ Restaurant
☕ Café
🍺 Pub/Bar
☀ Daytime opening only
🥖 Deli
🍸 Wine
🥖 Bakery
🍶 Gourmet/Farm Shop
🛁 Leisure Centre/Spa
CS Craft Shop
VC Visitor Centre

Les Routiers Awards

⭐ 2002 Award Winner
⭐ 2003 Award Winner
⭐ 2004 Award Winner
★ 2005 Award Winner

A LOT
TO LOAF
ABOUT

Caroline Workman talks to Les Routiers member Robert Ditty of

Ditty's Bakery about his family bakery and the tradition of craft baking in Northern Ireland.

Caroline Workman is a speciality food consultant and food writer. She spent five years working in the restaurant trade before setting up her own company, Food Stuff Ireland, a marketing and training consultancy dedicated to the speciality food trade.

Spreading butter on still-hot soda bread is one of life's real luxuries, as is a cup of tea with a slice of fruit loaf. Forgotten memories from the past? Not at all, these traditions are alive and kicking in Northern Ireland like never before.

When Robert Ditty took over the family home bakery in the seventies, he expected to witness the gradual disappearance of Northern Irish ethnic breads. However, thirty years on, while craft baking in the rest of the British Isles struggles, these speciality breads and over 150 home bakeries are thriving.

"We would be the envy of English bakers. We're still doing what they were doing 30 years ago and have lost. There isn't an ethnic English bread or an equivalent Scottish product and if there is, it is very, very localised. We're talking about the whole of Northern Ireland. Every craft baker in the country is making griddle breads, whereas the high street baker in England has become a fast food outlet.

"There are very few towns and villages outside Belfast that don't have a butcher, baker and a greengrocer. Northern Ireland people have a rural attitude to food, even in the city. If you meet people from Belfast in a supermarket, you'll find that they're only in there to buy certain items. They'll have bought their bread and bought their meat and they'll have bought their fish elsewhere."

"The Northern Irish housewife has a lot more in common with a French housewife, or an Italian housewife, than she does with an English housewife. She's more likely to buy food on a daily basis and there is a strong family tradition. It's slowly disappearing but families still eat, once a week anyway, around one table. Tea is a big thing in Northern Ireland too. You're more likely to be offered a cup of tea and a bun which has been either homemade or bought in a home bakery. Elsewhere you'll get a cup of coffee and a Penguin biscuit, or a mini Twix bar."

It's the unique character of the ethnic products themselves that has perhaps contributed most significantly to the unexpected success of the remaining bakers.

"Supermarkets can make a traditional English bloomer in house but they can't make things like soda bread. Northern Irish ethnic breads are labour intensive and require skills that the supermarkets are not prepared to invest in. They weren't able to turn them into a commodity." The combination of smart marketing and dedication to authentic craft expressed by the formation of a new collective of like-minded bakers, the Artisan Bakers of Northern Ireland, bodes well for the continued success of Northern Irish breads.

"The strength behind the group is people who are passionate about what they do, who have more than just a commercial interest in the future of Northern Irish baking. The bonus of being a group is that we can source and sell corporately, promote ourselves corporately and still be individuals.

"We're also looking at new ingredients. I think the ethnic bread range really needs a big change. It's been the same as long as I can remember - if anything it has decreased. We used to make things like Indian farls, based on maize flour, a yellow meal. They have a very distinctive, beautiful flavour. It's much easier to develop new products as a group than to work at it by yourself.

"Maybe there's a little in vogue thing to be making artisan bread. Maybe next year people will be taking night classes in darning socks but I do think more and more people will be going back to making things from scratch because of all the food scares, and because so many mass produced foods are so bland.

With passionate, driven bakers like Robert the future of craft baking is in good hands. "I enjoy it. I enjoy making something better than yesterday."

FIVE TYPICAL BREADS

Soda bread
Substantial, chunky farls with a fluffy consistency made with fresh buttermilk. Delicious toasted with melted butter and dolloped with home-made jam.

Potato bread
Dense, earthy farls with a dappled brown surface that fries deliciously crisp in butter. An essential element of a typical Ulster fry.

Batch bread
A springy, soft, sourdough bread with a toothsome crusty top, this square loaf is ideal for the ultimate Irish doorstep sandwich of honey roast ham or egg mayo and chives.

Wheaten bread
Light and nutty, buttered wheaten makes a great base for smoked salmon canapés.

Fruit loaf
A sweet tea bread with a glossy, chestnut brown surface and packed with juicy cherries, dried fruits, and nuts.

Carnlough Co Antrim

Londonderry Arms Hotel
Coastal Georgian hotel and restaurant

Glens of Antrim, 20 Harbour Road,
Carnlough, Co Antrim BT44 OEU
Tel. +44(0)28 2888 5255
Email. lda@glensofantrim.com
www.glensofantrim.com

Step into the old-fashioned village of
Carnlough and its lovely little harbour,
where this ivy-covered, 35-room former
coaching inn offers genuine Northern Irish
hospitality. Built by the Marchioness of
Londonderry in 1848, the inn passed to her
grandson, Herbert Vane Tempest, in 1865,
and subsequently to Sir Winston Churchill,
a second cousin, in 1921. The O'Neill
family have run the hotel for over 50 years.
Much of its original architecture remains
intact. The comfortable lounge, with its
ubiquitous turf fires, is a fine setting for
afternoon tea, and the good-sized, tastefully refurbished bedrooms are comfortable and quiet. The restaurant offers classic
fare such as homemade chicken liver paté
served with buttered toast and Cumberland
sauce, followed by locally caught grilled
fillet of salmon and sea bass on a nest of

Rooms: 35 ensuite. Double from £75.
Single from £40. Family from £80.
Prices: Lunch main course from
£10.95. Set Sunday lunch £15.95. Bar
snack from £7.95. Dinner main course
from £25. House wine from £9.95.
Food served: 12.00-21.00 Mon-Sat.
12.00-20.30 Sun.
Closed: 24, 25 December.
Cuisine: Modern Irish.
Other Points: No smoking area.
Children welcome. Car park.
Directions: On the Antrim coast road.

potato with a chive butter sauce, and fresh
raspberry and mint parfait served in a
tuille basket. A lovely base for exploring
the Antrim coast.

Queen's Arcade, Belfast

Carrick-a-Rede Rope Bridge | *Place to visit*

Ballintoy, Ballycastle, Co Antrim,
BT54 6LS
Tel. +44(0)28 2073 1582
Fax. +44(0)28 2073 2963
Email. carrickarede@nationaltrust.org.uk

After walking along the beautiful coast
path, you will find yourself confronted by
a precarious rope bridge, which crosses a
24m deep and 18m wide chasm to the tiny
Carrick Island. If you are bold enough to
cross, without thinking too much about
the sea swirling below you, then you will
receive your certificate. Enjoy watching the
birds and admire the stunning views over
the sea to the Scottish coast. We recommend appropriate footwear.

Other Points
Guided tours (by arrangement), Access
for visitors with disability (viewing plat-
form), Refreshments, Suitable for picnics,
Facilities for families, Learning, Dogs
welcome on leads (dogs not permitted to
cross bridge).

Admission Charged

Hours *(Weather permitting)*
04 Mar - 28 May 10.00 - 18.00 daily
29 May - 03 Sept 10.00 - 15.00 daily
04 Sept - 15 Oct 10.00 - 18.00 daily
Final access to Rope Bridge is 45 mins.
before closing time. Car Park and Coastal
Path open all year round.

Directions
On B15, 7ml from Bushmills, 5ml from
Ballycastle
Drive time: Belfast 1.15 hrs, Giant's
Causeway 10 mins.

St. George's Market | *Place to visit*

Oxford Street, Belfast City, Co Antrim
Tel. +44(0) 48 9032 0202
Fax. +44(0) 48 9027 0501
Email. markets@belfastcity.gov.uk
www.belfastcity.gov.uk

If you want to enjoy a real taste of Belfast, visit St. George's Market. One of the most colourful and vibrant destinations in Belfast, St. George's Market has been voted one of the UK's best markets in the prestigious Observer's Waitrose Food Awards 2004.

The Friday Variety Market opens at 6am every week and runs until approximately 1pm. This is a hugely vibrant retail experience of 248 market stalls selling diverse wares from apples to zips and antiques to shark meat. The fish section alone contains 23 fish stalls and holds the reputation for being the leading retail fish market on the island of Ireland. It is this eclectic mix that attracts thousands of 'punters' to probably the best market in Northern Ireland.

The City Food & Garden Market takes place in St. George's every Saturday from 9.00am until 3.00pm. Enjoy the best food taste and smells brought by local producers, including ostrich from Ballyclare, beef from Armagh, free range eggs from Limavady, venison, pheasant in season and local organic vegetables from Culdrum Farm. Added to these local delicacies the market now offers a huge range of continental and speciality foods such as wild boar, continental cheeses and cured meats, coffees from around the world, olive oils imported directly from Italy with traditional French Crepes and extraordinary French pastries to mention just a few.

Cookery demonstrations are provided on the first Saturday of each month by Michelin Star Chef Michael Deane from 12.00 noon. Customers can also sample the products; relax with a coffee and a newspaper against a backdrop of live jazz or flamenco music. Added to this plethora of tempting foods the Saturday market also encompasses a flower section with some of Northern Ireland's leading florists ensuring this Saturday market is a kaleidoscope of colour. This market is a real Saturday treat.

Other Points

A free market bus runs every 20 minutes between the City Centre (outside Boots the Chemist, Donegal Place or HMV, Castle Place) and the market. Bus departs 8am on Friday and every 20 minutes thereafter. Bus departs 9.00am on Saturday and every 20 minutes thereafter. Subsidised Customer Parking on a Friday at Stewart Street Car Park: £1 per 2 hours. Subsidised Customer Parking on a Saturday at Hilton Car Parks: £1 per hour. Max charge £5.00.

Hours

Friday Variety Market
Fri 6.00 - 13.00
The City Food & Garden Market
Sat 9.00 - 15.00

Directions

St. George's Market is located opposite Belfast Waterfront Hall and the Hilton Hotel in Oxford Street, which runs parallel to the River Lagan. From the rear of Belfast City Hall walk eastwards down May Street for few minutes, cross over Victoria Street and St. George's directly in front of you.

The Giant's Causeway | *Place to visit*

Causeway Road, Bushmills,
Co Antrim BT57 8SU
Tel. +44(0)28 2073 1582 or 2972
Fax. +44(0)28 2073 2963
Email.
giantscauseway@nationaltrust.org.uk

The North Antrim Coast is a designated
Area of Outstanding Natural Beauty. Along
its beautiful coast is the world famous
Giant's Causeway, an icon of Northern
Ireland and its only World Heritage Site.

Other Points
Guided tours by arrangement for
groups over 15 (Tel. 028 2073 1582
for details). Country walk, Suitable for
picnics, Shop, Refreshments, Available
for functions, Programme of events,
Access for visitors with disability,
Facilities for families, Learning, Dogs
welcome on leads.

Admission Charged

Hours
Stones & Coastal Path open all year
Trust Shop
Open all year -except 25 & 26 Dec
For opening times please contact
property directly.
Tea Room
Open all year - except 25 & 26 Dec
For opening times please contact
property directly.

Directions
On B146, 2ml from Bushmills.
Drive time: Belfast 1.15hr.

Ulster Museum | *Place to visit*

Botanic Gardens, Belfast, BT8 5AB
Tel. +44 (0) 28 9038 3000
www.ulstermuseum.org.uk

Unlock your imagination in the welcoming
environment of the Ulster Museum, where
the superb range of collections and friendly
staff will ensure that you enjoy a quality
experience, whatever your age or interests.
Enjoy a visual feast of fine and decorative
arts - from Irish, British and international
paintings and sculptures to stunning displays of glass, silver and ceramics, as well
as international touring shows. Discover
the richness of the heritage in the unfolding
story of the north of Ireland and its people
from as far back as the end of the Ice
Age. Explore the diversity of the natural
history of the island - its geology, animals
and plants - in the sciences galleries. As
well as permanent galleries and temporary
exhibitions, the Museum has lots of family
trails and activities to interest children,
year-round workshops, weekend events and
holiday activities - all the ingredients for a
fascinating voyage of discovery.

Other Points
Café, Gift Shop, Bureau de Change,
Family/Baby Care Room, Access and
facilities for visitors with disabilities,
Guide dogs welcome and Portable loop
systems for hearing-impaired visitors.

Admission Free

Hours
Mon - Fri   10.00 - 17.00
Saturday   13.00 - 17.00
Sunday   14.00 - 17.00
Closed   24-27 Dec

Directions
By train - Nearest station Botanic
By bus - No. 69 from city centre
By car - Balmoral exit from M1/M2.

W5 - whowhatwherewhenwhy | *Place to visit*

W5 at Odyssey, 2 Queen's Quay,
Belfast BT3 9QQ
Tel. +44(0) 28 9046 7700
www.w5online.co.uk.

W5 is Ireland's first and only purpose-built interactive discovery centre and is located at the Odyssey complex, Belfast. As one of Northern Ireland's premier visitor attractions the centre has over 130 amazing unique, hands-on exhibits, which offer hours of fun for visitors of all ages. There are five action-packed interactive exhibition areas called WOW, START, GO, SEE & DO with attractions including a laser harp, animation stations, cloud rings, a lie detector and lots more! In addition to the exhibits, W5 also present live science shows and have a changing programme of special events. New for Summer 2005; Myths and Monsters, a Natural History Museum travelling exhibition. Opens 2 July 2005. Exhibition is free with admission to W5

Other Points

W5 is fully accessible, educational workshops, corporate hire facilities, birthday party package, coffee shop available, admission charged, season pass, group and family ticketing options available.

Hours

Mon - Sat 10.00 - 18.00
Sun 12.00 - 18.00
Last admission 17.00
Please note, during school term time W5 will close one hour earlier Mon - Thur at 17.00 with last admission at 16.00.

Directions

From Belfast City Centre - follow signs for the A2 Bangor onto Queen Elizabeth Bridge. Keep in the left lane and immediately after crossing the River Lagan turn left onto Queen's Island. Follow the road for 1/4 mile, the car park is on your right.

Portadown Co Armagh

The Yellow Door
Bistro, deli, bakery and patisserie

74 Woodhouse Street, Portadown,
Co Armagh BT62 1JL
Tel. +44(0)28 3835 3528
Email. info@yellowdoordeli.co.uk
www.yellowdoordeli.co.uk

This fine addition to the Portadown food scene has won a deserved reputation for its imaginative, freshly cooked food, including an impressive range of breads from its in-house bakery. The Woodhouse street branch has a convivial, licensed bistro and café alongside the deli and patisserie - a great spot for a laid-back lunch. Start the day with fresh waffles with maple syrup, or Moyallon sausage with bacon, egg, soda bread and vine tomatoes. Chef Michael Donaghey produces a daily-changing lunch menu, which might take in fresh soups such as creamy roast root vegetable; gourmet sandwiches such as home-roasted turkey with cranberry and cracked pepper mayo, and tortilla wraps, including Feta cheese and pesto. Among the delicious main courses are home hot-smoked salmon with steamed baby

Prices: Lunch main course from £5-£8. House wine from £9.50 .
Food served: 9.00-17.00 Mon-Sat.
Closed: Sundays. 25, 26 Dec. May day. 12,13 July.
Cuisine: Modern Irish/French.
Other Points: No-smoking area. Children welcome. In-house bakery and French patisserie.
Directions: M1 exit 11 into town centre. On high street turn left only one street on left going downhill away from church, one way system.

potatoes in pimento beurre blanc sauce and Yellow Door chicken pie. If you're not stopping for lunch, consider stocking up for a gourmet picnic - don't miss the French apple tart.

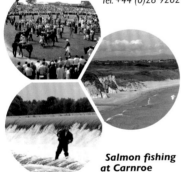

Nearest Racecourse
Down Royal
Tel. +44 (0)28 9262 1256

White Rocks Beach

Salmon fishing at Carnroe
on the River Bann

Armagh County Museum | *Place to visit*

The Mall East, Armagh BT61 9BE
Tel. +44 (0)28 37523070
Fax. +44 (0)28 37522631
Email. acm.um@nics.gov.uk
www.armaghcountymuseum.org.uk

Strolling along the tree-lined Mall, near the centre of St Patrick's cathedral city, a visit to Armagh County Museum is an ideal way to experience a flavour of the orchard county. Built in 1834 to a classical design, its impressive columns dominate the entrance, making it one of the most distinctive buildings in the area. The Museum's extensive collections and displays reflect the lives of people who have lived and worked in Armagh or have been associated with the county. Discover a rich and varied legacy revealed in objects ranging from prehistoric artefacts to household items from a bygone age. There are military uniforms, wedding dresses, ceramics, natural history specimens and railway memorabilia. An impressive art collection includes works by many well-known Irish artists. The Museum also has an extensive reference library, rich in local archive material, along with photographic and map collections. With a range of changing exhibitions throughout the year, it is an ideal place to see and explore the fair county of Armagh

Other Points
Museum Shop, Baby Changing Facilities, Access and Facilities for Disabled Visitors, Group Visits by prior arrangements for Adults, Community and School Groups, and Friends Association.

Admission is free

Hours
Mon - Fri 10.00 - 17.00 Sat 10.00 - 13.00 & 14.00 - 17.00

Directions
From Belfast exit and junction 11 from M1. Follow the signs through Portadown for Armagh. On entering the city the Museum is located about half way along the Mall, between the old gaol and the courthouse.

Londonderry Co Derry ✕ ✦ ⬛ ★

Browns Restaurant, Bar & Brasserie
City centre restaurant & bar

1 & 2 Bonds Hill, Londonderry,
Co Derry BT47 6DW
Tel. +44(0)28 7134 5180
Email. eat@brownsrestaurant.com
www.brownsrestaurant.com

Ivan Taylor's eponymous restaurant sits at the end of a pretty pastel-painted terrace in the waterside area of town, opposite the old railway station. Taylor - an engaging character - is known for his consistently original and adventurous menus which have attracted glowing reviews in the sixteen years or so he's been open. Lunch includes a coarse duck paté with sweet pepper salsa and crumbled chicken satay with fragrant rice and coriander bread, while dinner might bring herb-seared loin of lamb with taboulleh and roasted baby courgettes, or mature Irish Cheddar soufflé with roasted baby veg and fondue sauce. Puddings such as chocolate truffle cake with thick cream and raspberry coulis are luxury incarnate. The stylish interior, designed by Taylor himself, combines good lighting and comfortable seating with funky foliage

Prices: Lunch main course from £5.95. Dinner main course from £8.25. House wine from £12.95.
Food served: 12.00-14.30 Tue-Fri and 17.30 till late Tue-Sat.
Closed: Sun & Mon. First two weeks in August.
Cuisine: Modern Irish with a twist.
Other Points: Children welcome. Car park. A private dining/ function/ meeting room. Winner - Newcomer of the Year 2005.
Directions: In the Waterside area of town, opposite the old railway station.

and natural textures. There's a good-value, promptly served lunch menu, pre-theatre and children's menus, gluten-free dishes and a private dining room.

Derry City at night

Magherafelt Co Derry

Ditty's Home Bakery & Coffee Shop
Bakery and coffee shop

3 Rainey Street, Magherafelt,
Co Derry BT45 5AA
Tel. +44(0)28 7963 3944
Email. dittybky@aol.com
www.dittysbakery.com

The focus at Robert and Helen Ditty's family-run local bakery is on traditional, handmade breads from Northern Ireland. Fluffy, griddle-baked soda and potato farls, delicious wheaten bread and pastries, freshly made sandwiches and a diverting range of 'wee buns' are a huge draw for customers of Ditty's. There's also a thriving wholesale business which supplies Ditty's delectable oatcakes and breads to prestigious outlets such as Fortnum and Mason and Paul and Jeanne Rankin's Gourmet Ireland. The lunch menu includes homemade soups, burgers, pasta and toasted sandwiches, as well as traditional hot dishes such as baked gammon with parsley sauce. All ingredients are sourced locally, and bespoke hampers and special occasion

Prices: Main course from £5.
Food served: 8.00-17.30 Mon-Sat.
Closed: Sundays. 25, 26 Dec. 1 Jan. Easter Mon & Tue. First Mon in May. 12,13 July.
Cuisine: Traditional Irish.
Other Points: Non-smoking. Children welcome.
Directions: From Belfast: M22/M2 (by pass Toomebridge), follow A6 until you reach Derry/Magherafelt/Castledawson roundabout, take left to Magherafelt, go to centre of town, taking a right at top of hill in Rainey Street. The shop is located on corner roundabout.

cakes are also part of the service.

Magherafelt Co Derry

Laurel Villa Townhouse
Town centre bed and breakfast

60 Church Street, Magherafelt,
Co –Derry BT45 6AW
Tel. +44(0)28 7963 2238
Email.info@laurel-villa.com
www.laurel-villa.com

A gracious ivy-covered Victorian villa
in the centre of Magherafelt, Laurel
Villa oozes hospitality. Proprietors
Gerardine and Eugene Kielt took over
the guesthouse from Eugene's mother,
who started the business in 1962. The
house is old-fashioned in the best sense:
lots of period furniture and Victorian and
Edwardian collectables, and an "Ulster
Fry" for breakfast, but individually
decorated, comfortable bedrooms with
"power shower"-equipped bathrooms.
Gerardine is a fine home baker whose
specialties include organic wheaten
focaccia. Eugene is a Northern Ireland
Tour Guide Association-qualified "Blue
Badge" who offers a special-interest
"Seeing Things" tour, inspired by Nobel
Laureate Seamus Heaney, who was
born nearby. Other customised tours of
the region are available. Recalling the
area's rich cultural history, the Kielts
have loads of literary memorabilia on
the walls, an extensive collection of old
medicine bottles, and a reference room
devoted to books of genealogical and
Irish interest. Excellent golf and hill-
walking are easily accessible.

Rooms: 5 ensuite. Double from £50.
Single from £35. Family room from £60.
Closed: Christmas
Other Points: Non-smoking bed-
rooms. Garden. Children welcome. Car
Park. Reference library with Genealogi-
cal and Local Studies source material.
Directions: Conveniently situated
along A31 in Magherafelt Town Centre.
From M2/A6/Belfast/Airports/Ports,
take A31 into town. Straight through
first mini roundabout. House is 50
yards further along on right opposite
St. Swithin's Church. From A29/Money-
more/Tobermore go into town centre.
Follow signs for Belfast/M2. House
is 200 yards from Bridewell Tourist
Information Office, on left opposite St
Swithin's Church.

Laurel Villa Townhouse

The Tower Museum | *Place to visit*

6 Union Place, Derry City, Co Derry,
BT486AF.
Tel. +44 (0) 28 71377331
www.derrycity.gov.uk/museums

The Tower Museum uniquely houses two exhibitions relating to the city's history and development. The award winning Story of Derry exhibition chronicles the City's history from it's geological formation to present while An Armada Shipwreck - La Trinidad Valencera, a new interactive exhibition, tells the story of the discovery and excavation of the many artefacts recovered from the sunken ship.

Other Points

Wheelchair accessible. Interactive facilities for children. Educational resources for schools and state of the art audiovisual presentation. Multiple language interpretation also available for the Armada Shipwreck exhibition.

Hours

For more information on opening hours, prices, events and programmed activities please view www.derrycity.gov.uk/museums or telephone 0044 (0) 28 71377331.

Directions

From Belfast follow the A6 route, via Dungiven, to Derry/ Londonderry and follow signs for City Centre. From Dublin follow the M1 route towards Belfast. Take turn off at Ardee, following N2 to Derry via Strabane. From Dublin follow the M1 route towards Belfast. Take turn off at Ardee, following N2 to Derry via Strabane. From Dublin follow the M1 route towards Belfast. Take turn off at Ardee, following N2 to Derry via Strabane.

Hillsborough Oyster Festival

Comber Co Down

The Old Schoolhouse Inn
Guesthouse and restaurant

100 Ballydrain Road, Comber,
Co Down BT23 6EA
Tel. +44(0)28 9754 1182
Email. info@theoldschoolhouseinn.com
www.theoldschoolhouseinn.com

Situated on the picturesque shores of Strangford Lough, the largest sea inlet in the British Isles, and adjacent to Castle Espie Wildfowl and Wetlands Centre, the Old School House Inn is just eight miles from Belfast. Owners Avril and Terry Brown rescued the Ballydrain Primary school after it closed in 1985; the result is a charmingly atmospheric restaurant with 12 comfortable and simply furnished ensuite rooms, each named after an American president of Ulster descent. Avril is committed to using seasonal produce from local growers, and her French-inspired menu is traditional and assured. Dinner, taken by candlelight, could include dressed crab and tomato mayonnaise followed by noisettes of lamb with a rosemary and redcurrant jus or crispy roast duckling with plum and cognac jus. There are homemade puddings and locally grown strawberries for dessert.

Rooms: 12 ensuite. Double from £65. Single from £45.
Prices: Dinner main course from £16.95. Set Sunday Lunch £14.95. House wine from £12.95.
Food served: Sunday lunch 12.30-15.00. Dinner 19.00-21.30 Mon-Sat.
Closed: 25 December.
Cuisine: French, Grande Mère.
Other Points: No-smoking area. Garden. Children welcome. Car park.
Directions: From Comber on the A22 turn left at the Brown signposts. The Old Schoolhouse is well sign-posted; follow the signs for approximately two miles.

Set menus are reasonably priced, and there's a decent wine list, divided into an old, new and connoisseur's selection.

Dundrum Co Down ✕ 🍸 🍺

The Buck's Head Inn
Village restaurant and bar

77 Main Street, Dundrum,
Co Down BT33 0LU
Tel. +44(0)28 4375 1868
Email. buckshead1@aol.com

Alison and Michael Crother's eighteenth-century inn, in the centre of historic Dundrum, is known for its excellent food and warm welcome. Diners can choose from the cosy, cherry-panelled bar to the front, with its convivial atmosphere - stoked up in season by a good mix of regulars and holiday-makers - and the contemporary restaurant to the rear, decorated in neutral colours and over-looking a pretty walled garden through large, arched windows. Alison's modern menu brings together local ingredients, especially seafood, with flavours from the East and closer to home. Starters range from oven-baked oysters with a Parmesan soda and garlic gratin, to bang bang chicken salad with a peanut dipping sauce. Main courses bring a good variety of meat, fish and vegetarian dishes, including slow-cooked Mourne lamb

Prices: Lunch main course from £8. Bar snack from £4. Dinner main course from £16.50. House wine from £12.95.
Food served: Lunch 12.00-14.30 daily. 17.00-21.30 Mon-Sat. 19.00-20.30 Sun. Booking essential.
Closed: 24, 25 Dec. Mondays from October to March.
Cuisine: Modern Irish.
Other Points: Garden. Children welcome. Car park. No smoking policy in all internal areas.
Directions: Located on main Belfast to Newcastle road, 20 miles from Belfast, 4 miles from Newcastle.

shank with root vegetables and champ, and penne pasta with purple sprouting broccoli, Cashel Blue and roast pinenut cream. The wine list has some interesting French and antipodean bottles.

Holywood Co Down ✕ 🍸 ☕ CS

The Bay Tree
Coffee shop, restaurant, craft shop & gallery

118 High Street, Holywood,
Co Down BT18 9HW
Tel. +44(0)28 9042 1419
www.baytreeholywood.com

Sue Farmer's courtyard coffee house, restaurant and craft shop is something of an institution, a place, says Sue, where you might meet someone you know, or get to know someone you don't. Inventive homecooking is key to the experience - only the freshest ingredients are used, and the creative menu brings together a range of exotic influences as well as more homely comforts. Fabulous cinnamon scones, and toasted banana and bacon sandwiches are perfect breakfast treats, while dinner, on Fridays only, might bring Soulienka - a Russian beef and olive soup - poached hake with a Thai coconut sauce and rice, and rhubarb jelly with ginger ice cream. Lunch includes familiar favourites such as spicy chicken wings, pork casserole, broccoli and blue cheese flan, herb-laden salads and delectable chocolate and pecan brownies. There are also wheat- and gluten-free 'honest cakes' for guilt-free indulgence.

Prices: Lunch main course from £3.45-£7. Dinner 2 courses & coffee £19.50; 3-courses & coffee £22.50.
Food served: 8.00-16.30 Mon-Fri. 9.30-16.30 Sat. 19.00-23.00 Fri (last sitting 21.30). Pottery and Gallery open 9.30-16.30 Mon-Sat.
Closed: 25, 26 Dec. Easter 2 days & 12 July (possibly for one week).
Cuisine: Modern Irish.
Other Points: Non-smoking. Children welcome. Craft shop. Pottery and Gallery. Car Park.
Directions: From Belfast take the Bangor Road, turn off at Palace Barracks. The Bay Tree is opposite the police station.

The craft shop stocks Nicholas Mosse and Stephen Pearce pottery and designer jewellery.

Kircubbin Co Down ✕ ☘

Paul Arthurs Restaurant
Town centre restaurant

66 Main Street, Kircubbin,
Co Down BT22 2SP
Tel. +44(0)28 4273 8192
www.paul-arthurs.co.uk

Local man Paul Arthurs' contemporary dining room has recently seen the addition of five ensuite rooms next to the restaurant. This may prove to be a huge boon to those who prefer to linger until well after bedtime over the refreshingly no-fuss menu. Arthurs crams plenty of local produce into his spot-on dishes, including plump Strangford Lough prawns, Portaferry mussels, Finnebrogue venison and Kircubbin Bay crab claws. Beef comes direct from Paul's father's farm. Dinner might start with a chunky smoked haddock chowder, followed by oven-roast partridge with red wine, foie gras and redcurrant sauce, and raspberry pavlova with homemade vanilla ice cream. Arthurs is to be applauded for offering regular vegan dishes - sweet tomato couscous with roasted vegetables and harissa - alongside the vegetarian choices, which include

Prices: Sunday lunch main course from £12.95-£25. Dinner main course from £12.95-£25. House wine from £10.
Food Served: 12.00-14.30 Sun. 17.00-21.00 Tue-Thur. 17.00-21.30 Fri-Sat.
Closed: Mondays. January.
Cuisine: Modern Irish.
Other Points: No-smoking area. Children welcome.
Directions: From Newtownards follow the A20 for 14 miles to Kircubbin, restaurant situated on the left hand side in the middle of the main street.

potato gnocchi with saffron. The wine list offers eight by the glass - a great way to broaden your wine-drinking horizons - or, you can bring your own.

Warrenpoint Co Down ✕ ☘ ▯

The Duke Restaurant
Town centre restaurant

7 Duke Street, Warrenpoint
Newry, Co Down BT34 3JY
Tel. +44(0)28 4175 2084
www.thedukerestaurant.com

Ciaran Gallagher's restaurant is situated in the centre of Warrenpoint. The menu is based around some popular classics - scampi, chicken Maryland - all of which are lifted above the ordinary by Gallagher's skilful cooking and careful sourcing. Seafood is fresh from Kilkeel and beef locally raised. Main ingredients are listed first, so that the impression is of a self-assured core of primary produce. Elegant starters include fresh crab with avocado, vine tomato, lemon crème fraîche and balsamic syrup; while grilled turbot fillet with kol rabi fondant is a typical special. A generous seafood grill - hake, gurnard, monkfish, mackerel and squid - successfully unites contrasting tastes and textures. Vegetarians are treated to a surprise - the dish of the day is left a deliberate mystery on the typed menu. Desserts such as plum and ginger crème brûlée finish the meal with a flourish.

Prices: Dinner main course from £13.50. House wine from £9.95. 3 course menu £13.50 Tue-Thur.
Food served: 18.30-22.00 Tue-Fri. 18.30-23.00 Sat. 17.30-21.00 Sun.
Closed: Mondays except bank holidays. 24,26 Dec. 1 Jan.
Cuisine: Modern European. Seafood and steak a speciality.
Other Points: Non-smoking. Children welcome up to 20.00.
Directions: Newry is nearly equidistant from Belfast and Dublin. From there direct road to Warrenpoint. In town square take left at roundabout, the restaurant is 4 doors up on the left

Castle Ward & Strangford Lough Wildlife Centre | *Place to visit*

Strangford, Downpatrick, Co Down,
BT30 7LS
Tel. +44(0)28 4488 1204
Fax. +44(0)28 4488 1729
Email. castleward@nationaltrust.org.uk

Castle Ward was built, inside and out, in
two distinct architectural styles, Classical
and Gothic. It gives a full flavour of how a
house and estate worked with its upstairs
downstairs tales, its Victorian laundry and
the water-driven cornmill. Inside the beautiful 750 acre walled estate you will find an
exotic sunken garden, paths that wind their
way through woodland and suddenly open
onto the quiet shores of the Lough. Look
out for the Artists in Residence programme
working in a traditional cottage with studio.
Children will adore the paradise of fun at
the adventure play area.

Other Points
Historic house, Industrial heritage, Farm,
Garden, Park, Countryside, Coast,
Nature Reserve, Adventure Playground,
Shop, Refreshments, Guided tours, Suitable for picnics, Country walk, Available
for functions, Programme of events, Access for visitors with disability, Facilities
for families, Learning, Dogs welcome on
leads in grounds/garden only.

Admission Charged

Hours
Grounds
Oct - Apr: 10.00 - 16.00 daily
Ma - Sept: 10.00 - 20.00 daily
House & Wildlife Centre
17 Mar 1.00 - 18.00
01 Apr - 25 Jun 1.00 - 18.00 w/ends &
BH/PH
Easter 14 Apr - 23 Apr: 1.00 - 18.00 daily
1 Jul - 31 Aug: 1.00 - 18.00 daily
2 Sept - 30 Sept: 1.00 - 18.00 w/ends
Last tour 1hr before closing
Tea room & shop open as per House and
close at 5.30pm

Directions
On A25, 7ml from Downpatrick and 1.5ml
from Strangford.
Drive time: Belfast 45 mins, Dublin 2.5 hrs

Mount Stewart House & Gardens | *Place to visit*

Portaferry Road, Newtownards,
Co Down, BT22 2AD
Tel. +44(0)28 4278 8387
Fax. +44(0)28 4278 8569
Email.
mountstewart@nationaltrust.org.uk

Home of the Londonderry family, the
house and its contents reflect the remarkable history of the family. The house tour
includes world famous paintings and stories
about the prominent guests and the people
who have worked there over the centuries.
From the manicured formal terraces to the
grandeur of the lake and the views from
the Temple of the Winds, Mount Stewart's
breathtaking gardens over-flow with the
vibrant colour of the rare plants that thrive
in the mild climate of the Ards Peninsula.

Other Points
Historic house, Gardens, Shop, Restau-
rant, Guided tours, Suitable for picnics,
Lakeside walks, Available for functions,
Programme of events, Access for visitors
with disability, Facilities for families,
Learning, Dogs welcome on leads in
grounds/garden only.

Admission Charged

Hours
For opening times please contact property
Lakeside Gardens: Open all year daily 10.00
- sunset
Formal Gardens : 11- 26 Mar: w/ends & BH/
PH only. Apr - Oct: daily
House: 11 Mar - 30 Apr: w/ends & BH/PH
Easter 14 - 23 Apr: daily. May: daily (except
Tues). Jun - Aug: daily. Sept: daily (except
Tues). Oct: w/ends. Nov - Feb: closed.
Last admission to House & Formal Gardens
1 hour before closing
Temple of the Winds: 2 Apr - 24 Sept
Sun & BH/PH only

Directions
Bus: Ulsterbus no 10 between Belfast &
Portaferry, bus stop at garden gates.
Car: On A20, 5ml from Newtownards
on the Portaferry Road. Drive time: 25
mins from Belfast.

St Patrick Centre | *Place to visit*

Downpatrick, Co Down
Tel. +44 (0) 2844619000
Fax. +44 (0) 2844619111
Email. director@saintpatrickcentre.com
www.saintpatrickcentre.com

The St Patrick Centre is situated beside the Patron Saint's Grave in Downpatrick, medieval capital of County Down. This award winning building, within the shadow of the Mourne Mountains houses Ireland's newest visitor attraction. Bold graphics, sculptures and interactive videos allow visitors to explore the fascinating story of Patrick and how his legacy helped develop the Irish Golden Age which brought the light of Christianity to Dark Age Europe. Finally, take a flight through Ireland to all of the sites associated with Patrick in our 180 degree cinema. The St Patrick Centre is an essential destination for those who believe that Ireland really is the land of Saints and Scholars.

Hours
Oct to Mar: Mon-Sat 9.30 - 19.00
Apr, May & Sep: Mon-Sat 9.30 - 17.30.
Sunday 13.00 - 17.30
Jun to Aug: Mon-Sat 9.30 - 18.00
Sunday 10.00 - 18.00

Admission Charged

Directions
From Dublin: M1 Dublin to Newry and take A25 through Castlewellan and Clough. First left turn in Downpatrick at St Patrick's Square.
From Belfast: Take A24 to Carryduff and A7 at the roundabout through Saintfield and Crossgar. Turn Right at Roundabout in Downpatrick and follow signs.

Other points
Guided Tours, Craft Shop, Restaurant, Art Gallery, Tourist Information Centre, Gardens, Euro Notes Accepted.

Ulster Folk and Transport Museum | *Place to visit*

Cultra, Holywood, Co Down,
BT18 0EU
Tel. +44 (0)28 90 428428
Fax. +44 (0)28 90 428728
Email. louise.willis@magni.org.uk
www.uftm.org.uk

The Ulster Folk and Transport Museum, Irish Museum of the Year, illustrates the way of life and the traditions of the people of the north of Ireland. At the open air Folk Museum 60 acres are devoted to illustrating the way of life of people in the early 1900s. The Transport Museum boasts the most comprehensive transport collection in Ireland. The Museum has a full programme of major events from Vehicle Days in the spring to Halloween and Christmas events in the winter. For the full programme of Events and Exhibitions please contact the Museum +44(0)2890428428 or visit the web site www.uftm.org.uk .

Hours
Mon - Sat 10.00 - Closing.
Sun 11.00 - Closing. (Times vary from 16.00pm to 18.00pm according to the season).

Directions
The Museum is situated on the main Belfast to Bangor Road, just ten minutes outside Belfast with excellent access by road, rail and bus and close to Belfast City Airport. Nearest rail station to the Museum is Cultra Halt. Buses stop outside the Museum entrance.

Other Points
Tea Rooms, Shop, Tours by arrangement, Disabled Access, Family Facilities, Educational Programmes, Picnic Area, Parking, Guide Dogs welcome, Dogs welcome on a lead, Baby Changing Facilities, Corporate Hire.

Enniskillen Co Fermanagh ✕ ✦ ⭐

Oscar's Restaurant
Town centre restaurant

29 Belmore Street, Enniskillen,
Co Fermanagh BT74 6AA
Tel. +44(0)28 6632 7037
www.oscars-restaurant.co.uk

Dermot Magee's art deco-style restaurant, the exterior an attractive shade of blue, is dedicated to Oscar Wilde, who was educated at the town's Portora Royal School. Hundreds of books, architectural salvage, handcrafted furniture and paintings by a local artist all play into a depiction of the life and times of Wilde, with images of the writer and quotations from him and other Irish literary giants. The eclectic menu is wide-ranging, and never dull - no doubt Wilde would approve. Aside from daily vegetarian and fish specials, dishes range from the homegrown - Cooneed goat's cheese and cherry tomato tartlet, Dundrum garlic mussels, roast oak-smoked rack of Fermanagh lamb, for example - to the global, with chilli beef fajita, crispy oriental duck and a range of pizzas. Dermot prides himself on using locally sourced organic produce as well as local lamb,

Prices: Dinner main course from £7.50-£19.95. House wine from £9.95.
Food Served: 17.00-22.00 daily.
Closed: 25, 26 December.
Cuisine: Contemporary Irish, with emphasis on use of fresh local produce.
Other Points: No-smoking area. Children welcome. Highly commended-Restaurant of the Year 2003.
Directions: From the South African War Memorial, branch in to Belmore Street; restaurant on the left at the traffic lights.

duck and bacon. Desserts are homemade and the well-chosen wine list offers good value for money.

The Symbols

🂠 Accommodation

✕ Restaurant

☕ Café

🍺 Pub/Bar

☀ Daytime opening only

🥄 Deli

🍷 Wine

🥐 Bakery

🍶 Gourmet/Farm Shop

📶 Leisure Centre/Spa

CS Craft Shop

VC Visitor Centre

Les Routiers Awards

⭐ 2002 Award Winner

⭐ 2003 Award Winner

⭐ 2004 Award Winner

★ 2005 Award Winner

Belleek Pottery | *Place to visit*

Belleek, Co Fermanagh, BT3 3FY
Tel. +44(0)28 68659300
Fax. +44(0)28 68658625
Email. visitorcentre@belleek.ie
www.belleek.ie

Leave the hustle and bustle of modern life
behind and immerse yourself in the Belleek
experience. We invite you to join us on a
guided tour of Ireland's oldest and most
historic pottery. Established over 143 years
ago, a visit to Belleek offers a fascinating
insight into the life and times of a company
that has come to represent the highest
standard of Irish craftsmanship at home and
abroad. A Tour of the Pottery is like a step
back in time. The methods and techniques
developed by the very first Belleek craftsmen are still meticulously followed today.

Jul - Sept: Mon - Fri. 9.00 - 18.00
Sat 10.00 - 18.00. Sun 12.00 - 18.00
Oct - Dec: Mon - Fri. 9.00 - 17.30
Sat 10.00 - 18.00. Sun 14.00 - 18.00

Other Points
Guided Pottery Tours, Museum, Audio
Visual Theatre, Restaurant, Showroom.

Directions
Take the M1 to Dungannon. Continue on
the A4 for approximately 9 miles to the
Ballygawley roundabout. Follow the A4
through Augher, Clogher and Fivemiletown
until you reach Enniskillen. In Enniskillen
follow the signs for Belleek (A46). Travel
time by car - 2 hours.

Hours
Jan - Feb: Mon - Fri. 9.00 - 17.30
Sat & Sun Closed.
Mar - Jun: Mon - Fri. 9.00 - 18.00
Sat 10.00 - 18.00. Sun 14.00 - 18.00

Castle Coole | *Place to visit*

Enniskillen, Co. Fermanagh, BT74 6JY
Tel. +44(0)28 6632 2690
Fax. +44(0)28 6632 5665
Email.
castlecoole@nationaltrust.org.uk

Situated in a stunning landscaped parkland
on the edge of Enniskillen this majestic
18th century house built by James Wyatt
was created to impress. We highly recommend the house tour to soak up the opulent
Regency interior with its rich decoration,
furnishings and furniture, including the
ornate state bedroom prepared for George
IV in 1821. You can also walk through the
servants' tunnel and see the stableyard and
coaches. Castle Coole is one of the finest
neo-classical houses in Ireland. **Other**

Points
Historic house, Park, Shop, Refreshments, Guided tours, Suitable for picnics, Country walk, Available for functions, Programme of events, Access
for visitors with disability, Facilities for
families, Learning, Dogs welcome on
leads in grounds/garden only.

Admission Charged

Hours
Grounds
30 Oct - 31 Mar: 10.00 - 16.00 daily
1 Apr - 29 Oct: 10.00 - 20.00 daily
House
17-19 Mar: 1.00 - 18.00
1 Apr - 31 May: 1.00 - 18.00 w/ends &
BH/PH
Easter, 14 Apr - 23 Apr: 1.00 - 18.00 daily
1 - 30 June: 1.00 - 18.00 daily (except Thur)
1 Jul - 31 Aug: 12.00 - 18.00 daily
1 - 30 Sept: 1.00 - 18.00 w/ends
Last tour 1 hr before closing
Tea room & shop open as per House and
close at 5.30pm

Directions
On A4, 1.5 ml from Enniskillen, on main
Enniskillen to Belfast road. Drive time:
Enniskillen 5 mins, Belfast 1.5 hrs, Dublin
2.5 hrs.

Dungannon Co Tyrone

Grange Lodge
Period country house

7 Grange Road, Dungannon,
Co Tyrone BT71 7EJ
Tel. +44(0)28 8778 4212
Email. stay@grangelodgecountryhouse.com
www. grangelodgecountryhouse.com

Twenty years on, the Browns, Nora and Ralph to those of you not familiar with Grange Lodge, have a relaxed but confident way about them, which helps to put the weary traveller at their ease on arrival. The beautiful, stone Georgian house, which originates back to 1698 has been revamped (but not too much!) over the years, and is situated on three and a half acres of well established gardens with the most magnificent, almost regal pines and horse chestnuts. This in turn is surrounded by another seventeen acres of parklands, so you are never far from nature! The bedrooms are individually decorated, country cottage in style, with en suite bath or shower room. When it comes to dining, the elaborately decorated, formal dining room, which hosts various photos and trophies that Nora has won for her food is the place to be. Focusing on local produce is important to Nora, and she sources the speciality beef, lamb, pork and chicken from the farm shops and markets in the Dungannon area. Apart from the evening meal, the Bushmills Porridge that Nora cooks with organic oats and salt and water on the Aga the night before, and boasts

Rooms: 5 ensuite. Double from £78. Single from £55.
Prices: Set dinner from £26. House wine from £10.
Food Served: Sit down 7.30-20.00 for residents (must be booked in advance).
Closed: 20 Dec - 1 Feb.
Cuisine: Traditional Irish with a modern flavour with emphasis on using fresh local produce.
Other Points: Bedrooms non-smoking. Garden. Children welcome over 12 years old. Car park. Snooker table. Private dining for small groups by prior arrangement.
Directions: One mile from M1 Junction 15 on A29 Armagh Turn left at Grange Lodge sign, almost immediately right, then white walled entrance on right.

a healthy shot of Bushmills will put a smile on your face! Combine that with free range eggs, dry cured bacon, home made bread, the local apple juice (another speciality of the house!) and you are set up for the day.

Nearest Golf Courses

Portstewart Golf Club *Tel. + (028) 70834543*
Royal County Down *Tel. + (028) 43723314*
Royal Portrush Golf Club *Tel. + (028) 70822260*

| Ulster American Folk Park | *Place to visit* |

2 Mellon Road, Castletown, Omagh,
Co Tyrone BT78 5QY
Tel. +44(0) 28 8224 3292
Fax. +44 (0) 28 8224 2241
Email. info@uafp.co.uk

An outdoor museum of emigration which tells the story of millions of people who emigrated from these shores throughout the 18th and 19th centuries. The Old World and New World layout of the Park illustrates the various aspects of emigrant life on both sides of the Atlantic. Traditional thatched buildings, American log houses and a full-scale replica emigrant ship and the dockside gallery help to bring a bygone era back to life. Costumed demonstrators go about their everyday tasks including spinning, open-hearth cookery, printing and textiles. The museum also includes an indoor Emigrants Exhibition and includes a Centre for Migration Studies/library. A full programme of special events is organised throughout the year.

Hours
Oct - Mar: Mon - Fri 10.30 - 15.30
Museum closes at 17.00
Closed weekends and public holidays.
Apr- Sep: Mon - Sat 10.30 - 16.30
Museum closes at 18.00
Sun and public holidays 11.00 - 17.00
Museum closes 18.30

Directions
3 miles north of Omagh on A5 Road to Strabane. M1 to A5 from Belfast. N2 from Dublin on main North West Passage route.

Other Points
Guided Tours available, Residential Centre, Gift Shop, Restaurant, Coffee Shop, Bureau de Change, Free Car and Coach Parking, Cycle Shelter, Wheelchair Accessible

Carrick-a-Rede Rope Bridge, Antrim

Key Events

Equestrian Hennessy Cognac Gold Cup	Leopardstown Feb 12	
Music Feis Ceoil	Dublin March 7 - 20	
Equestrian Dublin Horse Show	Dublin Aug 3 - 07	
Sport All Ireland Hurling Final All Ireland Football Final	Dublin Sept Sept	
Theatre Dublin Theatre Festival	Dublin Oct 03 - 15	
Sport Dublin City Marathon	Dublin Oct 30	

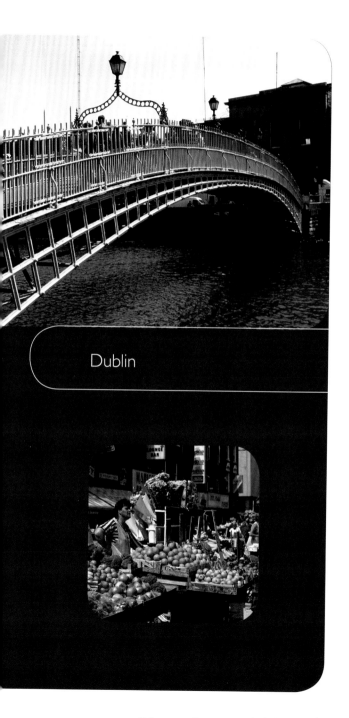

Dublin

Dublin I ✕ 🍷 ★

Chapter One Restaurant
City centre restaurant

18-19 Parnell Square, Dublin I
Tel. +353(0)1 8732266
Email. info@chapteronerestaurant.com
www.chapteronerestaurant.com

This excellent northside restaurant, under the Dublin Writers Museum, continues to impress for its fine, modern European cooking and excellent sourcing of raw materials. Producers are credited on the menu, where classically inspired dishes are driven by the seasons. Chef proprietor Ross Lewis and co-owner Martin Corbett run a sophisticated dining room, where excellent service and elegant surroundings make eating here a memorable occasion. Dinner might begin with Ardsallagh goat's cheese ravioli with warm asparagus, asparagus purée and lemon butter, and proceed with Roast Challans duck breast with buttered cabbage and sage, roast apple and walnut crumble. Desserts such as fig bread and butter pudding with almond anglaise, are as tempting as they are stylish. Chapter One offers a great value pre-theatre menu and the Gate Theatre is a short walk away - and the extensive wine list, weighted towards France and with six by the glass, is comparable with the best in the city.

Prices: 3 course lunch menu from €31 + 10% service charge. Dinner main course from €28.50. House wine from €22.50.
Food served: 12.30-14.30. Tue-Fri. 18.00-22.45 Tue-Sat.
Closed: Sun, Mon, 2 weeks at beginning of August, 2 weeks at Christmas.
Cuisine: Modern European.
Other Points: Children welcome over 10 years. Private dining areas (14 and 20). Winner - Wine Person of the Year 2005.
Directions: Top of O'Connell Street, North side of Parnell Sq. Basement of the Dublin Writers Museum.

Nearest Golf Courses
Glen of the Downs *Tel. + 353 (0)1 287 6240*
Malahide Golf Club *Tel. + 353 (0)1 8461611*
Royal Dublin Golf Club
Tel. + 353 (0)1 8336346
**St Margaret's Golf &
Country Club**
Tel. + 353 (0)1 8640400

Gate Theatre
Tel. + 353 (0)1 8744045

Mint, Dublin 6

Local Farmers' Markets

Temple Bar Food Market
Saturday mornings & Wednesdays 11am-3pm
**Dun Laoghaire People's
Park Market**
Sundays 11am-4pm
Leopardstown Racecouse Market
Fridays 10am-3pm
Dun Laoghaire Harbour Market
Saturdays 10am-4pm
Howth Market at the Harbour *Sundays 10am-3pm*
Malahide, GAA Facilities *Saturdays 10am-3pm*

Dublin 2

✕ ❤ ▼ 🍸 ☀ CS

Avoca Café
Daytime café and shop

11-13 Suffolk Street, Dublin 2
Tel. +353(0)1 6726019
Email. info@avoca.ie
www.avoca.ie

The Pratt family's flagship Avoca store is a 7-level, mini-department store located in the heart of Dublin, just off Grafton Street, across from Trinity College. Awash with colour and imagination, it carries a full range of exclusive woven throws, rugs, scarves, clothing, gifts, home furnishings, children's wear, jewellery, crafts and cookery books - and even boasts a secret rooftop garden. An extensive basement food hall is chock-a-block with specialist gourmet foods, giftware and kitchen gear, as well as home-baked products and freshly made salads that can be purchased for takeaway. The light-filled Avoca Café on the second floor has table service, dramatic floral arrangements and is hugely popular. Wholesome, healthy, home-cooked dishes might include sweet potato and lemongrass soup; chicken Caesar salad; shepherd's pie, chicken skewers with cous cous; and

Prices: Main course from €7.95-€13.95. House wine from €17.
Food Served: 10.00-17.30 Mon-Sat. 11.00-17.30 Sun.
Closed: 25, 26 Dec.
Cuisine: Traditional and modern Irish with international influences.
Other Points: Children welcome. Craft shop.
Directions: Turn left into Suffolk Street from the bottom of Grafton Street.

a range of impeccably fresh salads. Save room for a slice of chocolate and raspberry tart or a strawberry-orange tartlet with fresh cream.

Dublin 2

✕ 🍸

Botticelli
City centre Italian restaurant

1-3 Temple Bar, Dublin 2
Tel. +353(0)1 6727289
Email. botticelli@eircom.net

This casual Italian restaurant, in the heart of Temple Bar, seems to draw from the lively atmosphere on the streets visible through its large windows. The menu features classic pasta dishes such as rigatoni puttanesca and lasagne al forno, while starters such as antipasto all'italiana and caprese salad are a quintessentially Italian introduction. There are plenty of meat, fish and chicken dishes, including vitello ai funghi, saltimbocca al romana and swordfish with capers, olives, garlic and tomato sauce. Owner Piero Cosso believes in using the best ingredients to produce the best food, and chef Luigi Palmieri's pizzas are a case in point. A thin, crispy homemade crust arrives laden with tomatoes, cheese and a wide choice of extra toppings. Homemade ice creams come in nearly a dozen flavours, including green apple and champagne and strawberry. Set lunches are good value, and there is a wide

Prices: Lunch (starter/main course & tea/coffee) from €8.80.
Dinner main course from €10-€20. House wine from €18.
Food served: 13.00-24.00 daily.
Closed: Good Friday, 25, 26 Dec.
Cuisine: Italian
Other Points: Children welcome.
Directions: Just off the square in Temple Bar.

selection of mostly Italian wines. Service is courteous and professional.

Dublin 2   ✕ ☕ 🍸

Cornucopia
City centre vegetarian restaurant and café

19 Wicklow Street, Dublin 2
Tel. +353(0)1 6777583
Email. cornucopia@eircom.net

Conveniently located just off Grafton Street, this "cheap and cheerful" - in the best sense of the words - vegetarian café is relaxed and inviting. Clientele is primarily students, shoppers and alternative types who appreciate its easygoing self-service counter, wooden tables with tall stools, and owner Deirdre McCafferty's emphasis on wholesomeness. Most ingredients are organic, and many food intolerances and allergies are accommodated. Tasty soups include a smooth sweet-and-spicy Moroccan carrot soup served with a choice of homemade brown, tomato, wholewheat, gluten-free, or dairy-free bread; or an earthy lentil, chicory and coriander soup. Other reasonably priced dishes are garlicky hummous with pitta bread, marinated Kalamata olives and a choice of salad; or grilled polenta topped with roast pumpkin, fennel, sweet peppers and an almond pesto. Ten salads are available,

Prices: Lunch/dinner main course from €9.50. House wine from €18.50.
Food Served: 8.30-20.00, until 21.00 on Thursdays and 12.00-19.00 Sundays.
Closed: 25, 26 Dec. 1 Jan. Easter Sunday and Monday.
Cuisine: Modern and traditional Irish
Other Points: Children welcome.
Directions: Just off Grafton Street, take the turn at Brown Thomas.

five of which change daily. Vegetarian breakfasts are a specialty, as are rich desserts such as raspberry cheesecake brownies, or blackberry and apple crumble tarts.

Dublin 2   ✕ ☕ 🍸 🥄

Dunne & Crescenzi
Italian restaurant, café wine bar and deli

14 & 16 South Frederick Street, Dublin 2
Tel. +353(0)1 6759892

With their ever-expanding empire of charming small Italian café-restaurants Eileen Dunne and Stefano Crescenzi have nailed a winning formula. Authentic is a word much used about D&C, and indeed this is the kind of place you could bring a visiting Italian without batting an eyelid. The South Frederick Street branch has a large selection of Italian wines (some organic), and artisan ingredients - including olive oils, pastas and preserved fruits - to purchase and take away. The atmosphere is relaxed, the service brisk but friendly, and the simple menu a reminder that the best ingredients - buffalo mozzarella, fragrant basil, ripe tomatoes - can and should stand alone. The generous antipasti (misto and vegetariano) are particularly good, and there are daily changing pasta dishes, as well as side orders of delicious breads, olives and tomato or bean salad. The com-

Prices: A La Carte Menu available throughout the day - dishes from €5.50. House wine from €12.
Food Served: Deli 12.00-22.00, 12.00-17.00 Mon. Restaurant 9.00-23.00, 12.00-18.00 Sun.
Closed: Sundays. 25 Dec for 2 weeks.
Cuisine: Italian.
Other Points: Children welcome.
Directions: Close to Grafton Street and parallel to Dawson Street.

petitively priced wine list gives a regional tour of Italy.

Dublin 2 ✕ ☨

Eden
City centre restaurant

Sycamore Street, Templebar, Dublin 2
Tel. +353(0)1 6705372
Email. eden@edenrestaurant.ie
www.edenrestaurant.ie

With its knock-out location overlooking the vibrant Meeting House Square in the heart of Dublin's cultural quarter, Temple Bar, and its light, bright modern Irish cuisine, Eden attracts a buzzy crowd of artists, musicians, business types, and out-of-towners. Its two-storey, light-filled interior, awash with amazingly lush plants, sleek white tables and chairs, and its breezy outdoor dining terrace (perfect for watching movies shown in the square) are great for lazy weekend brunches, as well as lunch and dinner, anytime. Opened in 1997, its ultra-seasonal menus, under chef Michael Durkin's direction, rely on locally sourced produce, meat, seafood, game and cheeses; breads and ice creams are homemade. Try an exotic cocktail such as an espresso martini or a cosmopolitan before tucking into a starter of gratineed asparagus with hollandaise sauce and Parmesan crisp,

Prices: Lunch main course from €14.50. Dinner main course from €17.50. House wine from €23.
Food served: Lunch 12.00-15.00 daily. Dinner 18.00-22.30 Mon-Sat & 18.00-22.00 Sun.
Closed: Bank Holidays.
Cuisine: Modern Irish.
Other Points: Children welcome.
Directions: Next to the Irish Film Centre.

followed by pan-fried loin of venison, with Puy lentils, leek champ and crispy shallot rings. The wine selection is diverse and well-balanced.

The Symbols

☄ Accommodation

✕ Restaurant

☕ Café

🍺 Pub/Bar

☀ Daytime opening only

🧀 Deli

☨ Wine

🥐 Bakery

🍶 Gourmet/Farm Shop

🛁 Leisure Centre/Spa

CS Craft Shop

VC Visitor Centre

Les Routiers Awards

⭐ 2002 Award Winner

⭐ 2003 Award Winner

⭐ 2004 Award Winner

⭐ 2005 Award Winner

Dublin 2 ⚔🍸 ★

Ely Wine Bar
City centre restaurant and wine bar

22 Ely Place, Dublin 2
Tel. +353(0)1 6768986
Email. elywine@eircom.net
www.elywinebar.ie

Michelle and Erik Robson are the young, hardworking couple behind this easygoing, perennially popular wine bar, now with a newly extended basement. Upstairs, the marble fireplace, wooden floors and small bar with flattering lighting create an intimate atmosphere which induces you to linger. And what a great place this is to do just that; there are 400 wines to choose from, over 70 of them by the glass, so a spot of self-education is perfectly affordable. A delightful, uncomplicated menu melds seamlessly with the enjoyment of wine; lunch dishes such as a divine organic chicken liver and red berry terrine partner perfectly a recommended Californian red. A cold charger heaped with meats and Irish cheeses is ideal for large groups. All meat is organic and from the family farm in the Burren. Berry crumbles, baked cheesecakes and plum pies are simply crying out to be matched with the dessert wines which follow.

Prices: Lunch main course from €8.50. Dinner main course from €12.95. Wine from €24.
Hours: 12.00-24.30.
Food served: 12.00-23.30 Mon-Fri. 13.00-23.30 Sat.
Closed: Sundays and one week over Christmas.
Cuisine: Contemporary Irish.
Other Points: Winner - Wine List of the Year 2004.
Directions: At the junction of Baggot Street/Merrion Row, off St Stephen's Green.

Dublin 2 ⚔☕🍸🥄◉

La Maison des Gourmets
Restaurant, café and bakery

15 Castle Market, Dublin 2
Tel. +353(0)1 6727258

Tucked away on a pedestrians-only street in the heart of Dublin's smartest shopping area, this charming four-year-old café and boulangerie offers a true taste of France. Managing director Penny Plunkett earned her stripes as a chef at Guilbaud's restaurant in Dublin, and her talent is evident in her freshly baked sourdough boule, walnut and raisin bread, baguettes, focaccia, and bacon and onion bread, and pastries that include pain au chocolat, almond croissant, apple slice, frangipane and fruit tart, and chocolate lunette. The Maison does a great frothy cappuccino and offers a full range of teas. Light lunch dishes, served in a chic, understated space at the top of a winding staircase, include salad of barbeque smoked salmon with sun-dried tomato and sauce vierge; tartine of duck confit with onion marmalade and gherkins; and beef Bourguignon with potato purée. Wines are available, and the shop also does a brisk

Prices: Main course from €9.50-€14. Wine from €19.
Food served: 9.00-18.00 Mon-Sat. Lunch only served 12.00-16.00.
Closed: Sundays and 1 week after Christmas.
Cuisine: French.
Other Points: Children welcome. French language lessons at breakfast.
Directions: Between Georges St. Arcade and Powerscourt Shopping Centre or between Dury St. and South William St.

trade in custom-made, ultra-rich special-occasion cakes.

Dublin 2   🍽 ✕ 🍸

O'Neill's
City centre pub

2 Suffolk Street, Dublin 2
Tel. +353 (0)1 679 3656
Email. mike@oneillsbar.com
www.oneillsbar.com

This historic pub, owned by the O'Neill family since 1927, has been doing a brisk business for over 300 years. It's a great favourite with Dubliners for its central location and sustaining, reasonably priced food. There's an à la carte menu, carvery and sandwich bar, and the focus is on roasts and traditional meat dishes. Starters, such as the Nachos platter with spicy chilli, or blue cheese in won-ton pastry with a plum ginger dip are substantial. Meaty main courses include honey-baked Limerick ham, sticky ribs and Irish stew. Pasta, salads and fish dishes vary the pace, but desserts such as toffee apple cake bring yet more temptation. There are five bars and numerous alcoves and snugs in which to nurse a pint of Darcy's Dublin stout or Revolution Red Beer, both from the Dublin brewing company. A short wine list offers a good number of wines by the glass.

Prices: Lunch main course from €9.50. Dinner main course from €9.75. Bar snack from €3.20. House Wine from €14.95
Opening hours: 10.30-23.30 Mon-Thur. 10.30-00.30 Fri-Sat. 12.30-23.00 Sun.
Food served: 11.30-22.00 Mon-Fri. 11.30-21.00 Sat. 12.30-22.00 Sun.
Closed: Good Friday and 25, 26 Dec.
Cuisine: Modern and traditional Irish and European.
Other Points: Live traditional music every Sun and Mon night.
Directions: Opposite Dublin Tourism Centre on Suffolk Street.

Dublin 2   ✕ 🍸 🍽   ★

Shanahan's on the Green
Steakhouse and seafood restaurant

119 St Stephen's Green, Dublin 2
Tel. +353(0)1 4070939
www.shanahans.ie

Occupying a beautifully restored Georgian townhouse on St. Stephen's Green, Shanahan's is one of Dublin's most luxurious restaurants. The ground-floor Oval Office bar is decorated with memorabilia from 18 American presidents, including John F. Kennedy's rocking chair. The elegant dining room has butter-coloured walls; soft, plush crimson and gold carpeting; crystal chandeliers; large gilt mirrors; and crisp white linen-covered tables set well apart. The ambiance matches the restaurant's star attraction: fabulous, American-style steaks from certified Angus beef, that are cooked in a special broiler at 1600 - 1800F, to sear the outside and keep the inside meltingly tender. Sizes range from 8 ounces to a massive 24 ounces. Start with opulent chilled jumbo lump crab salad or broiled Galway oysters Rockefeller, and wind up the meal with a rich "Balboa" chocolate brownie. The wine list is high on quality, with over 370 selections, including

Prices: Set lunch from €45-€50. A La Carte during December. Dinner main course from €38. Wine from €30.
Food served: 12.30-14.00 Fridays only. 18.00-22.30 daily.
Closed: Over Christmas & New Year.
Cuisine: American steak house.
Other Points: Winner - Wine List of the Year 2003.
Directions: On the west side of St Stephen's Green.

16 champagnes. Come with a large wallet, and an appetite to match.

Dublin 2 Co Dublin

The Tea Room at The Clarence
City centre restaurant

The Clarence Hotel,
6-8 Wellington Quay, Dublin 2
Tel. +353(0)1 4070813
Email. tearoom@theclarence.ie
www.theclarence.ie

With its high, coved ceilings, double-height windows and sensitive use of Portland stone and American white oak, there are few prettier dining rooms in Dublin than the Tea Room, located in this landmark Temple Bar hotel famously reopened by Bono and The Edge of U2 in 1996. Executive chef Fred Corvonnier rises to the challenge of creating a menu to match the dining room's understated elegance by inventively combining luxury ingredients with the finest seasonal produce in his contemporary Irish cuisine. Tortellini of wild mushrooms with peanut cappuccino might be followed by caramelised monkfish with Serrano ham, creamed root vegetables and rosti potatoes; followed by a dessert of hot Valrhona chocolate fondant with black cherries and milk ice cream. A three-course

Prices: Lunch from €26 (2 courses); €30.00 (3 courses). Dinner from €47 (2 courses); €55.00 (3 courses). Set Sunday lunch €34.50 (3 courses) House wine from €23.50.
Food served: Breakfast 7.00-11.00 Mon-Fri. 7.30-11.30 Sat-Sun. Lunch 12.30-14.30 (except Sat). Dinner 18.30-22.30 Mon-Sat. 18.30-21.30 Sun.
Cuisine: Traditional with a continental twist.
Other Points: Children welcome.
Directions: The hotel overlooks the River Liffey at Wellington Quay, southside. The Tea Room has its own entrance on Essex Street.

Sunday lunch, at €34.50, is a fine option for families.

Dublin 2

Unicorn Restaurant
Italian restaurant and café

12B Merrion Court
Merrion Row, Dublin 2
Tel. +353(0)1 6762182
Email. unicorn12b@eircom.net
www.unicornrestaurant.com

Walk into the Unicorn on a busy Friday night and you feel your spirits lift; the unique atmosphere of this laid-back, buzzy Italian restaurant - which first opened in 1938 - has made it the place to be seen in Dublin year after year. The food offers no great surprises, but it's all incredibly civilised, and the service is exceptionally friendly and efficient. At lunchtime, the signature antipasto plates are particularly conducive to long, lingering grazing. Classic dishes include linguine with fresh clams, rognoncini trifolati - calf kidneys - and fritto misto with calamari and Dublin Bay prawns. All vegetables in season are organic, and meat is Irish and fully traceable. On the dessert menu, house specials include a wickedly rich chocolate biscuit cake, tiramisu and an Italian cheeseboard with homemade onion marmalade. Many of the Italian wines are exclusive to the

Prices: Lunch main course from Antipasto Bar from €9.50-€16.50. Dinner main course from €12.80-€42.50. House wine from €23.50.
Food served: 12.30-16.00 and 18.15-23.00 Mon-Sat.
Closed: Sundays. Good Friday. 25 Dec to 10 Jan. All Bank Holidays.
Cuisine: Contemporary Italian.
Other Points: Piano Bar open Thursday, Friday and Saturday nights - 19.30 'till late. Private dining.
Directions: East of St Stephen's Green.

Unicorn and there are some interesting and affordable wines by the glass.

Dublin 4

Aberdeen Lodge
Period guesthouse

53 Park Avenue, Ballsbridge, Dublin 4
Tel. +353(0)1 2838155
Email. aberdeen@iol.ie
www.halpinsprivatehotels.com

Pat Halpin's elegant Edwardian house stands in a smart, residential area of south Dublin, close to the city centre and a few minutes' drive from Lansdowne rugby ground and the RDS. The three-storey, redbrick building is a haven of peace and tranquillity with comfortable, softly lit public rooms, fresh flowers and antique furniture. Staff are well presented and efficient and plentiful enough to be always on hand. Bedrooms, including suites with a whirlpool spa, are spacious, with mini-bars, fluffy white towels, bathrobes, slippers and crisp white linen. Some of them overlook an old-fashioned walled garden. Breakfast - homemade soda bread and scrambled eggs with smoked Irish salmon are among the treats - is taken in the airy restaurant at tables laid with white linen. Light snacks, such as crab claws tossed in garlic butter, and honeyglazed ham sandwiches with

Rooms: 17 ensuite. Double from €140. Single from €99. Suite from €189 Some have spa bath.
Food served: Drawing Room Menu available throughout the day until 21.00.
Cuisine: European.
Other Points: Non-smoking. Complimentary wireless internet access. Garden. Children welcome. Car park.
Directions: Minutes to the city centre by Dart. By car take the Merrion Road towards Sydney Parade Dart Station and then first left into Park Avenue.

country relish, are served in the drawing room and library, along with afternoon tea, homemade scones and fine wines.

Dublin 4

Ariel House
Period guesthouse

50-54 Lansdowne Road, Ballsbridge, Dublin 4
Tel. +353(0)1 6685512
Email. reservations@ariel-house.net
www.ariel-house.net

This charming guesthouse is in a listed Victorian building on a pretty terrace, a few minutes from the heart of the city. The wide stone staircase which leads to the front door echoes the grand proportions of the interior, with its large bay windows and high ceilings. The reception area and drawing room feature ornate plasterwork, Waterford glass chandeliers, large mirrors and outsize antique furniture. The surroundings are impressive, but the welcome is still intimate - on arrival, guests are served tea and homemade scones, and each of the 37 ensuite bedrooms is elegantly decorated with every comfort in mind. All rooms feature mahogany four-poster, half-canopy or elaborate headboard beds, fresh Irish linen and large period wardrobes. Breakfast is served on antique tables in the conservatory-style dining room. Choose from a full Irish or continental breakfast, with freshly

Rooms: 37 ensuite. Double from €89. Single from €79.
Other Points: Totally non-smoking. Garden. Car park.
Directions: From Dublin city centre and Stephen's Green go straight down Baggot Street on to Pembroke Road. Pass over the junction on to Lansdowne Road.

squeezed juices, homemade brown breads, grilled prime cut Irish bacon and free-range eggs.

Dublin 4 ✕ 🍸 ★

O'Connells in Ballsbridge
City centre restaurant

Bewley's Hotel, Merrion Road,
Ballsbridge, Dublin 4
Tel. +353(0)1 6473304
Email. info@oconnellsballsbridge.com
www.oconnellsballsbridge.com

Owner and chef Tom O'Connell's commitment is to fresh, Irish ingredients and affordability. Pleasantly situated at ground level in front of Bewley's hotel, the restaurant offers something for everybody. Lunches are a particular point of pride; Sunday lunch is a real family affair, with a groaning buffet of meats, salads and fish, including smoked and poached Irish salmon. Fresh fish from Kilmore Quay is grilled before your eyes. Traditional roasts such as rib of prime Irish beef with fresh horseradish cream, or half a spit-roast chicken are all carefully sourced, as are desserts such as north Kilkenny apple pie. Dinner brings a similar roll-call of Irish producers, with grilled Ballybrado organic pork chop, and roast duck from the Hickey farm in Cork. Coeliacs are well accommodated with gluten-free 'little desserts' such as orange jelly and warm bitter chocolate mousse. The impressive wine list offers a commendable range of wines by the half bottle and glass.

Prices: Buffet lunch main course from €10.85. Dinner: 3-courses inclusive of first course, main course, two of O'Connell's little desserts and tea/coffee and Tipperary mineral water from €27.50. House wine from €19.85.
Food Served: 12.30-22.00. 12.30-21.00 Sun.
Closed: After lunch 24 Dec to 27 Dec at 15.00.
Cuisine: Traditional and modern Irish.
Other Points: Coeliac friendly. Carpark. Winner - Wine List of the Year 2002.
Directions: On the junction of Simmonscourt and Merrion Road in Ballsbridge.

Locks Restaurant, Dublin 8

Dublin 4

Raglan Lodge
Suburban guesthouse

10 Raglan Road, Ballsbridge,
Dublin 4, Co Dublin
Tel. +353(0)1 6606697

A magnificently restored, mid-19th-century, red brick Victorian residence with a sweeping front stairway, high ceilings, marble fireplaces and elegant proportions, Raglan Lodge evokes an older, more genteel Dublin. Conveniently located on leafy, quiet Raglan Road in the heart of elegant Ballsbridge, near Herbert Park, the US Embassy, and the city centre, the area is associated with the famous ballad, On Raglan Road, by the poet Patrick Kavanagh, who lived close by at number 19 from 1940 - 1943. Opened in 1991 by owner Helen Moran, the guesthouse has 7 quiet, tastefully appointed ensuite bedrooms that are exceptionally comfortable. Helen's hospitality encourages many return visitors. Her breakfasts, served from a massive white linen-covered sideboard, include fresh-squeezed orange juice, fresh and stewed fruits, assorted cereals, porridge, homemade muesli, toast, yogurt and

Rooms: 7 ensuite. Double from €120. Single from €70. Family from €150.
Closed: 20 Dec to 6 Jan 2006. Easter week and last week in October 2006.
Other Points: Garden. Car park. Children welcome.
Directions: Follow the signs for South City to Baggot Street, which becomes Pembroke Road, then turn right on to Raglan Road.

cheeses, followed by a choice of traditional Irish breakfast, kippers or smoked salmon - served under silver dome covers.

Dublin 4

The Douglas Food Company
Gourmet food shop and deli

53 Main Street, Donnybrook, Dublin 4
Tel.+353 (0)1 2694066
Email.
grainne@thedouglasfoodcompany.ie

This gourmet deli and catering company provides chic south Dublin with a classy spot for an over-the-counter lunchtime bite, as well as a one-stop shop for delectable takeaway meals. Owner Grainne Murphy takes pride in her hands-on approach and the midday rush finds her, along with her small team, serving up sandwiches, soup, coffee and delicious desserts to a busy and appreciative crowd. Then, and throughout the day, hot meals such as beef stroganoff and Mediterranean fish casserole are available, as well as colourful salads including couscous with roasted pepper, courgettes, coriander and basil dressing. Treats such as Normandy apple tart and banana and Bailey's loaf are perfect just with coffee. The shop is smart and bright, with a large window frontage in which the dishes of the day are displayed. Some

Opening hours: 10.00-19.30 Mon-Fri. 9.30-18.00 Sat.
Closed: 25 Dec to first Monday after New Year (open for catering orders on 31 Dec). Closed bank holiday Sundays and Mondays.
Cuisine: Modern Irish/Mediterranean.
Directions: Directly opposite Donnybrook rugby grounds on the Main Street.

unusual deli products can be found among the cheeses, wines, chocolates and coffees for sale. The top-notch catering service can accommodate special diets.

Dublin 6   ✕ ▼

Mint Restaurant
Restaurant

47 Ranelagh Village, Dublin 6
Tel. +353(0)1 4978655
Email. info@mintrestaurant.ie
www.mintrestaurant.ie

Trish Courtney's restaurant is fresh and modern with its understated minimalist look of white linen tablecloths, brown suede banquettes and punches of colour from single stems of crimson gerbera. Young French chef Oliver Dunne has worked alongside top British chefs Gary Rhodes and Gordon Ramsay, and his sophisticated, French-accented dishes bear the hallmark of this experience. A starter of venison and foie gras sausage with parsnip purée, truffle and port cappuccino showcases fine ingredients and finely honed skills, while a main course of fillet of hake with cod brandade, fennel crisps and watercress coulis exemplifies the clean flavours one might expect from a restaurant called Mint. The wine list has a concise but wide-ranging selection of French bottles, as well

Prices: Lunch main course from €15. Dinner main course from €21. House Wine from €20.
Food Served: Lunch 12.00-15.00. Dinner 18.00-22.00, Tues-Sun.
Closed: Mondays & all Public Holidays.
Cuisine: Classic French.
Other Points: Children welcome.
Directions: Located in the centre of Ranelagh Village.

as some new world examples. There are good value lunches for the corporate crowd, and locals pack the place at night.

Dublin 8   ✕ ▼

Locks Restaurant
Canal side restaurant

1 Windsor Terrace, Portobello, Dublin 8
Tel. +353(0)1 4543391

Facing the Grand Canal on a quiet residential street, Locks brims with charm and old Dublin character. Owned and run by Claire Douglas for over 25 years, it was featured in the film, My Left Foot, and was allegedly the birthplace of the Northern Ireland peace plan, reportedly hatched over lunch. Inside, linen tablecloths, cream chairs and red banquettes combine with huge palm fronds, open fires and dark wood to give a soothing old-world feel. Chef Alan Kinsella, who recently published a cookbook with Locks, incorporates the best Irish regional ingredients into his modern European cuisine. Dishes such as smoked duck breast and wild mushroom risotto, or crisp fillet of sea bass with crab and salmon ravioli, are imaginatively conceived and beautifully presented. Desserts, including peach clafoutis with apple and coconut ice cream, are small works of art. Food such as this deserves good wine, and the restaurant offers a carefully selected, predominantly French list.

Prices: Lunch main course from €28.95. Dinner main course from €38.95. House wine from €28. Service charge 12.5%.
Food served: 12.30-14.00 Mon-Fri. 18.30-22.00 Mon-Sat.
Closed: 25 December for 1 week.
Cuisine: Modern European.
Other Points: Children welcome. Private dining rooms.
Directions: Half way between Portobello and Harold's Cross on the city centre side of the Grand Canal. 10 minutes from the city centre.

Dublin 9

Andersons Food Hall and Café
Café, restaurant and deli

3 The Rise, Glasnevin, Dublin 9
Tel. (01) 8378394
Email. info@andersons.ie
www.andersons.ie

Noel Delany and Patricia van der Velde's two-year-old gem of a café/food hall features delicious Irish and continental cheeses, charcuterie, gourmet sandwiches, soups, pates, homemade breads, and cakes to eat in or take away, at reasonable prices, in a charmingly restored butcher shop that has been in Noel's family since the 1930s. The couple have preserved the shop's original tiled floor and facade, added a smart black-and-white striped canopy, under which there are outdoor tables, and installed handsome oak floor-to-ceiling wine racks that showcase some 180 wines, available at retail or to drink in the café for a corkage of €6 per bottle. The rear dining area, with its cream-coloured walls, subtle lighting, wooden tables and chairs, and background jazz is stylish and serene. Specialties include an Iberian selection featuring Serrano ham, chorizo, salamis, Mediterranean vegetables, olives

Prices: Lunch main course from €6.95. Dinner main course from €12.95. House wine from €15.95.
Food Served: 9.00-19.00 Mon-Wed. 9.00-20.30 Thur-Sat. 10.00-19.00 Sun.
Cuisine: Continental café style.
Closed: Good Friday & Christmas (3/4 days).
Other Points: Garden. Children welcome.
Directions: Just off Griffith Avenue. Near Drumcondra/Airport Road. Coming from the airport, turn right onto Griffith Avenue, then 2nd right.

and Manchego sheep's cheese. Excellent coffees, teas, wines by the glass, and a childrens' menu round off the selection.

Dun Laoghaire Co Dublin

Caviston's Food Emporium
Seafood restaurant, deli and fish shop

59 Glasthule Road, Glasthule, Dun Laoghaire, Co Dublin
Tel. +353(0)1 2809245/2809120
Email. info@cavistons.com
www.cavistons.com

Located in charming Glasthule, south of Dublin, Caviston's has, over the last 50 years, gained a reputation for high-quality food and friendly service. It's particularly known for its beautifully displayed selection of fresh seafood, as well as European salamis, farmhouse cheeses, organic vegetables, speciality breads, salads and pre-cooked meals. Garrulous Peter Caviston, a booming presence in the shop, has also instituted an annual celebration of Bloomsday on June 16th, fun for all ages. Since 1996, the diminutive restaurant next door, with its colourful murals depicting an underwater fantasy world, has produced an imaginative range of seafood dishes, prepared simply and expertly by Noel Cusack. The handwritten menu might include spaghettini with Boston shrimp chive sauce or grilled marinated mackerel fillet with hot

Prices: Main course from €10.50-€26. House wine from €20.
Food served: Three sittings (Tue-Fri) 12.00-13.30, 13.30-15.00, 15.00 last orders. 12.00-13.45 & 13.45-15.15 Sat.
Closed: Sundays & Mondays. 2 weeks from 22 December.
Cuisine: Seafood only.
Other Points: Children welcome.
Directions: First village after Dun Laoghaire going towards Dalkey approximately 8 miles from Dublin City.

cucumber pickle to start, then seared king scallops with sweet chilli sauce and crème fraîche, followed by homemade tiramisu or hazelnut chocolate and raspberry mousse. The short, comprehensive wine list is reasonably priced.

Andersons Food Hall and Café, Glasnevin

CELEBRATING THE REAL IRELAND

Charlotte Coleman-Smith meets a man with a mission to change the way we feed ourselves. Look to our own green land, says Terry McCoy, something he has been doing for years.

'My restaurant is all about being naughty,' laughs Terry McCoy, owner of the Red Bank restaurant in Skerries since 1983, and one of Ireland's most recognisable and established chefs.

'I'm a butter and cream man. Put it this way - you wouldn't come to my restaurant seven nights a week!' The same could be said for many great restaurants. You would, though, go to the Red Bank as often as your pocket and waistline could afford to sample a wonderfully imaginative menu filled with terrific seafood dishes, some classically restrained, some  more exuberant, but all utterly original to McCoy - who adds, hastily, that plainly cooked food can be prepared on request.

In his time, Terry has done his bit to break the rules. In the late 'seventies and early 'eighties, he claims to have been among the first wave of chefs to rebel against hotel dining rooms dishing up boiled bacon and cabbage. There were a handful of restaurants in those days, mostly in Dublin, and Myrtle Allen of Ballymaloe was starting to have an influence, but the food scene - well, there wasn't one. Things were beginning to change, though; people were going abroad and realising that there was more to eating out than meat and potatoes, and that stodgy hotel dining rooms shouldn't be the only alternative to dinner at home. McCoy and his contemporaries knew that a brave step was needed, despite straightened economic climate, to put Ireland on the culinary map.

Nearly twenty-five years have passed since McCoy and his late wife Margaret set up in Skerries, a pretty seaside town just north of Dublin. It hasn't always been easy - as McCoy points out, there aren't any customers in the sea. But despite occasional lean times, McCoy has stuck to his guns and is now well known as a dedicated champion of local produce. The Red Bank menu reads like a rollcall of the freshest local seafood - razorfish from Balbriggan, Dublin Bay prawns, rock pollock, sole, skate. Despite witnessing seismic changes in the restaurant business since the early 'eighties, McCoy still has issues with the way things are going. His biggest gripe is the fashion followed by so many chefs to ape cooking from other countries using exotic ingredients, while ignoring the rich harvest offered by our native land and sea. 'Sundried tomatoes? Wouldn't touch 'em!' is his indignant cry. 'We should use our raw materials. We have hedgerows full of wonderful elderflowers. In autumn there are rosehips to make syrup. This is what stimulates me and what I'm passionate about. You can pick dandelion leaves if you know what you're doing-never mind shipping in curly endive from Rungis market!'

The difficulty is when you get a glut of one thing - you have to be experienced to know how to use things when they are there. Farmers' markets are wonderful, but their usefulness is limited because most people just don't have enough knowledge of cooking.'

McCoy sees one of the biggest threats in the competition from 'cheap' food. 'Consumers don't understand the cost of food. They're unwilling to pay the price we should be charging. They'll go to a big hotel and pay 20 euros a head for a forgettable meal, but won't pay a little more to have something really unique and different.' Hotels - the large, corporate, 300-bed type, erected hastily by business people with little relevant experience - are, according to McCoy, responsible for much of the blandness and lack of imagination in catering today. Young chefs, he says, are lured by big paypackets to head up enormous kitchens, and flounder under the pressure. 'The food is usually mediocre, but people are lapping it up.'

McCoy is impressed, though, by the creative spirit shown by many other young chefs, particularly those under his own tutelage. A good number come from abroad - Poland and France - and bring with them a rich culture and knowledge of food. But shouldn't we be nurturing homegrown talent? 'The shame is that the training isn't there,' says McCoy. 'So I'm just trying to inspire the younger guys working with me. I'm 60 now, so there's no point in it being all about me any more. I should be reaping, not sowing. I'm just hoping the next generation will run with it.' ∎

Charlotte Coleman-Smith

Caviston's Food Emporium
Dun Laoghaire

Dun Laoghaire Co Dublin

Janet's Coffee House Deli
Daytime town centre coffee shop & restaurant

70 Upper George's Street,
Dun Laoghaire, Co Dublin
Tel. +353(0)1 6636871
Email. janetscoffeehousedeli@eircom.net

Located near People's Park in the seaside town of Dun Laoghaire in County Dublin, Janet's Coffee House Deli is a cheerful, homely and affordable place, featuring a spacious split-level interior, two large front windows, bright lighting, quarry-tiled floors, and unornamented pine tables. Opened in July, 2004, it has already gained a solid clientele of local residents and business people. Owner Janet Hosgood, and her husband/chef Roberto Morsiani offer an all-day flexible menu. You can order a full Irish breakfast at 4 p.m., or pasta in a creamy mushroom sauce with seasoned bacon at 10 a.m. There's an array of celebrity-inspired hot panini: the Kim Basinger, for example, features ciabatta bread, chicken, baked ham, peperonata sauce and mayonnaise. To accompany, try

Prices: Main course lunch from €6. House Wine from €3 per glass.
Food Served: 8.00-16.30. Mon-Fri 9.00-16.30 Sat.
Closed: Sundays.
Cuisine: Irish, Italian and European.
Other Points: Children welcome but no high chairs available.
Directions: On the left as you leave Dun Laoghaire centre heading south. Near to the People's Park.

one of Janet's specialty coffees, smoothies, or Italian wines by the glass or bottle. And if you've room left, there are homemade scones with jam, French apple tart, or Janet's zesty lemon cake.

Dun Laoghaire Co Dublin

Passion
Town centre gourmet food shop and deli

104 Patrick Street, Dun Laoghaire,
Co Dublin
Tel. +353(0)1 2846300
Email.info@passion.ie
www.passion.ie

The bright pink lips painted on its black shopfront say everything about owner Hermione Winters' passion for artisanal Irish foods at her 18-month-old jewel-box of a gourmet shop located just off the main street of bustling coastal Dun Laoghaire. An incredible aroma of Ivan's extra-rich chocolate brownies, delicate Ardsallagh soft goat's cheese, Gubbeen Smokehouse bacon and salami, Ariosa coffee, and fresh baguettes from La Boulangerie des Gourmets fills this little oasis. You will be hard-pressed to decide on exactly which organic ice cream, Italian extra-virgin olive oil or family-owned vineyard wine selection to choose amidst the shop's abundant displays - that's where Hermione's expertise comes in. For pure and natural "foodie" gifts, pantry staples, ready-prepared ingredients for Instant Gourmet Meals for Two, Indian

Opening Hours: 9.00-18.00 Mon,Tue, Sat & 9.00-19.00 Wed,Thurs & Fri.
Closed: Sundays & Bank Holidays.
Cuisine: Irish Artisan.
Other Points: Takeaway coffee and sandwiches made to order. Outside catering service.
Directions: Town centre loction just off Georges Street.

blended-spice mixtures, hampers and takeaway made-to-order sandwiches and coffee, this is your one-stop shop. They also do tastings and outside catering for any occasion.

Glencullen Co Dublin   🅿 🍴 🍸

Johnnie Fox's
Country pub & restaurant

Glencullen, Dublin Mountains,
Co Dublin
Tel. +353(0)1 2955647
Email. info@jfp.ie
www.jfp.ie

The quintessential "Irish pub," Johnnie Fox's is situated in the scenic Dublin Mountains, just 30 minutes from Dublin city. Founded in 1798, its warren of atmospheric rooms are chock-a-block with rustic wooden tables and chairs, peat and log fireplaces, and shelves and cupboards groaning with antique farm tools, books, bottles, signs, and other ornaments. Tourists and local residents alike enjoy its live Irish music 7 nights a week, while the popular "Johnnie Fox's Hooley Experience" is an entertaining evening featuring a four-course meal, traditional Irish music and a troupe of spirited Irish dancers clacking their heels. Head chef Paul Davies specialises in seafood, with signature dishes including home-made smoked salmon paté; fresh wild mussels steamed in white wine, garlic, onions and parsley; and Cajun-style sea-

Prices: Lunch main course from €11.95. Dinner main course from €11.95. Bar snack from €6.50. House wine from €19.50.
Opening hours: 10.30-23.30. 12.00-23.00 Sun.
Food served: 12.30-21.45 daily.
Closed: Good Friday. 24, 25 Dec.
Cuisine: Traditional & Seafood.
Other Points: Highest pub in Ireland. 3 Car Parks, Heli-pad.
Directions: Located in the Dublin mountains, approx. 30 minutes drive from the city centre.

food jambalaya with jumbo prawns, scallops and fish served over rice. Non-seafood eaters and vegetarians are accommodated; and a wide range of after-dinner drinks and coffees will round off any evening.

Malahide Co Dublin   🍴 🍸 🅿

Cruzzo Restaurant
Waterside restaurant and bar

Marina Village, Malahide, Co Dublin
Tel. +353(0)1 8450599
Email. info@cruzzo.ie
www.cruzzo.ie

This fashionable waterfront restaurant has an enviable position on Malahide marina. A buzzing ground floor bar opens out on to a terrace overlooking gin palaces and assorted boats - a great place to sip a gin-and-tonic and spot a celebrity or two. Inside, the design is sleek and contemporary with light reflected from the sea bringing a fresh, clean edge. From the piano bar, an impressive staircase leads up to the spacious restaurant, where chef Tom Meenaghan serves up a seasonal menu combining native and European cooking styles. A typical selection from the carte could include seared fillet of bream with garlic and lemon green beans and sauce vierge, or pan-fried chicken with champ, wild mushrooms and garlic cream. Sunday lunch - slow roast leg of lamb followed by pecan and treacle tart, for example - and an early bird menu offer reasonable value.

Prices: Lunch main course from €9. Dinner main course from €19.95. House wine from €19.50.
Opening hours: Open daily from 12.30 till late.
Food served: 12.30-14.45 & 18.00-22.00 Tue-Fri. 12.30-15.45 & 18.30-22.00 Sun. 18.00-22.00 Sat & Mon.
Cuisine: Contemporary. Seasonal emphasis on seafood.
Other Points: Car park. Children welcome.
Directions: From M50 follow sign to Malahide, take right at lights in village, straight to end of marina.

The global wine list has a decent selection of half bottles.

Skerries Co Dublin

Redbank House & Restaurant
Coastal guesthouse and restaurant

5-7 Church Street, Skerries,
Co Dublin
Tel. +353(0)1 8491005
Email. info@redbank.ie
www.redbank.ie

Terry McCoy has been running his famous restaurant for over 20 years. It includes 18 smart and comfortable rooms, making the prospect of an overnight stay in the pretty harbour town of Skerries - just north of Dublin airport - a most appealing one. Terry is a well-known TV chef with a passion for local ingredients, particularly seafood. Main courses such as rock pollock Milberton, served with wild crabapples and horseradish sauce, make the most of an unusual fish, while black sole on the bone with lemon butter is a classic dish perfectly executed. Starters might include Howth smokehouse salmon with horseradish sauce, or sparklingly fresh oysters cooked three ways. There are plenty of delicious meat options and the dessert trolley is legendary. The diverse wine cellar - created from the vaults of the bank which once stood here - is diligently researched and well priced. The value menu represents a particularly good deal.

Rooms: 18 ensuite. Double from €120. Single from €75. Family from €170.
Prices: Dinner main course from €20. Set Sunday lunch €29. House wine from €20.
Food served: 18.30-21.45 Mon-Sat 12.30-16.00 Sunday lunch.
Closed: 24-27 December.
Cuisine: Progressive Irish.
Other Points: Totally Non-smoking. Winner - Locally Produced Food Supporters Award 2005.
Directions: From Dublin Airport take N1 north through Lissen Hall Interchange following N1 to Blakes Cross turning right and follow signs to Skerries. From Dublin take the M1 to Lissen Hall Interchange & exit north to Skerries, Rush, Lusk, follow signs. From North on M1 take exit to R222 through Balbriggan turning right at the T-junction and follow signs to Skerries.

Nearest Racecourses

Fairyhouse Racecourse *Tel. + 353 (0)1 8256167*
Leopardstown Racecourse
Tel. + 353 (0)1 2893607

City Hall - The Story of the Capital | *Place to visit*

Dame St, Dublin 2.
Tel. +353(0) 1 222 2936
Fax. +353(0) 1 222 2620
Email. cityhall@dublincity.ie
www.dublincity.ie/your_council

The Story of the Capital in Dublin's City Hall is an exciting multimedia exhibition tracing the history of Dublin City. It tells of the city's founding, from Viking times, through prosperity and oppression, into the unique and vibrant city of today. Treasures of the city, from the original city seal to the chains of the Lord Mayor are on display, together with medieval manuscripts, costumes from various periods and contemporary art. Newsreel clips and interactive screens offer fascinating insight about the city's evolution.

City Hall itself is a spectacular piece of architecture, designed by Thomas Cooley and built as the Royal Exchange for a then prosperous Dublin's merchant population between 1769-1779. Dublin City Council has owned the building since 1851 and have recently restored it to it original beauty.

Other Points
Wheelchair accessible, small café and shop, free guided tours and multi-lingual audio guides, Banqueting and Conference Facilities,

Hours
Mon - Sat 10.00 - 17.15
Sun & Bank holidays 14.00 - 17.00

Admission charged

Directions
On Dame Street in Dublin's City Centre, just outside the Gates of Dublin Castle.

Dublinia & The Viking World | *Place to visit*

St Michael's Hill, Christchurch, Dublin 8
Tel. +353 (0) 1 6794611
Fax. +353 (0) 1 6797116
Email. info@dublinia.ie
www.dublinia.ie

The Dublinia & The Viking World exhibitions are amongst Dublin's most popular visitor attractions. The exhibitions reveal fascinating glimpses of the Viking and medieval past using reconstructions, audiovisual and interactive displays. Superbly researched and imaginatively presented there is something here to interest everyone. The exhibition is housed in a beautiful neo Gothic building, formerly the Church of Ireland Synod Hall, linked to Christ Church Cathedral by an elegant covered bridge, one of the city's landmarks. Owned by The Medieval Trust, a charitable trust, income generated from the Dublinia exhibitions is used to fund the ongoing preservation of this beautiful building.

many related to Viking and medieval themes. Guided tours available by prior arrangement. Wheelchair Accessible, Coach Parking, Toilets.

Hours
Apr -Sept: 10.00 - 17.00 Daily
Oct - Mar: 11.00 - 16.00 Mon - Fri
10.00 - 16.00 Sat, Sun & Bank Holiday
Closed 23rd, 24th, 25th & 26th Dec
and 17th Mar.

Directions
Beside Christ Church Cathedral, located half way between Trinity College and the Guinness Storehouse.

Other Points
Discounted admission tickets to Christ Church Cathedral can be purchased by visitors to Dublinia & The Viking World. A gift shop features a wide range of books, gifts and souvenirs

Dublin Writers Museum | *Place to visit*

18 Parnell Square, Dublin 1
Tel. +353(0)1 8722077
Fax. +353(0)1 8722231
Email. writers@dublintourism.ie
www.writersmuseum.com

Situated in a magnificent 18th century mansion in the north city centre, the collection features the lives and works of Dublin's literary celebrities over the past three hundred years. Swift and Sheridan, Shaw and Wilde, Yeats, Joyce and Beckett are among those presented through their books, letters, portraits and personal items. In 1991, the Dublin Writers Museum was opened to house a history and celebration of literary Dublin. The splendidly restored Georgian house is a pleasure in itself with its sumptuous plasterwork and decorative stained-glass windows. The museum holds exhibitions, lunchtime theatre and readings and has a special room devoted to children's literature. Dublin is famous as a city of writers and literature, and the Dublin Writers Museum is an essential visit for anyone who wants to discover, explore or simply enjoy Dublin's immense literary heritage.

Other Points
Multi-lingual Tours, Specialist Bookshop, Calendar of Events, Café & Conference Facilities.

Hours
Jan to Dec: Mon - Sat 10.00 - 17.00
Sun & Public Holidays:11.00 - 17.00
Late opening Jun, Jul & Aug
Mon - Fri   10.00 - 18.00

Admission Charged

Directions
North end of O'Connell Street on Parnell Square, opposite the Garden of Remembrance.

Malahide Castle Demesne | *Place to visit*

Malahide, Co Dublin
Tel. +353(0)1 8462184
Fax. +353(0)1 8462537
Email. malahidecastle@dublintourism.ie
www.malahidecastle.com

Set on 250 acres of parkland in the pretty seaside town of Malahide, the Castle was both a fortress and a private home for nearly eight hundred years, and is an interesting mix of architectural styles. The Talbot family lived here from 1185 to 1973. The history of the family is recorded in the Great Hall, with portraits of generations of the family telling their own story of Ireland's stormy history. One of the more poignant legends concerns the morning of the Battle of the Boyne in 1690, when fourteen members of the family breakfasted together in this room, never to return, as all died during the battle. Adjacent to the Castle is the Fry Model Railway, one of the largest model railways in Europe.

Hours
Jan to Dec: Mon - Sat 10.00 - 17.00
Apr to Sep: Sun & Public Holidays 10.00 - 18.00
Oct to Mar: Sun & Public Holidays 11.00 - 17.00

Admission Charged

Directions
North of the city centre (8 miles), go to Fairview take the turn for the Malahide Road on your left, follow the signs for Malahide and then signs for Malahide Castle.

Other Points
Multi-lingual Tours, Talbot Botanic Gardens, Craft Shop and Restaurant, Banqueting Facilities.

Skerries Mills | *Place to visit*

Skerries, Fingal, Co Dublin.
Tel. +353 1 8495208
Fax. +353 1 8495213
Email skerriesmills@indigo.ie
www.indigo.ie/skerries

The coastal town of Skerries boasts a
brace of windmills and a large watermill,
fine examples of Ireland's industrial
heritage and now the focus of a town
- centre park. The mills were monastic
property until the mid 16th-century while
the following 400 years saw succeeding
proprietors run a thriving business grind-
ing for the locality and selling foodstuffs.
A bakery which was added in the mid
19th century, flourished until the 1980's.
In 1989, new owners, the local County
Council initiated a conservation project
to restore the mills and machinery to
working order and breath life back into
the buildings. Skerries Mills is a Fingal
County Council project in association
with F.Á.S.

Other Points
Guided tours, Watermill Café all bak-
ing & cooking in-house, Craft Shop,
Exhibition space.

Admission charged

Hours
Open daily from 10.30
1 Oct -31 Mar: 10.30 - 16.30
1 Apr - 30 Sept: 10.30 - 17.30
Closed: 20 Dec - 1 Jan inclusive &
Good Friday.

Directions
30km north of Dublin City on East
Coast. Signposted off M1.
Bus 33 from Dublin City/ Suburban
train to Skerries Train Station.

Blackcurrant harvesting, Ballykelly Farms, Wexford

ONE FOR THE ROAD

Stops along the way

Listings in BLUE denote
places to visit

Rosslare to Cork

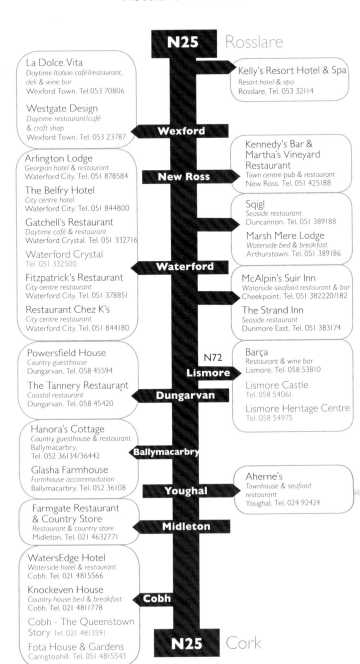

N25 Rosslare

La Dolce Vita
*Daytime Italian café/restaurant,
deli & wine bar*
Wexford Town. Tel.053 70806

Kelly's Resort Hotel & Spa
Resort hotel & spa
Rosslare. Tel. 053 32114

Westgate Design
*Daytime restaurant/café
& craft shop*
Wexford Town. Tel. 053 23787

Wexford

Arlington Lodge
Georgian hotel & restaurant
Waterford City. Tel. 051 878584

New Ross

**Kennedy's Bar &
Martha's Vineyard
Restaurant**
Town centre pub & restaurant
New Ross. Tel. 051 425188

The Belfry Hotel
City centre hotel
Waterford City. Tel. 051 844800

Gatchell's Restaurant
Daytime café & restaurant
Waterford Crystal. Tel. 051 332716

Sqigl
Seaside restaurant
Duncannon. Tel. 051 389188

Marsh Mere Lodge
Waterside bed & breakfast
Arthurstown. Tel. 051 389186

Waterford Crystal
Tel. 051 332500

Fitzpatrick's Restaurant
City centre restaurant
Waterford City. Tel. 051 378851

Waterford

McAlpin's Suir Inn
Waterside seafood restaurant & bar
Cheekpoint. Tel. 051 382220/182

Restaurant Chez K's
City centre restaurant
Waterford City. Tel. 051 844180

The Strand Inn
Seaside restaurant
Dunmore East. Tel. 051 383174

Powersfield House
Country guesthouse
Dungarvan. Tel. 058 45594

N72
Lismore

Barça
Restaurant & wine bar
Lismore. Tel. 058 53810

The Tannery Restaurant
Coastal restaurant
Dungarvan. Tel. 058 45420

Dungarvan

Lismore Castle
Tel. 058 54061

Lismore Heritage Centre
Tel. 058 54975

Hanora's Cottage
Country guesthouse & restaurant
Ballymacarbry.
Tel. 052 36134/36442

Glasha Farmhouse
Farmhouse accommodation
Ballymacarbry. Tel. 052 36108

Ballymacarbry

Youghal

Aherne's
*Townhouse & seafood
restaurant*
Youghal. Tel. 024 92424

**Farmgate Restaurant
& Country Store**
Restaurant & country store
Midleton. Tel. 021 4632771

Midleton

WatersEdge Hotel
Waterside hotel & restaurant
Cobh. Tel. 021 4815566

Knockeven House
Country house bed & breakfast
Cobh. Tel. 021 4811778

Cobh

**Cobh - The Queenstown
Story** Tel. 021 4813591

Fota House & Gardens
Carrigtoohill. Tel. 051 4815543

N25 Cork

Dublin to Wexford to Rosslare

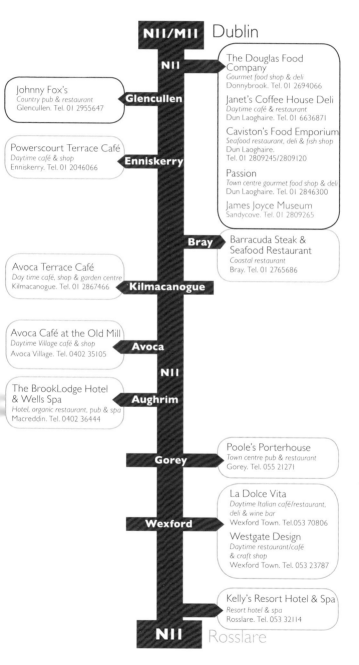

NII/MII — Dublin

NII

Glencullen

Johnny Fox's
Country pub & restaurant
Glencullen. Tel. 01 2955647

The Douglas Food Company
Gourmet food shop & deli
Donnybrook. Tel. 01 2694066

Janet's Coffee House Deli
Daytime café & restaurant
Dun Laoghaire. Tel. 01 6636871

Caviston's Food Emporium
Seafood restaurant, deli & fish shop
Dun Laoghaire.
Tel. 01 2809245/2809120

Passion
Town centre gourmet food shop & deli
Dun Laoghaire. Tel. 01 2846300

James Joyce Museum
Sandycove. Tel. 01 2809265

Enniskerry

Powerscourt Terrace Café
Daytime café & shop
Enniskerry. Tel. 01 2046066

Bray

Barracuda Steak & Seafood Restaurant
Coastal restaurant
Bray. Tel. 01 2765686

Kilmacanogue

Avoca Terrace Café
Day time café, shop & garden centre
Kilmacanogue. Tel. 01 2867466

Avoca

Avoca Café at the Old Mill
Daytime Village café & shop
Avoca Village. Tel. 0402 35105

NII

Aughrim

The BrookLodge Hotel & Wells Spa
Hotel, organic restaurant, pub & spa
Macreddin. Tel. 0402 36444

Gorey

Poole's Porterhouse
Town centre pub & restaurant
Gorey. Tel. 055 21271

Wexford

La Dolce Vita
Daytime Italian café/restaurant, deli & wine bar
Wexford Town. Tel.053 70806

Westgate Design
Daytime restaurant/café & craft shop
Wexford Town. Tel. 053 23787

Kelly's Resort Hotel & Spa
Resort hotel & spa
Rosslare. Tel. 053 32114

NII — Rosslare

Belfast to Derry

From the North dial 028. From the Republic dial 048

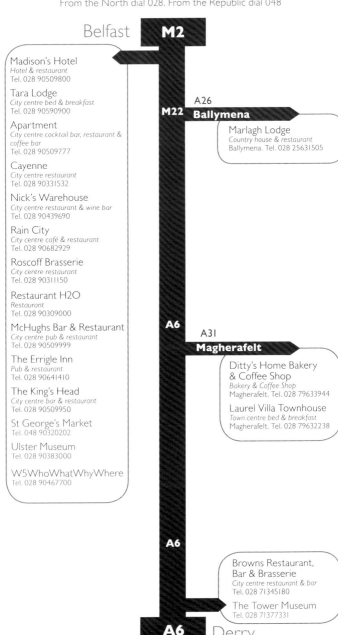

Belfast

M2

Madison's Hotel
Hotel & restaurant
Tel. 028 90509800

Tara Lodge
City centre bed & breakfast
Tel. 028 90590900

Apartment
City centre cocktail bar, restaurant & coffee bar
Tel. 028 90509777

Cayenne
City centre restaurant
Tel. 028 90331532

Nick's Warehouse
City centre restaurant & wine bar
Tel. 028 90439690

Rain City
City centre café & restaurant
Tel. 028 90682929

Roscoff Brasserie
City centre restaurant
Tel. 028 90311150

Restaurant H2O
Restaurant
Tel. 028 90309000

McHughs Bar & Restaurant
City centre pub & restaurant
Tel. 028 90509999

The Errigle Inn
Pub & restaurant
Tel. 028 90641410

The King's Head
City centre bar & restaurant
Tel. 028 90509950

St George's Market
Tel. 048 90320202

Ulster Museum
Tel. 028 90383000

W5WhoWhatWhyWhere
Tel. 028 90467700

M22   A26   **Ballymena**

Marlagh Lodge
Country house & restaurant
Ballymena. Tel. 028 25631505

A6   A31   **Magherafelt**

Ditty's Home Bakery & Coffee Shop
Bakery & Coffee Shop
Magherafelt. Tel. 028 79633944

Laurel Villa Townhouse
Town centre bed & breakfast
Magherafelt. Tel. 028 79632238

A6

Browns Restaurant, Bar & Brasserie
City centre restaurant & bar
Tel. 028 71345180

The Tower Museum
Tel. 028 71377331

A6   Derry

Belfast to Sligo

From the North dial 028. From the Republic dial 048

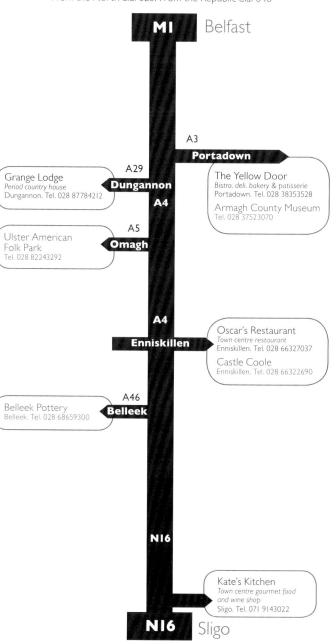

MI Belfast

A3
Portadown

A29
Dungannon

A4

Grange Lodge
Period country house
Dungannon. Tel. 028 87784212

The Yellow Door
Bistro. deli. bakery & patisserie
Portadown. Tel. 028 38353528

Armagh County Museum
Tel. 028 37523070

A5
Omagh

Ulster American
Folk Park
Tel. 028 82243292

A4
Enniskillen

Oscar's Restaurant
Town centre restaurant
Enniskillen. Tel. 028 66327037

Castle Coole
Enniskillen. Tel. 028 66322690

A46
Belleek

Belleek Pottery
Belleek. Tel. 028 68659300

N16

Kate's Kitchen
*Town centre gourmet food
and wine shop*
Sligo. Tel. 071 9143022

N16 Sligo

Dublin to Sligo

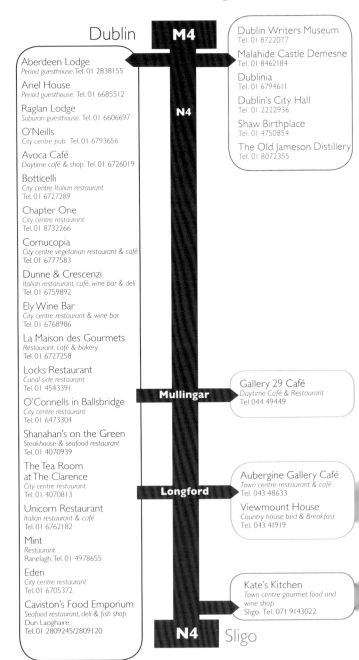

Dublin

M4

Aberdeen Lodge
Period guesthouse. Tel. 01 2838155

Ariel House
Period guesthouse. Tel. 01 6685512

Raglan Lodge
Suburan guesthouse. Tel. 01 6606697

O'Neills
City centre pub. Tel. 01 6793656

Avoca Café
Daytime café & shop. Tel. 01 6726019

Botticelli
City centre Italian restaurant
Tel. 01 6727289

Chapter One
City centre restaurant
Tel. 01 8732266

Cornucopia
City centre vegetarian restaurant & café
Tel. 01 6777583

Dunne & Crescenzi
Italian restaurant, café, wine bar & deli
Tel. 01 6759892

Ely Wine Bar
City centre restaurant & wine bar
Tel. 01 6768986

La Maison des Gourmets
Restaurant, café & bakery
Tel. 01 6727258

Locks Restaurant
Canal-side restaurant
Tel. 01 4543391

O'Connells in Ballsbridge
City centre restaurant
Tel. 01 6473304

Shanahan's on the Green
Steakhouse & seafood restaurant
Tel. 01 4070939

The Tea Room
at The Clarence
City centre restaurant
Tel. 01 4070813

Unicorn Restaurant
Italian restaurant & café
Tel. 01 6762182

Mint
Restaurant
Ranelagh. Tel. 01 4978655

Eden
City centre restaurant
Tel. 01 6705372

Caviston's Food Emporium
Seafood restaurant, deli & fish shop
Dun Laoghaire.
Tel. 01 2809245/2809120

N4

Dublin Writers Museum
Tel. 01 8722077

Malahide Castle Demesne
Tel. 01 8462184

Dublinia
Tel. 01 6794611

Dublin's City Hall
Tel. 01 2222936

Shaw Birthplace
Tel. 01 4750854

The Old Jameson Distillery
Tel. 01 8072355

Mullingar

Gallery 29 Café
Daytime Café & Restaurant
Tel 044 49449

Longford

Aubergine Gallery Café
Town centre restaurant & café
Tel. 043 48633

Viewmount House
Country house bed & Breakfast
Tel. 043 41919

Kate's Kitchen
*Town centre gourmet food and
wine shop*
Sligo. Tel. 071 9143022

N4 Sligo

Galway to Sligo

N17 Galway

O'Grady's on the Pier
Oyster & seafood restaurant
Barna. Tel. 091 592223

N59 via Clifden/Westport

Kirwan's Lane Restaurant
City centre restaurant
Tel. 091 568266

McDonaghs Seafood House
Seafood restaurant & fish & chip bar
Tel 091 565001

Goyas
City centre café & bakery
Tel. 091 567010

Royal Tara
Tel. 091 705602

Killeen House
Country house bed & breakfast
Galway. Tel. 091 524179

White Gables Restaurant
Cottage restaurant
Moycullen. Tel. 091 555744

Abbeyglen Castle
Seaview hotel
Clifden. Tel. 095 21201

Kylemore Abbey & Garden
Daytime coffee shop & restaurant
Clifden. Tel. 095 41146

Renvyle House Hotel
Coastal hotel & restaurant
Connemara. Tel. 095 43511

Delphi Lodge
Lakeside country house
Leenane. Tel 095 42222

Blackberry Café
Waterside café & restaurant
Leenane. Tel 095 42240

Quay Cottage
Waterside restaurant
Westport. Tel. 098 26412

National Museum of Ireland
Castlebar. Tel 094 9031755

Knock

Knock House Hotel
Hotel & restaurant
Tel. 094 9388088

Kate's Kitchen
*Town centre gourmet food
and wine shop*
Sligo. Tel. 071 9143022

N17 Sligo

Dublin to Limerick to Tralee

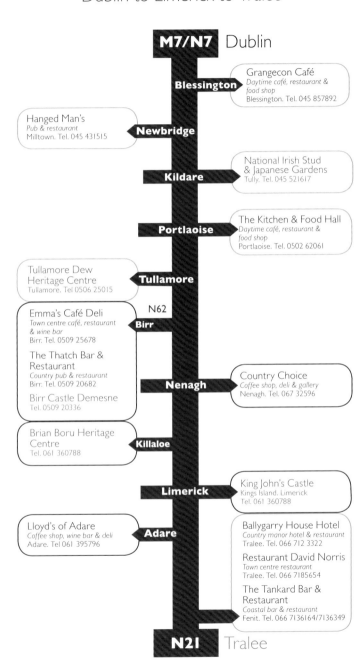

M7/N7 Dublin

Blessington

Grangecon Café
Daytime café, restaurant & food shop
Blessington. Tel. 045 857892

Hanged Man's
Pub & restaurant
Milltown. Tel. 045 431515

Newbridge

Kildare

National Irish Stud
& Japanese Gardens
Tully. Tel. 045 521617

Portlaoise

The Kitchen & Food Hall
Daytime café, restaurant & food shop
Portlaoise. Tel. 0502 62061

Tullamore Dew
Heritage Centre
Tullamore. Tel 0506 25015

Tullamore

N62

Emma's Café Deli
Town centre café, restaurant & wine bar
Birr. Tel. 0509 25678

Birr

The Thatch Bar &
Restaurant
Country pub & restaurant
Birr. Tel. 0509 20682

Birr Castle Demesne
Tel. 0509 20336

Nenagh

Country Choice
Coffee shop, deli & gallery
Nenagh. Tel. 067 32596

Brian Boru Heritage
Centre
Tel. 061 360788

Killaloe

Limerick

King John's Castle
Kings Island. Limerick
Tel. 061 360788

Lloyd's of Adare
Coffee shop, wine bar & deli
Adare. Tel 061 395796

Adare

Ballygarry House Hotel
Country manor hotel & restaurant
Tralee. Tel. 066 712 3322

Restaurant David Norris
Town centre restaurant
Tralee. Tel. 066 7185654

The Tankard Bar &
Restaurant
Coastal bar & restaurant
Fenit. Tel. 066 7136164/7136349

N21 Tralee

Dublin to Belfast

From the North dial 028. From the Republic dial 048

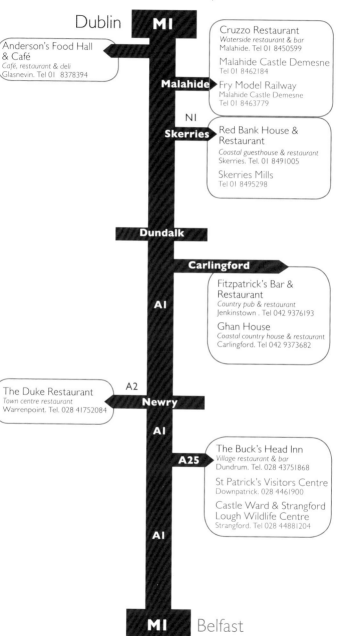

Dublin

M1

Anderson's Food Hall & Café
Café, restaurant & deli
Glasnevin. Tel 01 8378394

Cruzzo Restaurant
Waterside restaurant & bar
Malahide. Tel 01 8450599

Malahide Castle Demesne
Tel 01 8462184

Malahide

Fry Model Railway
Malahide Castle Demesne
Tel 01 8463779

N1

Skerries

Red Bank House & Restaurant
Coastal guesthouse & restaurant
Skerries. Tel. 01 8491005

Skerries Mills
Tel 01 8495298

Dundalk

Carlingford

A1

Fitzpatrick's Bar & Restaurant
Country pub & restaurant
Jenkinstown . Tel 042 9376193

Ghan House
Coastal country house & restaurant
Carlingford. Tel 042 9373682

A2

The Duke Restaurant
Town centre restaurant
Warrenpoint. Tel. 028 41752084

Newry

A1

A25

The Buck's Head Inn
Village restaurant & bar
Dundrum. Tel. 028 43751868

St Patrick's Visitors Centre
Downpatrick. 028 4461900

Castle Ward & Strangford Lough Wildlife Centre
Strangford. Tel 028 44881204

A1

M1 Belfast

Dublin to Cork to Killarney

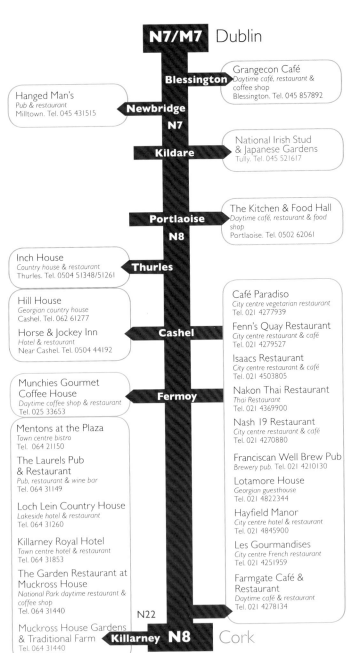

N7/M7 Dublin

Blessington

Grangecon Café
Daytime café, restaurant & coffee shop
Blessington. Tel. 045 857892

Hanged Man's
Pub & restaurant
Milltown. Tel. 045 431515

Newbridge

N7

Kildare

National Irish Stud & Japanese Gardens
Tully. Tel. 045 521617

Portlaoise

N8

The Kitchen & Food Hall
Daytime café, restaurant & food shop
Portlaoise. Tel. 0502 62061

Inch House
Country house & restaurant
Thurles. Tel. 0504 51348/51261

Thurles

Hill House
Georgian country house
Cashel. Tel. 062 61277

Horse & Jockey Inn
Hotel & restaurant
Near Cashel. Tel. 0504 44192

Cashel

Café Paradiso
City centre vegetarian restaurant
Tel. 021 4277939

Fenn's Quay Restaurant
City centre restaurant & café
Tel. 021 4279527

Isaacs Restaurant
City centre restaurant & café
Tel. 021 4503805

Munchies Gourmet Coffee House
Daytime coffee shop & restaurant
Tel. 025 33653

Fermoy

Nakon Thai Restaurant
Thai Restaurant
Tel. 021 4369900

Mentons at the Plaza
Town centre bistro
Tel. 064 21150

Nash 19 Restaurant
City centre restaurant & café
Tel. 021 4270880

The Laurels Pub & Restaurant
Pub, restaurant & wine bar
Tel. 064 31149

Franciscan Well Brew Pub
Brewery pub. Tel. 021 4210130

Lotamore House
Georgian guesthouse
Tel. 021 4822344

Loch Lein Country House
Lakeside hotel & restaurant
Tel. 064 31260

Hayfield Manor
City centre hotel & restaurant
Tel. 021 4845900

Killarney Royal Hotel
Town centre hotel & restaurant
Tel. 064 31853

Les Gourmandises
City centre French restaurant
Tel. 021 4251959

The Garden Restaurant at Muckross House
National Park daytime restaurant & coffee shop
Tel. 064 31440

Farmgate Café & Restaurant
Daytime café & restaurant
Tel. 021 4278134

N22

Muckross House Gardens & Traditional Farm
Tel. 064 31440

Killarney **N8**

Cork

Limerick to Galway

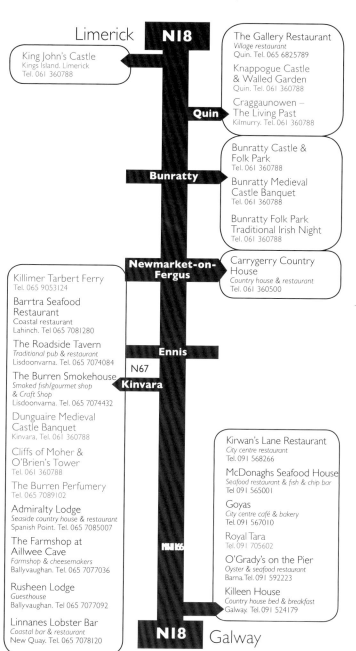

Limerick

N18

King John's Castle
Kings Island. Limerick
Tel. 061 360788

Quin

The Gallery Restaurant
Village restaurant
Quin. Tel. 065 6825789

Knappogue Castle
& Walled Garden
Quin. Tel. 061 360788

Craggaunowen –
The Living Past
Kilmurry. Tel. 061 360788

Bunratty

Bunratty Castle &
Folk Park
Tel. 061 360788

Bunratty Medieval
Castle Banquet
Tel. 061 360788

Bunratty Folk Park
Traditional Irish Night
Tel. 061 360788

Newmarket-on-Fergus

Carrygerry Country
House
Country house & restaurant
Tel. 061 360500

Killimer Tarbert Ferry
Tel. 065 9053124

Barrtra Seafood
Restaurant
Coastal restaurant
Lahinch. Tel 065 7081280

The Roadside Tavern
Traditional pub & restaurant
Lisdoonvarna. Tel. 065 7074084

The Burren Smokehouse
*Smoked fish/gourmet shop
& Craft Shop*
Lisdoonvarna. Tel. 065 7074432

Dunguaire Medieval
Castle Banquet
Kinvara. Tel. 061 360788

Cliffs of Moher &
O'Brien's Tower
Tel. 061 360788

The Burren Perfumery
Tel. 065 7089102

Admiralty Lodge
Seaside country house & restaurant
Spanish Point. Tel. 065 7085007

The Farmshop at
Aillwee Cave
Farmshop & cheesemakers
Ballyvaughan. Tel. 065 7077036

Rusheen Lodge
Guesthouse
Ballyvaughan. Tel 065 7077092

Linnanes Lobster Bar
Coastal bar & restaurant
New Quay. Tel. 065 7078120

Ennis

N67

Kinvara

Kirwan's Lane Restaurant
City centre restaurant
Tel. 091 568266

McDonaghs Seafood House
Seafood restaurant & fish & chip bar
Tel 091 565001

Goyas
City centre café & bakery
Tel. 091 567010

Royal Tara
Tel. 091 705602

O'Grady's on the Pier
Oyster & seafood restaurant
Barna. Tel. 091 592223

Killeen House
Country house bed & breakfast
Galway. Tel. 091 524179

N18 Galway

Dublin to Waterford

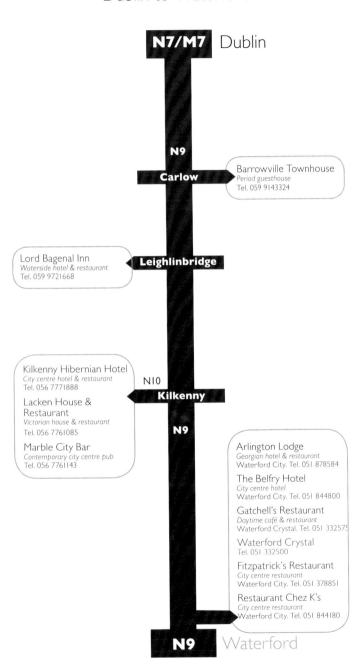

N7/M7 Dublin

N9

Carlow

Barrowville Townhouse
Period guesthouse
Tel. 059 9143324

Lord Bagenal Inn
Waterside hotel & restaurant
Tel. 059 9721668

Leighlinbridge

Kilkenny Hibernian Hotel
City centre hotel & restaurant
Tel. 056 7771888

Lacken House &
Restaurant
Victorian house & restaurant
Tel. 056 7761085

Marble City Bar
Contemporary city centre pub
Tel. 056 7761143

N10

Kilkenny

N9

Arlington Lodge
Georgian hotel & restaurant
Waterford City. Tel. 051 878584

The Belfry Hotel
City centre hotel
Waterford City. Tel. 051 844800

Gatchell's Restaurant
Daytime café & restaurant
Waterford Crystal. Tel. 051 332575

Waterford Crystal
Tel. 051 332500

Fitzpatrick's Restaurant
City centre restaurant
Waterford City. Tel. 051 378851

Restaurant Chez K's
City centre restaurant
Waterford City. Tel. 051 844180

N9 Waterford

Waterford to Limerick

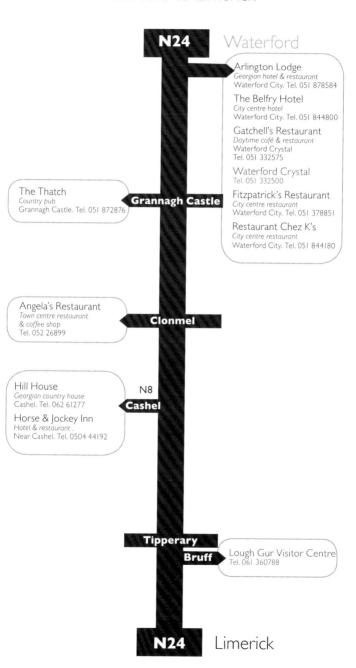

N24 Waterford

Arlington Lodge
Georgian hotel & restaurant
Waterford City. Tel. 051 878584

The Belfry Hotel
City centre hotel
Waterford City. Tel. 051 844800

Gatchell's Restaurant
Daytime café & restaurant
Waterford Crystal
Tel. 051 332575

Waterford Crystal
Tel. 051 332500

The Thatch
Country pub
Grannagh Castle. Tel. 051 872876

Grannagh Castle

Fitzpatrick's Restaurant
City centre restaurant
Waterford City. Tel. 051 378851

Restaurant Chez K's
City centre restaurant
Waterford City. Tel. 051 844180

Angela's Restaurant
Town centre restaurant
& coffee shop
Tel. 052 26899

Clonmel

Hill House
Georgian country house
Cashel. Tel. 062 61277

Horse & Jockey Inn
Hotel & restaurant .
Near Cashel. Tel. 0504 44192

N8
Cashel

Tipperary

Bruff

Lough Gur Visitor Centre
Tel. 061 360788

N24 Limerick

Westport to Sligo to Donegal

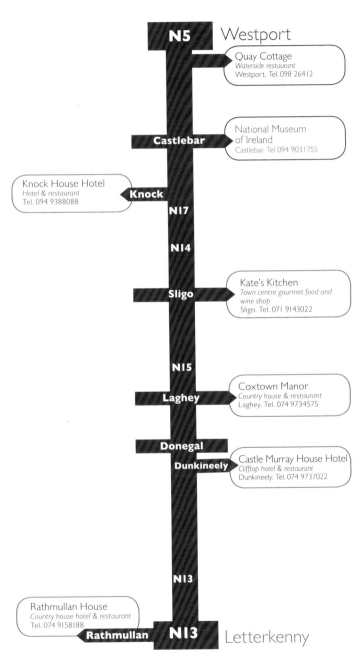

N5 Westport

Quay Cottage
Waterside restaurant
Westport. Tel. 098 26412

Castlebar

National Museum
of Ireland
Castlebar. Tel 094 9031755

Knock House Hotel
Hotel & restaurant
Tel. 094 9388088

Knock

N17

N14

Sligo

Kate's Kitchen
*Town centre gourmet food and
wine shop*
Sligo. Tel. 071 9143022

N15

Laghey

Coxtown Manor
Country house & restaurant
Laghey. Tel. 074 9734575

Donegal

Dunkineely

Castle Murray House Hotel
Clifftop hotel & restaurant
Dunkineely. Tel. 074 9737022

N13

Rathmullan House
Country house hotel & restaurant
Tel. 074 9158188

Rathmullan **N13** Letterkenny

Index of Establishments
A-Z

Les Routiers in Ireland Guide 2006

Did you enjoy your visit?

We would like to hear how the properties in the guide matched up to your expectations. Les Routiers Ireland has inspectors who visit each property in an effort to ensure that the experience we describe is accurate. Please let us know how you enjoyed your visit as your efforts will assist us in monitoring standards. If any property exceeded your expectations you may like to recommend them for an award. Quality, Value, Individual Hospitality and Good Food are the key principles of the Les Routiers ethos and we do hope our members live up to your expectations and ours.

We look forward to hearing from you.

Property Name
....

PLEASE PRINT IN BLOCK CAPITALS

Address
....

....

....

I had ☐ lunch ☐ dinner ☐ stayed there on (date)
....

Details
....

....

....

....

Reports received up to the end of May 2006 will be used in the research of the 2007 edition

Would you recommend this establishment for an award? ☐

Why?..

....

....

....

☐ I am not in any way connected to the proprietors.

Name
....

Address
....

....

....

As a result of your sending Les Routiers this form, we may send you information on Les Routiers in the future. If you would prefer not to receive such information. please tick this box ☐

Please send completed form to

GUEST COMMENTS
Les Routiers Ireland
Ballykelly House, Drinagh, Wexford, Ireland
Tel. +353 (0)53 58693. Fax. +353 (0)53 58688
Email. info@routiersireland.com

Les Routiers in Ireland Guide 2006
Did you enjoy your visit?

We would like to hear how the properties in the guide matched up to your expectations. Les Routiers Ireland has inspectors who visit each property in an effort to ensure that the experience we describe is accurate. Please let us know how you enjoyed your visit as your efforts will assist us in monitoring standards. If any property exceeded your expectations you may like to recommend them for an award. Quality, Value, Individual Hospitality and Good Food are the key principles of the Les Routiers ethos and we do hope our members live up to your expectations and ours.

We look forward to hearing from you.

Property Name

....
PLEASE PRINT IN BLOCK CAPITALS

Address

....

....

....

I had ☐ lunch ☐ dinner ☐ stayed there on (date)

Details

....

....

....

....

Reports received up to the end of May 2006 will be used in the research of the 2007 edition

Would you recommend this establishment for an award? ☐

Why?...

....

....

....

☐ I am not in any way connected to the proprietors.

Name

....

Address

....

....

....

As a result of your sending Les Routiers this form, we may send you information on Les Routiers in the future. If you would prefer not to receive such information. please tick this box ☐

Please send completed form to
GUEST COMMENTS
Les Routiers Ireland
Ballykelly House, Drinagh, Wexford, Ireland
Tel. +353 (0)53 58693. Fax. +353 (0)53 58688
Email. info@routiersireland.com

Les Routiers in Ireland Guide 2006
Did you enjoy your visit?

We would like to hear how the properties in the guide matched up to your expectations. Les Routiers Ireland has inspectors who visit each property in an effort to ensure that the experience we describe is accurate. Please let us know how you enjoyed your visit as your efforts will assist us in monitoring standards. If any property exceeded your expectations you may like to recommend them for an award. Quality, Value, Individual Hospitality and Good Food are the key principles of the Les Routiers ethos and we do hope our members live up to your expectations and ours.

We look forward to hearing from you.

Property Name
....

PLEASE PRINT IN BLOCK CAPITALS

Address
....

....

....

I had ❏ lunch ❏ dinner ❏ stayed there on (date) ....

Details
....

....

....

....

Reports received up to the end of May 2006 will be used in the research of the 2007 edition

Would you recommend this establishment for an award? ❏

Why?...

....

....

....

❏ I am not in any way connected to the proprietors.

Name
....

Address
....

....

....

As a result of your sending Les Routiers this form, we may send you information on Les Routiers in the future. If you would prefer not to receive such information. please tick this box ❏

Please send completed form to
GUEST COMMENTS
Les Routiers Ireland
Ballykelly House, Drinagh, Wexford, Ireland
Tel. +353 (0)53 58693. Fax. +353 (0)53 58688
Email. info@routiersireland.com

Les Routiers in Ireland Guide 2006
Did you enjoy your visit?

We would like to hear how the properties in the guide matched up to your expectations. Les Routiers Ireland has inspectors who visit each property in an effort to ensure that the experience we describe is accurate. Please let us know how you enjoyed your visit as your efforts will assist us in monitoring standards. If any property exceeded your expectations you may like to recommend them for an award. Quality, Value, Individual Hospitality and Good Food are the key principles of the Les Routiers ethos and we do hope our members live up to your expectations and ours.

We look forward to hearing from you.

Property Name

PLEASE PRINT IN BLOCK CAPITALS

Address

I had ❏ lunch ❏ dinner ❏ stayed there on (date)

Details

Reports received up to the end of May 2006 will be used in the research of the 2007 edition

Would you recommend this establishment for an award? ❏

Why?

❏ I am not in any way connected to the proprietors.

Name

Address

As a result of your sending Les Routiers this form, we may send you information on Les Routiers in the future. If you would prefer not to receive such information. please tick this box ❏

Please send completed form to
GUEST COMMENTS
Les Routiers Ireland
Ballykelly House, Drinagh, Wexford, Ireland
Tel. +353 (0)53 58693. Fax. +353 (0)53 58688
Email. info@routiersireland.com

Les Routiers Arrives in Ireland

Presented to Margaret Jeffares and Hugo Arnold by the members of Les Routiers Ireland on the first anniversary of Les Routiers in Ireland.